LEGO® AND PHILOSOPHY

T0311472

The Blackwell Philosophy and Pop Culture Series
Series editor William Irwin

A spoonful of sugar helps the medicine go down, and a healthy helping of popular culture clears the cobwebs from Kant. Philosophy has had a public relations problem for a few centuries now. This series aims to change that, showing that philosophy is relevant to your life—and not just for answering the big questions like "To be or not to be?" but for answering the little questions: "To watch or not to watch *South Park*?" Thinking deeply about TV, movies, and music doesn't make you a "complete idiot." In fact it might make you a philosopher, someone who believes the unexamined life is not worth living and the unexamined cartoon is not worth watching.

Already published in the series:

LEGO® AND PHILOSOPHY

CONSTRUCTING REALITY BRICK BY BRICK

Edited by

Roy T. Cook
and
Sondra Bacharach

WILEY Blackwell

Registered Office
John Wiley & Sons, Inc., 111 River Street, Hoboken, NJ 07030, USA

Editorial Office
9600 Garsington Road, Oxford, OX4 2DQ, UK

For details of our global editorial offices, customer services, and more information about Wiley products visit us at www.wiley.com.

Wiley also publishes its books in a variety of electronic formats and by print-on-demand. Some content that appears in standard print versions of this book may not be available in other formats.

Library of Congress Cataloging-in-Publication data is available for this book.

ISBN 9781119193975 (paperback)

Cover Design: Wiley
Cover Image: © photopia /Shutterstock

Set in 10.5/13pt SabonLTStd by Aptara Inc., New Delhi, India

10 9 8 7 6 5 4 3 2 1

Contents

Notes on Contributors

Sondra Bacharach is a Senior Lecturer in the philosophy department at Victoria University of Wellington (New Zealand). She works in philosophy of art, and is the coeditor of *Collaborating Now: Art in the Twenty-first Century* (with Jeremy Booth and Siv Fjaerstag, Routledge, 2016) and former coeditor of the American Society of Aesthetics Newsletter. When she's not doing philosophy, she can be found building Classic Spaceships (Spaceship, Spaceship, SPACESHIP!) with her kids' big box of LEGO.

Steve Bein is Assistant Professor of Philosophy at the University of Dayton. He is a regular contributor to Blackwell's Philosophy and Pop Culture series, including *Wonder Woman and Philosophy* and *The Ultimate Star Trek and Philosophy*. He's also a novelist and his sci-fi short stories have been used in philosophy and science fiction courses across the U.S. His books include *Purifying Zen* (University of Hawai'i Press, 2011), *Compassion and Moral Guidance* (University of Hawai'i Press, 2012), and the critically acclaimed *Fated Blades* trilogy from Penguin Roc. Steve is the proud owner of some 40,000 LEGO bricks. Don't judge.

Samantha J. Boardman is a public history and research consultant who received her PhD in American Studies from Rutgers University–Newark. Her projects have included research into expressions of U.S. nationalism in miniature tourist attractions, the digital preservation of Great Migration oral histories, short digital documentaries on civic and community institutions and curatorial services for a wide variety of exhibits. She has a five year-old daughter with whom she builds bangin' LEGO pirate ships.

Eric Chelstrom is Assistant Professor of Philosophy at St. Mary's University. Tacos in San Antonio are so awesome, they aren't just for Tuesdays. He worries about things like oppression and whether his children will share their LEGOs. Sure, they have been told to keep away from their father's precious LEGOs. He might sometimes also wonder if it's okay to make his kids share a double-decker-couch so that there's more space for LEGOs. In this he struggles with being maybe too much like The Man Upstairs, even if his students probably think he's way more like Emmet, *before* Emmet got special.

Roy T. Cook is CLA Scholar of the College and Professor of Philosophy at the University of Minnesota Twin Cities, and Resident Fellow at the Minnesota Center for the Philosophy of Science. He is the author of *Paradoxes* (Polity, 2013) and *The Yablo Paradox* (Oxford, 2014), the editor of *The Arché Papers on the Mathematics of Abstraction* (Springer, 2007), and coeditor of *The Art of Comics: A Philosophical Approach* (with Aaron Meskin, Blackwell, 2012) and *The Routledge Companion to Comics* (with Frank Bramlett and Aaron Meskin, Routledge, 2016). No matter how much LEGO he buys, he never seems to have enough headlight bricks.

Ramon Das is a Senior Lecturer in philosophy at Victoria University of Wellington (New Zealand). He works mainly in normative ethics and political philosophy, and more recently has branched out into meta-ethics and philosophy of mathematics. An ex-patriot American, he occasionally (not often) wishes that he lived in a country where he could purchase a LEGO set for less than the cost of his monthly power bill.

Bob Fischer is an Assistant Professor of Philosophy at Texas State University. He is coeditor of two volumes—*The Moral Complexities of Eating Meat* (Oxford University Press, 2015) and *Modal Epistemology After Rationalism* (Springer, 2016)—the sole editor of *College Ethics: A Reader on Moral Issues That Affect You* (Oxford University Press, 2016), and the author of *Modal Justification via Theories* (Springer, 2017). In his spare time, he searches for vintage LEGO sets at garage sales. (The quest is quixotic, but he soldiers on anyway.)

Saul Fisher is Visiting Associate Professor of Philosophy at Mercy College (NY), where he serves as Executive Director for Grants and Academic Initiatives in the Office of the Provost. His work in philosophical aesthetics is centered on architecture, for which he was awarded a Graham Foundation grant (2009), and which includes the *Stanford Encyclopedia of Philosophy* article on philosophy of architecture (2015). The greatest works of his own architectural oeuvre, realized in the LEGO medium, are lost to the ages.

Michael Gettings is Associate Professor of Philosophy at Hollins University. Some of his philosophical work ranges from analyzing arguments for God's existence to developing new ontological categories for works of art. He has also contributed philosophical musings on topics from the Grateful Dead to the *Daily Show*. One of his proudest moments as a parent was the day his son presented him with a LEGO brick portrait of Ole Kirk Christiansen.

Rhiannon Grant is Tutor for Quaker Roles at Woodbrooke Quaker Study Centre (UK). Her work covers the philosophy of Wittgenstein, feminism in religion, and studies of British Quakers. She enjoys using tools from diverse academic disciplines, including philosophy, theology, sociology, and gender studies. If her career were a LEGO wall, it would be multicolored, with roof bricks dotted here and there in the middle and an upside-down door on the left-hand side.

Rebecca Gutwald is an Associate Professor of Philosophy at the University of Munich, Germany. Her main areas of research are political philosophy, feminism, and social ethics. Currently she is working on a book on the political philosophy of resilience and its role for future ethics. This includes gauging the potential of philosophy to solve problems in practice. She urges the philosopher to leave the armchair and visit the real world. As part of her own experience of doing so, she has taught philosophy outside of academia, especially to her children. Since her own children had to endure her philosophy lessons, she suspects that they are retaliating by leaving around their LEGOs for her to step on, which results in a severe form of pain which only parents know about. She has now bought some sturdy slippers and begun to wonder about the increasing gendering of toys, longing for the old days of LEGO in which boys and girls could just simply sit down, build a LEGO house, and dream of a better future.

David Kahn, PhD, is the author of *Case, Spandex, Briefcase: Leadership Lessons from Superheroes* (Starewell, 2015) and writes on ways to make leadership theories and research accessible through pop culture. David is a Leadership Expert, Human Resource Executive, Speaker, and Consultant concentrating on incorporating the principles of culture, leadership and organizational development to improve business strategies and, ultimately, performance. In his spare time, he is on a lifetime pursuit to "Create the Impossible" … or at least a life-sized LEGO Yoda.

Alice Leber-Cook has an MEd in Adult Education and an MA in Curriculum and Instruction, focusing on Family, Youth, and Community education, both from the University of Minnesota – Twin Cities. She keeps herself busy both as an educational researcher and as a very active Female Fan of LEGO (FFOL), LEGO User Group (LUG) member (go VirtuaLUG!), and coordinator for Brickworld, the largest Adult Fan of LEGO (AFOL) convention in North America. She breaks out in hives when she hears someone say "Legos."

Stephan Leuenberger is a Lecturer in Philosophy at the University of Glasgow, working mainly in metaphysics and philosophical logic. He likes to give his papers pretentious titles, preferably including Latin words. Representative examples are "Ceteris absentibus physicalism" and "De jure and de facto validity in the logic of tense and modality." He tried to do some clever word play with the Latin meaning of "lego," but failed.

David Lueth is a Professional Writing Tutor at Anoka Ramsey Community College. He is slowly collecting college degrees; his third and most recent is an MFA in Creative Writing from Hamline University, and he is pondering how a couple more degrees in cultural anthropology would look on his wall. When not tutoring students on the finer points of comma splices or subjecting all his friends to monologues on the increasing relevance of Jean Baudrillard's concept of the hyperreal, he reminds himself that he really ought to finish that novel he's been working on for the past twelve years. Sometimes, to avoid the guilt those reminders bring up, he plays with his LEGO collection.

Robert M. Mentyka grew up as a fervent "LEGO Maniac" during the 1990s and long considered going into engineering or architecture thanks to the influence of these addictive little blocks. Although his attention was eventually won over by the charms of philosophy, he is still a lifelong LEGO fan and part-time builder of the "most radical" of spaceships. Having earned both his Bachelors and Masters in Philosophy at the Franciscan University of Steubenville, Ohio, he currently works nights as a Legal Document Processor and spends his days constructing arguments about Bioethics, Personalism, and the Philosophy of Warfare.

Ellen Miller is Associate Professor and Chair in the Department of Philosophy and Religion Studies at Rowan University where she has taught for fifteen years. Her book, *Releasing Philosophy, Thinking Art: A Phenomenological Study of Sylvia Plath's Poetry* (Davies Group Publishers), is the first full-length philosophical examination of Sylvia Plath's poetry. Her other publications and scholarly presentations focus on topics in philosophy of art, feminist philosophy, and environmental ethics. In her current Plath studies, she is exploring how Sylvia Plath's writings can help us better understand medicine and mental health care. She loves tacos on Tuesdays, or any day of the week!

Alexander Quanbeck has studied philosophy at St. Olaf College, the Center for Medieval and Renaissance Studies at Oxford University, and the Howard and Edna Hong Kierkegaard Library. His interests lie especially in epistemology and the philosophy of religion. Some days he wishes to realize his childhood aspiration to create a life-size LEGO model of the Great Wall of China, but other days his preoccupation with philosophical idealism makes him wonder whether LEGOs really exist in the material world.

Jon Robson teaches at the University of Nottingham in the UK. He has research interests in a bunch of different areas including aesthetics, epistemology, ethics, metaphysics and the philosophy of religion. He has previously written a chapter for *Veronica Mars and Philosophy* (Wiley Blackwell 2014) and is coauthor of *A Critical Introduction to the Metaphysics of Time* (Bloomsbury 2016). Also, he's from the planet Duplo and he's here to destroy you.

Tyler Shores is a PhD student at the University of Cambridge and received his Master's Degree from the University of Oxford. At the University of California, Berkeley, he created and taught a course on *The Simpsons* and Philosophy (inspired by William Irwin's book of the same name). Tyler has contributed to other volumes in this series including *Alice in Wonderland and Philosophy*, *30 Rock and Philosophy*, and *Inception and Philosophy*. He previously worked at Google on the Authors@Google lecture series. Unlike Emmet in *The*

LEGO Movie, Tyler definitely does not think overpriced $37 coffee is awesome.

Fenner Tanswell is just starting as a postdoctoral researcher in Oxford, after receiving his PhD in the philosophy of mathematics and logic at St Andrews and Stirling. He grew up in both the UK and the Netherlands, where the Christmas celebrations are three weeks apart, so December was always a double whammy of LEGO presents.

Craig van Pelt is a doctoral student in sociology at the University of Oregon. He specializes in the sociology of food, environmental health, and food access issues. If he could build anything out of LEGO it would be a hoverboard, à la *Back to the Future II*. Yes, a fully functioning hoverboard would be the best LEGO set *ever.*

Ruth Wainman has recently completed a PhD in the School of History at the University of Kent. Most of the time she specializes in history of science but when this is not the case, she likes to build her childhood hobbies into her work, one brick at a time.

Mary Beth Willard is an Assistant Professor of Philosophy at Weber State University, where she teaches a little of everything and publishes primarily in metaphilosophy, metaphysics, and aesthetics. She wrote for this volume in the hope that she might have written something that will one day be interesting to her three-year-old son, whose research interests include LEGO, cars, and cars made with LEGO.

Introduction
Play Well, Philosophize Well!

Sondra Bacharach and Roy T. Cook

LEGO® is, of course, a children's toy. Or better yet, LEGO bricks and elements are the basic building blocks with which children, and adults, build such toys. But they are also the building blocks of a transgenerational multimedia empire. The LEGO Group is currently the largest toy manufacturer in the world, and the LEGO brand covers not just the basic bricks, but a massive multimedial empire including animated television shows, feature films, a vibrant adult fan base with over a dozen yearly conventions, an educational robotics program, an award-winning series of videogames, hundreds of books, magazines, and comics, a team-building workshop program for businesses, a clothing line, an endowed professorship at Cambridge University, and much, much more.

So, LEGO is much more than a mere toy—it's really big, and it involves a whole lot of different kinds of stuff. But is it philosophical? At first glance, one might not think so—after all, how deep and profound could a little plastic building block be? It turns out that the answer is "very"!

When we—especially adults—play or work with LEGO, it is natural to reflect on these iconic bricks and to ask questions about how we construct ourselves and our world, the difference between childhood and adulthood, and the role of sustainability and reusability in the modern industrial world. In addition, the LEGO Group's forays into business training (e.g., *Serious Play*®), robotics education (e.g., *Mindstorms*®), gender issues (e.g., *Friends*) and environmental

LEGO® *and Philosophy: Constructing Reality Brick By Brick*, First Edition.
Edited by Roy T. Cook and Sondra Bacharach.
© 2017 John Wiley & Sons Ltd. Published 2017 by John Wiley & Sons Ltd.

debates (e.g., the Greenpeace LEGO/Shell video, LEGO *Farm*) invite us to ask hard questions about this particular toy company—questions that we might not ask of Mattel or Hasbro. But why is that? What makes LEGO so special?

The simple reason is that LEGO, unlike Mattel or Hasbro, doesn't actually make *toys*. Strictly speaking, LEGO isn't a *toy*. We can *make* toys with LEGO, either by following the steps in the little instruction books, or by constructing our own original creations. And, lots of us do. But, we can make virtually *anything* with LEGO—not just toys. These little plastic bricks are more like a building material or medium, and probably have as much or more in common with bricks and paint than they have with most of the items in the toy aisle at the local megamart.

Indeed, lots of people treat LEGO as a building material, constructing practical artifacts like desks, pinball machines, and even full-sized houses out of these little bits of ABS plastic. LEGO is special in part *because* it's a building tool—one that opens up a new world of possibility for the builder. And as soon as we appreciate that LEGO is a tool for making things, we can see how it gives rise to a whole new way of appreciating these brightly colored little bricks. For tools can be used to make toys; and tools can be used to make tables; but tools can also be used to make art. Suddenly the domain of LEGO covers not only what is in our ordinary, quotidian world, but also encompasses the world of art—a world that ends only at the limits of our imagination.

Artists like Sean Kenney, Zbigniew Libera, Nathan Sawaya, Adam Reed Tucker, and Ai Weiwei have used LEGO bricks the way other artists use marble or paint, creating artworks that have been displayed in galleries and museums around the world. And, LEGO is well aware of this rich potential of those little ABS bricks—one of the LEGO Group's most successful advertisement campaigns carried the minimal tagline "Imagine."

Thinking about LEGO as part of the world of art—including the world of storytelling—explains why children can spend hours and hours lost in their imaginations, telling stories about their little ABS bricks: children know and appreciate how powerful LEGO, and the iconic minifigures so closely associated with the company, really are at storytelling! And, LEGO's narrative potential, when combined with vivid imaginations, explains how LEGO literally opens up new worlds of possibility for builders young and old. As a result, we can ask the same questions about LEGO creations that we might ask about artworks, narratives, and all the intimate connections between, and surprising combinations of, art, stories, and other creative endeavors.

This book explores just how far LEGO's reach into popular culture extends, and how that reach can help to illuminate philosophical problems old and new. The essays collected here highlight how LEGO has successfully infiltrated so many aspects of our popular culture, to say nothing of the pop-cultural ramifications of a toy that has enjoyed licensing deals with over a dozen hit Hollywood films. It turns out that properly understanding LEGO's rise to cultural pre-eminence is itself a deeply philosophical question—one that can be appreciated by coming back to our aesthetic roots with the ancient philosopher and playwright Aristophanes (c. 446–c. 386 BC). Aristophanes introduces the original concept of Cloud Cuckoo Land in his comic play *The Birds* in order to make a pointed critique of Athenian social life. It's no accident that Unikitty gives her chaotic, no-rules kingdom in *The LEGO Movie* the same name, since LEGO can also be used to make pointed commentary on, draw philosophical insights into, and learn more about the world we live in. Like Aristophanes and Unikitty, the essays included in this book attest to this variety of topics and approaches, ranging from the philosophy of architecture and the nature of autonomy to ApocaLEGO zombies and the Zen of LEGO, and pretty much everything in between.

As you are reading this volume, and thinking about your own past and future LEGO adventures, we only ask two simple things. First, as the very name of the company reminds us, "leg godt!," or "play well!" But equally importantly, we also ask you to philosophize well!

Part I
LEGO® AND CREATIVITY

Constructing Creativity

Mary Beth Willard

My toddler concentrates mightily, his tiny brow furrowed, his tongue poking ever so slightly out of the corner of his mouth. He fails to acknowledge my entry to the playroom, nor does he notice when I sit next to him cross-legged on the floor. His eyes lock on to each LEGO® DUPLO® square in turn as he deliberately presses them into a single layer on a flat green board. After several minutes, he looks up, startles as he notices me, and then breaks into a grin. "Mommy," he says, "I made you a pie!"

The pie is his first LEGO creation, and my heart swells with parental pride, but I would be lying if I said that such pride had not been leavened with a tiny scoop of self-congratulation. My spouse and I had ensured that one of his first toys was LEGO DUPLO because we believe, like many parents I know, that playing with LEGO encourages creativity. And look! It works! The moment of self-congratulation passes as my son encourages me to eat the pie, because as I dutifully pretend to nom away on raspberries (red bricks), blueberries (blue bricks), and bananas (you get the pattern), I wonder why the belief that LEGO contributes to creativity is so pervasive.

Originality and Creativity

We should pause here to distinguish between originality and creativity. True originality is rare, whether in art, science, or LEGO, because to

LEGO® and Philosophy: Constructing Reality Brick By Brick, First Edition.
Edited by Roy T. Cook and Sondra Bacharach.
© 2017 John Wiley & Sons Ltd. Published 2017 by John Wiley & Sons Ltd.

be truly original means to have done something that no one has ever done before, and that no one could have anticipated.[1] Most LEGO creations will not meet that condition, for with the exception of serious hobbyists who undertake massive builds, most players who make original creations are making creations that are commonplace. My son's DUPLO pie is not original, but it is creative, in the sense that constructing it was a new idea to him, and it is in this sense that we can ask whether playing with LEGO truly contributes to creativity.

On the one hand, LEGO allegedly encourages creativity by inviting us to build whatever we can imagine; on the other hand, actual LEGO play often involves following someone else's instructions or building meticulous scale models of real-world objects. Many LEGO enthusiasts, especially adult LEGO enthusiasts, enjoy building sets, and then displaying them. In such cases, the point is not to use the bricks in new ways; the point is to carefully follow the instructions so that every piece winds up in its proper place. Following the instructions might be challenging, but it is hardly creative to follow an exacting plan laid out by someone else.

Perhaps being creative with LEGO just means setting aside the instructions and striking off solo to build one's own creations. The system of play developed by the LEGO Group is commonly hailed as having the potential to contribute mightily to a child's creative development because even though many bricks are sold as sets, all of the bricks interlock, so they can be reused over and over. Moreover, the high quality of the ABS thermoplastic used in LEGO bricks ensures that the bricks can survive generations of use; my son's pie was made of DUPLOs that used to belong to his father. LEGO Batman® snaps into place happily alongside the original LEGO astronauts, and he may even borrow their space helmets; the only limits on Batman's adventures lie in the imagination of the child.

Yet even original LEGO creations must follow the constraints that result from the physical forms of the bricks. We might think of creativity as requiring significant artistic freedom to create whatever we want, and while the LEGO bricks facilitate stacking, the interlocking studs-and-bricks constrain what is possible. Working with LEGO requires working with edges and corners; it is no surprise that many large-scale creations are pieces that are well-suited to being built out of rigid plastic: cars, boats, buildings, and so forth.

Moreover, LEGO purists insist that only products produced by the LEGO Group should be used in an authentically original LEGO creation. Painting or remolding or placing stickers on the bricks counts against the spirit of LEGO creation.[2] Though a fan could exercise creativity while remolding LEGO, according to this line of thought, she would not be building with LEGO creatively. Rather, doing so would be creatively using LEGO as raw materials, as one might repurpose any other piece of plastic. As a result, while we often hear that playing with LEGO encourages creativity, the implicit rules of fan culture, as well as the material constraints imposed by the bricks themselves, limit significantly what may be created.

Herein lies the paradox of creativity: how can the freedom required for true creativity be compatible with a toy that *comes with incredibly detailed instructions for creating specific objects*, let alone with a fan culture that constrains what counts as a legitimately creative use of LEGO? Confronted with this paradox, I am cynically tempted to assume that I am nothing more than a dupe of marketing. "Creativity" perhaps means nothing more than "buy this toy, o conscientious parent; you will certainly get a lot of use out of it, and trust us, you will have more fun if you buy lots and lots of bricks."

Madmen, Oddballs, and Visionaries

The LEGO Movie embodies this paradox, presenting three conflicting models of creative LEGO play, illustrated by the Master Builders, Finn's father, and Emmet. *The LEGO Movie* winks knowingly at pop culture and LEGO fandom, so that I have to believe that the movie's creators were deliberately playing around with conflicting popular conceptions of creativity: creativity as *madness*, creativity as *thinking outside the box*, and creativity as *vision*.

Quite a lot of philosophical writing focuses on the experience of being creative as a kind of madness. The imagery is violent: we are seized by the Muse, or possessed by the Gods. The artist becomes a passive conduit as the madness works through him to produce something wholly novel.

In the Platonic dialogue *Ion*, Socrates likens the creativity of lyric poets, or rhapsodes, to divine possession or madness. When rhapsodes perform in front of an audience, the breath of the gods literally inspires ("breathes into") the poets so that they become a conduit for the brilliance of the Muse.[3] Centuries later, Kant argues that creativity resides in the free play of the imagination, consisting of the capacity to produce wholly original ideas. Yet, according to Kant, creativity remains mysterious to even the creative genius.[4] Likewise, Coleridge's preface to *Kubla Khan* describes creativity as coming unbidden to an artist, possessing him, and leaving him bewildered, as if coming down from a drug high, marveling at the work he has created.

In *The LEGO Movie*, the Master Builders depict the *madness* model of creativity, represented as unfettered recombination. The Master Builders work to thwart the nefarious President Business, who plans to fix all of the worlds of the LEGO universe in place with the Kragle (Krazy Glue) so that they may never again be taken apart and recombined to make new things. President Business is the bad guy; he stifles creativity because he wishes to have all of his LEGO worlds neat and tidy. Pirates sail on the ocean; citizens stay in the cityscape; the Old West never need fear an invasion by laser guns and spaceships.

The creations of the Master Builders transcend mere instructions. In psychedelic Cloud Cuckoo Land, Unikitty builds mad rainbow-colored creations and insists that there are no rules (or consistency!). The heroine Wyldstyle repeatedly saves the day by constructing elaborate vehicles out of spare parts on the fly; the movie visualizes her as seeing the exact pieces she needs in piles of discarded city bricks meant to represent junk. She is an inspired genius, and when she exhorts the citizens of Bricksburg to rebel against President Business's plan, they do so with whatever bricks they have at hand. We next see a plucky citizen attempting to insert a croissant into a steering wheel.

The second conception of creativity developed in *The LEGO Movie* lies with the hero Emmet, who in the early scenes devotedly follows not just instructions for building but all rules. He is a conformist. Yet the movie also suggests that the roots of creativity lie in the simple act of *thinking outside the box*. Emmet is an oddball, the Special with nothing special about him. Emmet's first original creation is a double-decker couch, roundly mocked by his new Master Builder friends because it does nothing more than fill a much-needed gap in conceptual space. Emmet thought outside the box, but *badly*. Emmet is redeemed, however. Not only does his double-decker couch, which floats, rescue his friends from the destruction of Cloud Cuckoo Land, but he eventually manages to save the day not by designing a new spaceship but by building an ordinary Octan corporation transport. His most creative moment lies not in the development of something new but in recognizing that building an ordinary ship according to the instructions is the last thing that their enemies will expect. He uses the ship design creatively, even though it is not itself a creative design.

If these were the only conceptions of creativity open to us, then clearly LEGO's claim to creativity would be nothing more than clever marketing. Madness has no aim, yet to develop one's own creation, whether it is something as simple as a DUPLO pie, as unimaginative as a double-decker couch, or as complex as Richter's Sitting Bull, with 1.75 million pieces, requires having a goal in mind, and some idea of how to accomplish it. The builder will adapt her plans as she works through the challenges that arise as she builds, of course; no plan completely survives first contact with the studs. But she will not be astonished or mystified at what she has produced. Moreover, merely *thinking outside the box* would not be sufficient reason to bother with LEGO, because the creativity demonstrated by Emmet in *using* his creations is completely divorced from the utter conformity he exhibits in *building* his creations.

Fortunately, the madness model has been challenged by psychologists and philosophers who have a more workmanlike focus on creativity. Even in ancient Greece, the philosopher Aristotle argued against his teacher Plato that poets did indeed possess a skilled art, and were not merely the subjects of divine whims. According to Aristotle, the poets have the skill to produce rhythmic and rhymed verse directly calculated to provide catharsis of negative emotions. It may sound obvious, but Aristotle's point is that provoking catharsis is an identifiable, repeatable process. It can be taught; it can be mastered. So much for waiting for divine inspiration![5]

Much more recently, the psychologist Robert Weisburg goes so far as to call the creative genius a myth. No genius is born; all are fired in the crucible of hard work. Simon Blackburn quotes with approval Thomas Edison's quip that genius is 1 percent inspiration and 99 percent perspiration, as well as Thomas Huxley's wry remark concerning Darwin's brilliant theory of evolution: "how extremely stupid not to have thought of that."[6] Scientists and engineers can be creative, but their genius sometimes lies in nothing more than having done the work necessary to be able to see the path for which everyone else is searching. Even Coleridge himself wrote drafts of *Kubla Khan*, and drew his inspiration from books that he read rather than the drugs he consumed. His preface is nothing more than conscious self-posturing, to advance the myth of the genius at the expense of the truth.[7] Creativity lies not in madness but in extraordinary *vision*.

In *The LEGO Movie*, the vision model of creativity is represented by Finn's father. Toward the end of the movie, we learn that Emmet's adventures are the work of the imagination of eight-year-old Finn, who is furtively playing with his dad's LEGO creations, immense vistas that correspond to the vibrant LEGO worlds visited by Emmet.

The movie implies that his uptight dad, who wears a coat and tie that eerily match those of the evil President Business, should recover his spirit of creativity and play by breaking down his meticulous yet static vistas and permitting Finn's free-for-all LEGO construction.

It's tempting to interpret the movie as implying that Finn's father isn't creative at all, merely following instructions, and that his future redemption lies in committing to unfettered recombination. Yet that's too quick.[8] The elaborate vistas, arguably consisting of millions of bricks, lie far beyond even the most expensive and intricate LEGO kits. No set of instructions could have guided Finn's father as he painstakingly constructed the roiling ocean in Pirate world. If you were to encounter one of these displays at Brickfest or Brickfair, you would never think: what a waste! If only he'd had the vision to put a croissant on a steering wheel!

The movie criticizes Finn's father, in other words, not for his lack of creativity but for the lack of joy and spontaneity in his creations. He wants to glue the bricks so they can never be enjoyed as building blocks again. Some philosophers have argued that even if we set aside the madness model, any theory of authentic creativity must account for the subjective experience of being creative.[9] Being creative does not feel like running mechanically through a series of algorithms; it feels like flying without a net, dangerous and thrilling and pregnant with expectation. All creative experiences share this feeling, for it is this feeling that separates working through a problem mechanically, as a computer might, and working through a problem as a fully creative being.

We might think that the subjective experience of creativity requires the cessation of conscious thought. Like Emmet, we must empty our minds if we are to become truly creative. Yet when solving a scientific or engineering problem, or even constructing an intricate LEGO display, we cannot afford the luxury of emptying our conscious minds.

Fortunately for science and LEGO, recent research indicates that the subjective experience of creativity does not require our conscious mind to be disconnected or idle. When guitarists are asked to engage their conscious minds by counting while they simultaneously are instructed to improvise a jazz composition, their creations are judged to be more creative than those of guitarists who were simply asked to improvise without also engaging their conscious minds. Artists who are instructed to count the occurrences of the word "time" in songs that they listen to while sketching produce drawings that are judged to be more creative than those who had no additional cognitive load. We do not need to empty our conscious minds in order to be creative, but instead, we need our conscious minds to be focused.[10]

This tantalizingly suggests that states of creativity bear striking similarities to flow states, intense states of concentration in which time seems to slow or stop. A baseball player in a flow state might experience the baseball as moving slowly and growing to the size of a pancake. For a brief flicker, he feels invincible; he knows that no matter the curve of the pitch, the ball will soar over the center field wall. In a flow state, we become like the master butcher Cook Ding from Daoist tales. Ding's skill at carving oxen is so great that he has never had to sharpen his knife, because he expertly slides his knife into the hollows at the joints. Yet at difficult points, Ding describes himself as focused, sizing up the situation, and proceeding carefully.[11]

According to the psychologist Mihaly Csikszentmihalyi, we may find these flow states anywhere, but particularly in areas where we meet a highly difficult challenge with a high level of skill. We do not reliably achieve a flow state by disengaging our minds, but by engaging them so fully that we become fully absorbed in the task at hand. It is pure concentration, not pure dissociation; we can think of it as concentrating so deeply that we lose even the feeling that we are consciously concentrating. In those moments, we may become truly creative.

Resolving the Paradox

Viewed in this light, a LEGO builder encountering a thorny design problem might well enter a state of flow as she works through the possible configurations of bricks. Suppose she wants to avoid having any studs on top so that viewers of her creation see only flat surfaces. To do so will require the clever usage of specialized pieces originally designed for other purposes. She will need to call on her experience with LEGO pieces, her ability to visualize the internal layout of her creation, and her knowledge of how best to achieve the overall effect. It is no surprise that many adult fans of LEGO find working through these problems to be relaxing, as they bask in the afterglow of a flow state.

Yet our LEGO builder will not be able to solve the problem if she lacks the experience with the fundamentals. In *LEGO: A Love Story*, Jonathan Bender recounts the first fumbling steps when he returns to constructing LEGO creations after some time away. Techniques that seem obvious to experienced builders baffle him. Because he has not regained his familiarity with the fundamentals, he cannot yet see the path to the problems he has set for himself.

The LEGO Movie's competing conceptions of creativity can be thus construed not as adversaries but as stages in the development of a creative builder. Everyone starts like Emmet, building from instructions and making small, novel modifications. As they become more skilled, they develop the vision, like Finn's father, to attempt larger, more complex projects: a cityscape, a mosaic portrait, a 100-stud-long spaceship (spaceship! Spaceship!). The true joy of LEGO, however, lies in following Wyldstyle and Unikitty, and building freely.

And so the resolution of the paradox snaps into place like a tiny LEGO windshield. Our initial error was to think that being creative meant having no idea of the purpose of our actions, building double-decker couches in the air, but we can see now that creativity also requires intense thoughtfulness, manipulating the resources at hand. Creativity lies in the joy of the mastery of the process.

To master the process, however, requires practice. What better way to practice than to learn how all of the little pieces fit together, building a database of moves that can be retrieved later? What better way to motivate someone to build that database than by providing them with a set of instructions that promises to result in a really cool spaceship? Following the instructions is as necessary in the initial stages of promoting creative construction as is doing basic math problems to the development of fractal geometry, or as practicing études is to the concert violinist.

Return to the playroom. My son is building a new LEGO creation. He soon informs me that he is making a DUPLO pot, so that he can cook some soup, which will undoubtedly require simmering tasty DUPLOs until they are tender. His tongue pokes out again as he loses himself in the flow, as he constructs his pot, and himself, brick by brick.

Notes

1. Margaret A. Boden is credited with this distinction. She calls what I've termed "creativity" "P-creativity," for "psychologically creative," which she contrasts with "historical creativity (H-creativity)," which results in something "new to the whole of human thought." See Margaret A. Boden, "Creativity and Artificial Intelligence: A Contradiction in Terms?" in Elliot Paul and Scott Barry Kaufman, eds., *The Philosophy of Creativity* (Oxford: Oxford University Press, 2014), 224–46.

2. See Jonathan Bender, *LEGO: A Love Story* (Hoboken: Wiley, 2010), 61.
3. See Plato, *Ion*, trans. Paul Woodruff, in *Plato: Complete Works*, ed. John Cooper (Indianapolis: Hackett, 1997), 937–49.
4. Kant's great work *The Critique of Judgment* (1790) discusses aesthetics and art at length, but a more accessible discussion of Kant and some of his insights can be found in Dustin Stokes, "The Role of Imagination in Creativity," in Elliot Paul and Scott Barry Kaufman, eds., *The Philosophy of Creativity* (Oxford: Oxford University Press, 2014), 157–84.
5. Christopher Shields provides an insightful discussion of Aristotle's *Poetics* in Chapter 10 of his *Aristotle* (New York: Routledge, 2007), 375–97.
6. Quoted in Blackburn, Simon, "Creativity and Not-So-Dumb Luck," in Elliot Paul and Scott Barry Kaufman, eds., *The Philosophy of Creativity* (Oxford: Oxford University Press, 2014), 157–84.
7. Ibid., 152–3.
8. After all, the adult fans of LEGO watching the film probably have a lot in common with Finn's father!
9. See Bence Nanay, "An Experiential Account of Creativity," in Elliot Paul and Scott Barry Kaufman, eds., *The Philosophy of Creativity* (Oxford: Oxford University Press, 2014), 17–38.
10. See Roy F. Baumeister et al., "Creativity and Consciousness: Evidence from Psychology Experiments," in Elliot Paul and Scott Barry Kaufman, eds., *The Philosophy of Creativity* (Oxford: Oxford University Press, 2014), 185–99.
11. Chuang-tzû, *The Inner Chapters*, trans. A.C. Graham (Indianapolis: Hackett, 2001), 63–4.

Building Blocks of Thought
LEGO® and the Philosophy of Play

Tyler Shores

> So now you see what I meant about Lego blocks. They have more or less the same properties as those which Democritus ascribed to atoms. And that is what makes them so much fun to build with. They are first and foremost indivisible. They have different shapes and sizes … These connections can later be broken again so that new figures can be constructed from the same blocks.[1]

When Sophie, the precocious fourteen-year-old protagonist of *Sophie's World*, begins her study of philosophy with LEGO®, we glimpse what LEGO can inspire:

> The best thing about them was that with Lego she could construct any kind of object. And then she could separate the blocks and construct something new … Sophie decided that Lego really could be called the most ingenious toy in the world. But what it had to do with philosophy was beyond her.[2]

Part of the ingenious quality of LEGO is that it is a system of play, fundamentally based on interconnecting sets of parts and open-endedness. As building blocks they are "abstractions of reality in a more comprehensible, miniature form" and LEGO as a system of play is "another level removed. In their unbuilt form they are ideas for ideas of things."[3]

We might even think of LEGO as a medium through which ideas can be expressed.[4] Much like philosophy, LEGO encourages us not only to look at the pieces, but also to examine relationships, patterns,

LEGO® and Philosophy: Constructing Reality Brick By Brick, First Edition.
Edited by Roy T. Cook and Sondra Bacharach.
© 2017 John Wiley & Sons Ltd. Published 2017 by John Wiley & Sons Ltd.

and underlying structures. While philosophy is made of thoughts and ideas that ultimately form the building blocks of our own worldviews and sense of self, LEGO helps to remind us of the importance of just how fun this kind of thoughtful play can be, too.

LEGO as a Thing You Think With

One of the defining characteristics of LEGO identified by Godtfred Kirk Christiansen was: "the more LEGO, the greater the value"— which serves as a useful metaphor for our own building of thoughts and knowledge. In fact, the unique properties of LEGO can provide a model for our ideas as conceptual building blocks that we piece together: "like the LEGO constructions, the conceptual ones, too, may be occasionally disassembled and turned into alternative constructions. This betokens the tremendous potential for change in our knowledge."[5]

We might consider LEGO as what Sherry Turkle calls "objects to think with."[6] It's often difficult to think about things we can't express. This is part of the premise of Serious Play®, a unique LEGO-based methodology that meets the needs of the corporate business world through use of LEGO bricks as a tool for thinking. The elegance of the LEGO system lies in how it can serve as a common language of hands-on thinking and physical representation of even abstract ideas:

> [LEGO] suggest[s] a human dimension which is not contained in the bricks themselves, with notions such as 'imagination', 'classic' and 'fun'. Inevitably, of course, the system is not just about objects but about what humans *do* with the objects.[7]

It's also no coincidence that the word "LEGO" is itself a combination of the Danish words "*leg*" and "*godt*," meaning "play well," although more coincidental is the fact that it is also the Latin word for "I put together." If LEGO has succeeded in making work more play-like, perhaps philosophers have in some cases sought to define play as more work-like.

Philosophy as Serious Play

In his *Republic*, Plato (427–347 BCE) treats the notion of play with no small amount of caution. The kinds of play that children engage in, according to Plato, have an important influence on the adults they become, and therefore on society—so play must be closely regulated. In other words, for Plato, play was serious business. Nonetheless, Plato's dialogues are filled with Socrates's singular type of "playful amusement,"[8] a sportive process involving philosophical questions and inversions: "Every man and woman should spend life in this way, playing the noblest possible games, and thinking about them in a way that is the opposite of the way they're now thought about."[9]

In Plato's philosophy, play served many functions: "play can be a childish game, an educational tool, or a metaphor for philosophical activity."[10] Rather than simply a game that can be won or lost, play is an important mindset, "a constant self-awareness, and a recognition of the provisionality of all philosophical claims. To approach philosophy dogmatically is to approach it with an inappropriate and excessive kind of seriousness—a grim or humorless attitude that precludes true learning."[11] An awareness of our humble limitations as philosophers can sometimes instill an optimistic, flexible outlook toward the pursuit of wisdom. More importantly, play and seriousness in philosophy needn't be mutually exclusive. Indeed, it is more helpful to think of philosophy as "serious play."[12]

There are also times when play is not playful, as seen in *The LEGO Movie*. Think of how Lord Business/The Man Upstairs plans to use that weaponized superglue, the Kragle, to freeze everything into his version of seeming perfection. In this instance, the Kragle is a reminder of what happens when play is taken *too* seriously: play becomes inert, lifeless. A binary opposition between play and seriousness is not helpful, implying more of an absolute division between the two than there really is. What happens when play becomes too work-like? The Irish playwright George Bernard Shaw (1856–1955) once noted: "We don't stop playing because we grow old, we grow old because we stop playing." Must play have a purpose? Perhaps play is simply its own purpose—we play because it's fun.

In one of the most well-known discussions of the central importance of play, *Homo Ludens* ("Man The Player"), historian Johan Huizinga (1872–1945) observes that play is "in fact an integral part of life in general. It adorns life, amplifies it and is to that extent a necessity both for the individual—as a life function—and for society."[13] To separate play and seriousness absolutely is to lose the enjoyment from what we think of as our work—that work becomes simply the absence of play, and play becomes no more than a brief escape from work. Likewise, to separate play from work is to miss out on the interstices, the little moments of playful thinking that can make life worth living.

There can be something profoundly generative and inventive about playful thinking. Play, like philosophy itself, is fundamentally about seeking alternatives, new ways of looking at something:

> While philosophers are not normally thought of as either childlike or playful, in fact the practice of philosophizing comes down to reconstructing deep historical constructs of meaning. It is innovative in the profoundest sense. Philosophy is not just a professional occupation but also an activity of being human.[14]

The psychologist Brian Sutton-Smith suggests, "that play is like language: a system of communication and expression, not in itself either good or bad."[15] Sometimes the best kind of philosophy comes from a certain approach of playfulness. *Does this thing have to be this way? Why this way, and not some other way?* And sometimes playful thinking means taking seriously the things that no one else would think to— as well as not taking seriously the things that everyone else would.

LEGO and Forms of Play

The Ancient Greek concepts of play (*paidia*) and education (*paideia*) were closely intertwined, and the English philosopher John Locke (1632–1704) was an early proponent of the possibility of play and learning not being mutually exclusive. Locke in this way demonstrated insights into the inner workings of human nature: a fundamental part of play is freedom, and what is imposed upon learners as a chore might instead be something freely sought and explored for its own sake.[16] A century later, Jean-Jacques Rousseau (1712–1778) would advocate for a kind of spontaneous free play for children as part of their formal and social learning, although within structured conditions. In that sense, play and learning are entangled in a positive sense: "as children, we learn how to interact with the world through playing."[17]

In fact, with its emphasis on the inherent value of creative free play, LEGO is connected to learning and education as perhaps no other toy company in the world. LEGO Education's global efforts have included the "LEGO School" in Billund, Denmark, a scientific research lab at MIT (the origins of LEGO Mindstorms® can be traced to MIT Media Lab in 1998), as well as a LEGO Professor of Play at the University of Cambridge. A prevailing theme in present-day educational philosophy is the study of how play is closely interwoven with our learning process; play is both a means to an end and an end in itself. The words of Mr. Rogers seem especially relevant: "Play is often talked about as if it were a relief from serious learning. But for children, play is serious learning."[18]

Play is a form of learning, and when we engage with play in its various forms, we push against the boundaries of the possible. We might think of creativity as being defined first and foremost by curiosity—creativity is also about asking the right kinds of questions. Creativity can sometimes mean not fixating on the one "right" answer to our questions but instead engaging with our imaginations to think laterally and from different angles and approaches. Sometimes the most important questions in life have no one answer, after all.

Creativity also means different kinds of play, including LEGO free-building, creating something new from nothing. In the memories of some longtime LEGO builders, it's interesting to note that even following instructions in a playset can become a compelling kind of constrained creativity in its own right:

> What excited me most was following the instructions. I loved watching how many small and simple steps resulted in a single beautiful and complicated piece. I found it thrilling that I could take the instructions—simple pieces of paper—and figure out what they were telling me to do.[19]

With instructions, or without, there is no single way to go about LEGO building. The same can be said of philosophical thinking. Curiosity inspires us to ask *"why?"* whereas playfulness moves us to wonder *"what if"*? Both LEGO and philosophy enliven our inner worlds by instilling a kind of structured free play through which we come to learn new ideas by trial and error, and new ways of looking at familiar things—and sometimes the mistakes we make along the way are when we learn the most.

In a related way, some fascinating recent research has suggested that free-building with LEGO leads to more creative thinking than following the instructions found in LEGO sets.[20] Of course, creative play can take on many forms: perhaps as the creation and recreation of experimentation; the systematic planning of breaking things down into their components and then creating something anew; or the free play of ideas by dreaming up connections in completely new and different ways. (Speaking of LEGO creativity, did you know that the first Google server rack was built out of LEGO bricks? LEGO represented a relatively inexpensive, heat-resistant and endlessly reconfigurable solution, and was thus the perfect tech geek life hack.[21])

The different forms of LEGO also encourage different kinds of play. Nowadays, themed and specialized LEGO playsets far outnumber the more free-form building oriented sets we might see on store shelves. Everything from the themed (and totally awesome) LEGO Space and LEGO City to extensions of the imaginary franchise universes of Star Wars®, Harry Potter®, and *The Simpsons*® suggest a kind of play experience where purely imagination-driven building becomes secondary to the kinds of storytelling and narrative play that LEGO playsets encourage.

Narrative is not only an essential component of play, but also a vital way in which we structure our thoughts. We make sense of so many things through stories (either real or imagined), which Sigmund Freud (1856–1939) observed as a type of play:

> Might we not say that every child at play behaves like a creative writer, in that he creates a world of his own, or, rather, rearranges the things of his world in a new way which pleases him? It would be wrong to think he does not take that world seriously; on the contrary, he takes his play very seriously and he expends large amounts of emotion on it. The opposite of play is not what is serious but what is real.[22]

A LEGO builder remembers her childhood experience of themed playsets compared to free building: "I didn't understand their appeal because you could make only one object with each kit, with only minor possible variations ... I did not enjoy playing with the finished product." For that builder, the nature of play was derived from the "heart of the analytical attitude I developed toward building." "Unlike my sister, I did not immerse myself in fantasy. I stayed on the outside."[23]

On the one hand, we can view the playset, narrative-driven kinds of play as a limitation on imaginative play. On the other hand, we can imagine play-as-narrative as a different sort of play within boundaries—the narrative structure of playsets can provide a sort of structure to our imaginative play. This is what Seth Giddings describes as the difference between "imagining how the bricks can be connected to solve it" and "LEGO's potential for the exercise of symbolic or performative imagination." "Children building towns or worlds through which to tell their own stories and invent their own characters would epitomize this preferred style of play."[24] But definitions of play in themselves are tricky to place within absolute categories, and one kind of play doesn't preclude the other. Just as boundaries or constraints do not necessarily hinder creativity, the same can be said of play.

We might compare the different kinds of play experience between, for example, LEGO Star Wars: The Video Game and the 3,803-piece LEGO Death Star (set #10188). Kevin Schut makes the case that the shift toward video game LEGO is a quite different kind of play, and different kinds of play result in different kinds of pleasure:

> But of course, restrictions are a fact of existence, and can even be pleasurable. When a puzzle or challenge in a video game cannot be re-imagined or wished away, it has a kind of solidity that makes conquest of it deeply satisfying. So there is a kind of trade-off here: in virtual form, LEGO becomes less of a free-form open toy, and more of a rigid, goal-directed item.[25]

These different kinds of play—LEGO playset building compared to LEGO video game playing—can be thought of as what the sociologist Roger Caillois calls *ludus* (more structured, goal-oriented play) and *paidia* (exuberant, spontaneous free play).[26] Not to mention the fact that the LEGO video game genre is best characterized as a puzzle and action-mode game, with a goal-oriented and linear narrative structure. It's also interesting to note how in addition to puzzle solving and LEGO building, the main game tasks alternate between building LEGO structures in order to advance levels, and destroying other LEGO structures that explode into a shower of LEGO studs (the in-game currency). This provides an opportunity to think about how different media influence our experience of play, noting how the "manual labor of assembling and disassembling bricks, so crucial to how most people play with the toy, is nothing like the video game action of simply pressing a button a few times or pressing and holding one."[27] As further evidence that LEGO is an interconnected play ecosystem, where everything truly does connect with everything else, consider that we can sometimes buy the plastic playset versions of what we digitally play with in LEGO video games.

All of this is of course a roundabout way of saying that our defining experience of LEGO is one of *fun*. Fun can be the happiness that LEGO inspires during the process of building with bricks—where that happiness might be due to the tangible quality of playing with LEGO that engages our senses, from the sound of rummaging through a pile of LEGO (an "incredibly evocative sound. This is the noise of a child's mind working, looking for the right piece"[28]) to the feel of using our teeth to pull apart LEGO bricks. As the LEGO Group perfectly describes it:

> Fun is the happiness we experience when we are fully engaged in something (hard fun) that requires mastery, when our abilities are in balance with the challenge at hand and we are making progress towards a goal.[29]

Likewise, when we are fully engaged in *doing* philosophy, it changes our mindset and how we look at the world and our sense of self. There's a truly unique kind of joy that comes from discovering connections between ideas that you never knew existed.

LEGO as a Metaphor for Philosophy

LEGO in many ways serves as a helpful analogy for how philosophical thinking can lead us toward new connections between our thoughts and ideas. LEGO and philosophy invite us to question the nature of play. When we think about it, LEGO is a fundamentally optimistic medium—with an ethos built on the notion that anything can be built, and that true meaning and inspiration comes from freedom and flexibility of thinking, as well as the meaningful engagement with LEGO and with thoughts and ideas. In this sense we intuitively understand how "building begets a love of building."[30]

As Jason Mittell aptly describes it, what we need in thinking about LEGO as well as philosophy is "fluidity and flexibility, the ability to put unlikely pieces together while also being able to dismantle and reconfigure what has already been done."[31] We can see this as an invitation for ourselves to bring a little bit of play into our thinking, and bring philosophy into play, or play into philosophy.

Notes

1. Jostein Gaarder, *Sophie's World: A Novel About the History of Philosophy*, trans. Paulette Møller (New York: Farrar, Straus and Giroux, 1994), 42.
2. Ibid., 42.
3. Norman Brosterman, "Potential Architecture: An Infinity of Buildings," in *Potential Architecture: Construction Toys from the CCA Collection* (Montreal, Canada: Centre Canadien d'Architecture, 1991), 7–14.

4.   Mark J.P. Wolf, "Prolegomena," in Mark J.P. Wolf, ed., *LEGO Studies: Examining The Building Blocks of a Transmedial Phenomenon* (New York: Routledge, 2014), xxii.
5.   Arie Kruglanski, *Lay Epistemics and Human Knowledge: Cognitive and Motivational Bases* (New York: Springer Science and Business Media, 1989), 11.
6.   Sherry Turkle, *Evocative Objects: Things We Think With* (Cambridge, MA: MIT Press, 2007).
7.   David Gauntlett, "The LEGO System as a Tool for Thinking, Creativity, and Changing the World," in Mark J.P. Wolf, ed., *LEGO Studies*, 189–205.
8.   Plato, *Plato: Complete Works*, ed. John M. Cooper (Indianapolis: Hackett, 1997), 554.
9.   Plato, *The Laws of Plato*, trans. Thomas Prangle (Chicago: University of Chicago Press, 1980), 207.
10. Kathryn Morgan, *Myth and Philosophy from the Presocratics to Plato* (Cambridge: Cambridge University Press, 2004), 168.
11. Daniel S. Werner, *Myth and Philosophy in Plato's Phaedrus* (Cambridge: Cambridge University Press, 2012), 224.
12. Armand D'Angour, "Plato and Play: Taking Education Seriously in Ancient Greece." *American Journal of Play* 5/3 (2013): 293–307.
13. Johan Huizinga, *Homo Ludens* (London: Routledge, 1980).
14. John Wall, "All the World's a Stage: Childhood and the Play of Being," in Emily Ryall, Wendy Russell, and Malcolm MacLean, eds., *The Philosophy of Play* (New York: Routledge, 2013), 40.
15. Brian Sutton-Smith, *The Ambiguity of Play* (Cambridge, MA: Harvard University Press, 2009), 219.
16. John Locke and James Axtell, *The Educational Writings of John Locke: A Critical Edition with Introduction and Notes.* Cambridge: Cambridge University Press, 1968).
17. Barry Dixon, "Gadamer and the Game of Dialectic in Plato's *Gorgias*," in Emily Ryall, Wendy Russell, and Malcolm MacLean, eds., *The Philosophy of Play* (New York: Routledge, 2013), 64.
18. Heidi Moore, "Why Play is the Work of Childhood." Fred Rogers Center, September 23, 2014. Available at http://www.fredrogerscenter.org/2014/09/23/why-play-is-the-work-of-childhood/ (accessed February 23, 2017).
19. Scott Brave, "LEGO Planning," in Sherry Turkle, ed., *Falling for Science: Objects in Mind* (Cambridge MA: MIT Press, 2008), 159.
20. Garth Sundem, "Building With LEGO Kit Instructions Makes Kids Less Creative." *Psychology Today*, June 16, 2015. Available at https://www.psychologytoday.com/blog/brain-candy/201506/building-lego-kit-instructions-makes-kids-less-creative (accessed December 7, 2015).

21. The center of the internet universe as we know it now began as ten 4GB hard drives, held together by LEGO bricks. See http://news.stanford.edu/news/2011/april/google-stanford-ties-042811.html (accessed August 18, 2016)

22. Sigmund Freud, "Creative Writers and Day-Dreaming," in Peter Gay, ed., *The Freud Reader* (New York: Norton, 1989), 437.

23. Sandie Eltringham, "LEGO Metrics," in Sherry Turkle, ed., *Falling for Science: Objects in Mind* (Cambridge, MA: MIT Press, 2008), 150–1.

24. Seth Giddings, "Bright Bricks, Dark Play: On The Impossibility of Studying LEGO," in Mark Wolf, ed., *LEGO Studies: Examining the Building Blocks of a Transmedial Phenomenon* (New York: Routledge, 2014), 252.

25. Kevin Schut, "The Virtualization of LEGO," in Mark Wolf, ed., *LEGO Studies: Examining the Building Blocks of a Transmedial Phenomenon* (New York: Routledge, 2014), 236.

26. Roger Caillois, *Man, Play, and Games*, trans. Meyer Barash (Urbana: University of Illinois Press, 1961).

27. Kevin Schut, "The Virtualization of LEGO," 235.

28. Seth Giddings, "Bright Bricks, Dark Play," 256.

29. The LEGO Brand. Available at http://www.lego.com/en-gb/aboutus/lego-group/the_lego_brand (accessed June 3, 2015).

30. Sherry Turkle, *Falling for Science: Objects in Mind*, 14.

31. Jason Mittell, "Afterword: D.I.Y. Disciplinarity—(Dis)Assembling LEGO Studies for the Academy," in Mark Wolf, ed. *LEGO Studies: Examining the Building Blocks of a Transmedial Phenomenon* (New York: Routledge, 2014), 272.

3
LEGO® Formalism in Architecture

Saul Fisher

My LEGO® is not your LEGO. I say this not in any supercilious purist way, but simply in the historical sense that the LEGO world I inhabit—in the mental space I allot to LEGO and in the box of LEGO that sits in my parents' closet—is of pre-1976 vintage. It is a world of fairly basic shapes and colors, and has no representative human figures (minifigs). There are some trees and bushes, true, and a handful of complex forms like fence work or shutters and mechanical parts like a crane or even a motor (none of which work anymore, except as structural elements). Yet if we strip out those few, assorted special elements, the remaining LEGO world is incredibly simple and archetypal in virtue of capturing the core and traditional aspects of LEGO construction and design. Indeed, that world—which I'll call *original*, and which LEGO refers to as *System i Leg*—merits our attention, telling us about not just LEGO architecture but architecture generally: its objects, its aesthetic properties, and how we judge them.

Three Scenarios

To see how thinking about LEGO can help us with such matters, consider three scenarios, the first two about real-world architecture:

- First, you tell a friend that you visited the *Eiffel Tower* and you realize that, oddly, she has never seen it and has no idea what it looks like. You describe the soaring steel structure and sketch it

LEGO® and Philosophy: Constructing Reality Brick By Brick, First Edition.
Edited by Roy T. Cook and Sondra Bacharach.
© 2017 John Wiley & Sons Ltd. Published 2017 by John Wiley & Sons Ltd.

out on a napkin. It's such an iconic design, you note, that folks think "Eiffel Tower"—and even "France"—no matter where they see anything like that shape or form. That would be true even of a shoddy replica built in your local park.

- Second, your friend now tells you about a special house by Frank Lloyd Wright where the building responds aesthetically to, and is integrated in, its surrounding environment. That sounds like *Fallingwater*, you say, where Wright designed the structure to look of a piece with the nature around it, suspended over a waterfall. The structure and environment seem so mutually responsive in their aesthetic natures, you and your friend agree, that it's hard to think of that building placed anywhere else.

- Third, you and your friend build a group of houses using only "original LEGO world" elements.[1] *You* look at your collaborative architectural creations and pronounce them as great models for houses that could be built anywhere. *Your friend*, however, claims to have imagined them specifically as built on the Greek island of Mykonos. You shake your head and protest that they would work equally well as houses in Milwaukee. Indeed, you continue, what era we built them in doesn't matter, nor the ways imagined people—or, in contemporary LEGO worlds, minifigs—might use the houses. What gives these houses their unique aesthetic identity is their design and the forms of the LEGO elements we used.

These scenarios illustrate two very different ways of thinking about architecture. On the one hand, we might think architectural objects (more commonly, "works of architecture"), like buildings, bridges, and aqueducts, have forms that stand on their own, and which thereby don't depend on historical, environmental, or any other contexts. We don't need to understand their contexts, in short, to create, visualize, or judge the architectural objects or their features. That seems like it might be true in the *Eiffel Tower* case. On the other hand, we might think that architectural objects are best understood (maybe *only* understood) if we have one or more kinds of contextual information, as in the *Fallingwater* case. The former view is some-times spurned in architectural circles, on the grounds that we pay great practical penalties by ignoring contextual information—such as environmental fit—when we put up buildings for real people to use in different environments. That said, a long line of architects from the twentieth century on deploy similar designs in many different contexts.

This is where the third case—houses built with original LEGO world elements—is of interest. Your friend is convinced that those houses are inspired by, or best suit, a specific Greek island setting, and it would be pointless to question her reported inspiration or imaginative conception. Yet your thought—that the location or other contextual factors do not matter to the aesthetic identity of the homes—if true, seems to undermine your friend's claim. For if we could imagine those LEGO structures as built *anywhere*, then the fact that your friend imagines them in Mykonos is a colorful, charming vision but not one that fixes the nature or identity of those houses. Two questions arise, then: whether it *is* true that structures we design with original LEGO world elements sustain the same aesthetic identities though we imagine them as located in varied contexts, and what that might entail for architecture in LEGO worlds or the real world.

LEGO and Formalism

To answer the first question, it's helpful to consider what we might mean by the aesthetic nature or identity of an architectural structure (LEGO or otherwise). A simple answer is that we mean whatever makes the structure distinctive or unique, relative to typical aesthetic properties like being beautiful, sublime, compelling, vibrant, and so on. These are the sorts of properties we associate with evaluation of architectural objects, their elements, or our experiences of them—much as with artworks more broadly, or as with anything we appreciate aesthetically.

So, your friend's context-bound view of aesthetic identity says that something about their context—perhaps their location—shapes the aesthetic nature or identity of our LEGO houses, as with *Fallingwater*. You take an opposing tack, suggesting that it's rather a set of internal, non-contextual properties—generally fundamental, standard, and quantifiable—of those LEGO houses or the *Eiffel Tower* that yields their aesthetic *properties*, and so determines those objects' aesthetic *identities*.

You are espousing, broadly, a version of *formalism*, a view that says aesthetic properties of an object arise from its formal properties. For example, color, shape, or organization, yield unity, symmetry, or balance. Formalism typically suggests that our experience and assessment of those properties *justifies* the aesthetic judgments we make about architecture. While formalism comes in many varieties,

I'll suggest a general version, pertaining to the original LEGO world of basic bricks and other architectural, non-figurative elements (pre-1976 designs), which accounts for how we identify and evaluate aesthetically its architectural creations (as opposed to, for example, its sculptural creations).

First, though, let's get a better idea as to why anyone might be a formalist in speaking of architecture of any kind, whether real world or LEGO world. So far, we have suggested that we might not need to take into account contextual information to understand architectural objects. As motivation goes, this would only provide us with a negative spur to formalism. For *positive* motivation, proponents of formalism take note of what makes architectural objects distinctive. Unlike objects of other artforms such as drawing or sculpture, architectural objects are not *representative*; they do not usually represent other things in the world. (One sort of exception are objects like *The Big Duck* of Flanders.[2]) Accordingly, we cannot judge them aesthetically in terms of how they relate to external reality, yet we can appreciate them aesthetically in terms of internal features. In addition, formalists highlight the key role of operations on forms, and relations among forms, in architecture. The architectural design enterprise revolves prominently around the manipulation, aggregation, arrangement, and association of constituent forms, in order to constitute greater forms. Formalists take this to indicate that what we primarily think about aesthetically when we think about architecture is its forms, their relations, and their properties.

These last motivations for formalism in architecture should have particular resonance with those who dwell, at least in spirit, in the "original LEGO world." That world, like other (more diverse, complex) LEGO worlds, constitutes a modular system for construction, and comprises forms with basic formal properties that lend themselves to creating larger forms with appreciable aesthetic qualities. Original LEGO elements are standardized, interlocking plastic bricks and other parts that fit together with the bricks. Further, such LEGO elements offer an exemplary uniformity in building forms. Designing or building architectural objects in the original LEGO world, consequently, is an exploration of how those forms are best combined to fashion larger forms constituting whole, independent structures.

Further hallmark features of original (and other) LEGO elements build on their *uniformity* of forms and facilitate—in a special, characteristic way—exploration of combinations into larger forms. One hallmark feature is *versatility*—their capacity for (a) joining with other components and (b) yielding extensive design and deployment possibilities. A second feature is *backwards compatibility* with existing components. A third feature is *ease of disassembly* for reuse—which also guarantees persistence of uniformity among the basic forms. Together, these features contribute to a design experience and universe of built structures where formal operations and relations play a core role in architecture in many LEGO worlds. Such operations and relations include brick stacking, serial concatenation (lining them up), shape composition, boundary definition, and much else. Each such operation or relation is central to designing LEGO architectural structures—whether at the macro-level of designing entire structures, or the creation of component parts of those structures. In this way, pursuit of architectural design for the original LEGO world assumes the hallmark features in each brick to be deployed.

We might well not expect to find beauty in any single brick or other formal element: *that* need not be a hallmark feature at the elemental level. (If we did, we should likely take every brick to be beautiful albeit *not* in its own special way.) But if, in virtue of hallmark features we *have* identified—and the constraints and direction they impose on LEGO design—we find beauty in architecture in the original LEGO world, then it might seem that we arrive at a classic formalism. In short: the nature of beauty in original LEGO world architecture, and our appreciation of it, is greatly or even solely shaped by the basic forms, their hallmark features, and their operations and relations. And the same should hold for other aesthetic properties—for example, balance, or gracefulness—in the original LEGO world.

The case for formalism is not, however, yet made. In the story so far, assembling basic parts of objects with the right sorts of features (e.g., LEGO bricks) results in whole objects (LEGO houses) that have aesthetic properties like beauty. So we may find tempting the idea that those basic forms and their attendant features, conditions, and principles are primary factors determining the nature or appreciation of aesthetic properties in the whole objects. But that story doesn't *guarantee* formalism because it doesn't identify those forms and their features as the *only* things that determine such aesthetic properties.

Looking in another direction, we might be formalists about LEGO architecture in the original LEGO world because of the partial similarity between original LEGO world elements as non-representative and the generally non-representative nature of architectural designs. Perhaps original LEGO world architecture tends to be non-representational because of, or as abetted by, the solidly non-representational nature of original LEGO elements. But that line of thought is a dead end. As the sculptures of Nathan Sawaya and others suggest, the standard, uniform forms of original LEGO elements make them useful for representative, as well as non-representative, possibilities.[3] This much parallels the range of design possibilities for real-world bricks for real-world buildings (which tend to be non-representational). Original LEGO world architecture, in this regard, is no more governed by formalism than is real-world architecture.

From a different angle, some might see formalism as a *better* fit with original LEGO world design than with real-world architectural design. LEGO elements have a generally fixed or non-malleable nature: they can't be bent, curved, or otherwise reshaped without a certain kind of engineering—such as heating to warp—that transgresses the spirit of the original LEGO world (however permissible such methods are in use or practice associated with some LEGO worlds). We are wedded to the edges that the basic elements define.[4] As a consequence, architectural design in the original LEGO world, insofar as it models the real world, is an art of approximation. And to the extent that the promise of fidelity is needed for optimal representation, original LEGO architecture can't aspire to optimal representation but is perfectly suitable as a non-representative medium. At this point, the formalist may insist on a small victory: if architectural objects have representational deficiencies, our appreciation of them best plays to their internal, formal features. Formalism in original LEGO world architecture, on this view, is a byproduct of LEGO architectural objects doing a poor job of representation because of the nature of their constituent elements.

There are, however, at least two problems. First, just because pure, uniform, or standard forms are fundamental to the nature of original LEGO world elements, we cannot land on formalism as the only or best account of aesthetic properties of original LEGO world architectural objects. That requires dismissing competing accounts of how such properties may be constituted. Second, we have not yet made a case for formalist *evaluation*. We might grant that aesthetic properties of original LEGO world architectural objects arise from formal features and yet hold that our aesthetic judgments are not *inescapably* formal in character or origin. For example, we might judge a LEGO built structure—say, a bridge—as bold or brash because it defies our expectations as to how we generally imagine bridges to look or how we generally imagine them to be designed with LEGO. Those prior expectations could be informed by our best understanding of LEGO forms and formal properties but they could also be informed by, say, our general familiarity with bridge structures.[5]

Contextualism, Functional Beauty, and LEGO

Some anti-formalists appeal to the importance of architectural history, styles, and contextual information and propose that, if we don't grasp the relevant contextual background, then we don't have full access to aesthetic properties of built structures. An original LEGO structure composed of all-white bricks might be considered stark or pure if simply considering formal color properties—whereas fuller aesthetic judgment might require familiarity with real-world architecture styles (for example, Le Corbusier, Meier, Mediterranean vernacular), or LEGO element production (for example, the early prominence of red and white bricks, or the post-2013 all-white and translucent LEGO Architecture Studio kit[6]), or the history of built structures in the original or alternate LEGO worlds.

Other anti-formalists appeal to functional beauty theory, suggesting that the aesthetic properties of architectural objects—as with other functional objects, like cutlery or clothes—are gauged in terms of the objects presenting a functional solution.[7] In real-world architectural settings, we might suggest that aesthetic successes or failures of a built structure are connected to the architect's intention to solve a particular problem, like designing housing for a given client or population in a specific location. In a contemporary LEGO world, we might point to built structures functioning to organize the spatial environment for one or another minifig population, and gauge the beauty or other aesthetic properties of the structure accordingly. In these cases, the functional beauty theorist maintains, formal properties alone don't determine the aesthetic properties of the structure or our judgments thereof; broader design features are gauged against the prescribed functional needs and the degree to which those needs are met. We find a LEGO village *delightful*, for example, because it features circulation paths fitting to the functions of its constituent structures, those structures fitting to the basic range of a village's functions, and all at a scale and in styles fitting to one or another concept we have of a well-working village—in contemporary LEGO worlds, as populated by minifigs.

To be sure, neither contextualism nor functional beauty theory is inconsistent with a moderate formalism. The aesthetic judgments we make of a structure in original LEGO world architecture as based on, say, context or function, are triggered because the structure has *forms* particularly fitting to such framing or judgment. The contextualist and functional beauty theorist will protest that, while we might need the forms of our LEGO structure to arrive at such aesthetic judgments, they are not sufficient to producing our delight (for example) in that structure. Conceding the necessity of the forms, though, is a step toward at least a moderate formalism.

Worse still, for these top brands of anti-formalism, is the strengthened case against your friend's initial claim that the aesthetic identity of the LEGO houses was reflective of a Mykonos context. For it turns out that any design in the original LEGO world can be built anywhere at any time for any function or user or, even more compellingly, for none at all. As we have seen, one reason for this broad robustness of possibilities, not anchored to context or functional intention, is the versatility of forms among the elements of the original LEGO world. A second reason is that original (and other) LEGO worlds feature very loose rules of use. In the original LEGO world of buckets of bricks, there are effectively no directions, hence no constraints or shaping influences. If I want to build a *Fallingwater*-like structure in the original LEGO world amid a LEGO model of the Aegean sea or Saharan dunes, no guidelines prevent me—and the structure's aesthetic properties likely arise from, and will be judged by, its forms.

We still might not think, per formalism, that we account for aesthetic properties and judgments in original LEGO world architecture in terms of forms and formal properties of structures built with elements of that world. What we have indicated, after all, is only that the most prominent alternative views do not hold. In the absence of a positive argument, we might opt for an agnostic stance. Yet given the dominant contribution of LEGO forms to aesthetic properties and judgments in original LEGO world architecture, the onus is on the anti-formalist to say in what other ways such properties and judgments might arise. The most likely candidates—for which better cases might be made in other LEGO worlds or perhaps real-world architecture—are not on the table or, in this case, the baseplate.

Other LEGO Worlds and the Real World

Admittedly, I dwell in the world of original LEGO world elements when few others do. The LEGO universe has certainly moved on. Thus, nostalgia aside, we may ask why we should care. We might think the formalism of the original LEGO world is limited to just this one antiquated design world, and worry that it has little broader relevance for architecture overall. I suggest this formalism has significantly broader relevance.

First, the original LEGO world is the base case for all LEGO worlds, at least those that contain a subset of LEGO *System i Leg* elements. Subsequent worlds enhance our overall capacity for representation (more complex forms, moving beyond basic bricks) and for recreating specific real-world structures (model kits), and they enrich narrative possibilities (minifigs). If, however, we remove all these enhancements and create structures in those domains with the limited universe of forms that remains we see a basic LEGO design character common to all such creations. This suggests that the *core* aesthetic properties and judgments we identify in a wide variety of, or perhaps all, such LEGO worlds are best characterized by some version of formalism—even if only a moderate version.

Second, formalism is not limited to original LEGO world architecture but has a counterpart in real-world architectural models. This is unsurprising, as real-world architectural models have a good deal in common with architectural structures in the original LEGO world, regardless of whether those LEGO structures represent real-world architectural objects. Like architectural models, original LEGO world architectural structures often preserve scale (in a given vignette); draw on fixed sets of material elements to create physical instances of designs; highlight, simplify, or abstract elements of designs by physically instancing them; and give us pictures of ("model") a system (here, a built environment system) that afford descriptions or depictions of behaviors of and in the system. Most importantly, and strongly suggestive of formalism, architectural models are like original LEGO world architectural structures in that we can appreciate them outside of context or history—they bear none of the actual architectural functions of the built objects they model.

As for real-world architecture generally, whether this LEGO formalism or anything like it applies depends in part on whether we think of architecture as consisting primarily of built structures, or as consisting primarily of the *ideas* for such built structures. In the latter view, architectural design concepts and their representations (modeled, drawn, or digitally rendered) look importantly similar to original LEGO world architectural structures. In particular, architectural design concepts may be shaped by context, yet subject to routine and trivial transformations. Nor are such concepts unalterably linked to specific functions. These features suggest that, as in the original LEGO world, real-world architecture is marked by at least a moderate formalism. For the proponent of concrete, built structures as the true and unique architectural domain, however, the parallel with structures in original LEGO architecture may be less compelling—and so, too, the case for formalism.

A further possibility is that architectural objects include built objects, corresponding underlying design ideas, *and* (in between) models or representations of those ideas, which may include LEGO architectural structures. Then we could imagine a formalist continuum: forms of real-world architectural objects might play a diminished (but non-negligible) role relative to aesthetic properties or judgments thereof, and forms in the original LEGO world a more prominent such role. In *this* moderate formalist scenario, too, original LEGO world architectural objects exhibit a feature central to—though not uniformly robust in—architecture broadly considered. If so, my LEGO tells us something important about your LEGO, and about architecture overall.

Notes

1. We can define LEGO worlds broadly as environments or narratives (real, virtual, or fantastical) in which we find or create LEGO built structures or diorama-like scenes. There are infinitely many such LEGO worlds but I am concerned instead with LEGO worlds more narrowly defined by the kinds of elements they include. The collection of such LEGO worlds is fairly small, corresponding to the evolution, over time, of LEGO designs and of LEGO traditions, usage, and practice.
2. On *The Big Duck* of Flanders, see Robert Venturi, Denise Scott Brown, and Steven Izenour, *Learning from Las Vegas: The Forgotten Symbolism of Architectural Form,* revised edition (Cambridge, MA: MIT Press, 1972/1977).
3. Nathan Sawaya, *The Art of the Brick: A Life in LEGO* (San Francisco: No Starch Press, 2015).
4. LEGO designers are endlessly inventive in response to this challenge; see Didier Enjary, *The Unofficial LEGO Advanced Building Techniques Guide.,* available at http://photos.freelug.org/main.php?g2_view=core .DownloadItem&g2_itemId=33732 (accessed February 23, 2017).
5. Consider another sort of case, where LEGO structures represent real-world structures, as models of, for example, the White House or the Roman Coliseum. These structures prompt historical or other contextually determined aesthetic judgments, at least partly independent of

formal properties of those structures. But use of LEGO in models representative of real-world architecture is a special case of original LEGO world architecture and doesn't speak to the broader realm of free play in non-representative, original designs.

6. In addition to the all-white-and-transparent Architecture Studio set, LEGO Architecture kits allow construction of models of iconic architectural works, such as Le Corbusier's *Villa Savoye*. As kits for building specific, actual works, these do not offer the robust design possibilities of the Architecture Studio elements, original System bricks and elements, or the original System as expanded in the Scale Model line (1962) with, among other elements, plate-shaped bricks. LEGO models of extant architectural works are documented, along with guidelines for *inventive* architectural LEGO modeling, in Tom Alphin, *The LEGO Architect* (San Francisco: No Starch Press, 2015).

7. Glenn Parsons and Allen Carlson, *Functional Beauty* (Oxford: Clarendon Press, 2008).

"That Was *My* Idea!"
LEGO® Ideas and Intellectual Property

Michael Gettings

On August 1, 2011, a long-time LEGO® fan from Japan posted a model of the *Back to the Future* DeLorean Time Machine to the website Cuusoo. At the time, Cuusoo and the LEGO Group were partnering to solicit ideas for new models from the public. After the DeLorean gained 10,000 supporters, the LEGO Group reviewed the model to consider it for commercial production. The project gained approval and on August 1, 2013, LEGO set #21103, the DeLorean Time Machine, was released to the public.

Set #21103 sold quickly, though controversy spread among LEGO fans once pictures of the final set were available. The controversy mostly revolved around the changes made to the original Cuusoo design. The original model had a single-piece smooth sloping hood, squared-off windshield struts, white rear fender accents, and more. The final LEGO-released set featured a blockier, stepped hood, angled windshield struts, and no white fender accents, among other modifications. The LEGO-produced set was also smaller overall (though it consisted of roughly the same number of pieces). Some LEGO fans decided to buy the new set but shared plans to modify it to look more like the original Cuusoo design, which they preferred. With all the changes we might ask the question: is LEGO set #21103 the product of the original Cuusoo designers, or is it a different model? And if it's a different model, can we credit the original Cuusoo designers, Masashi Togami and Sakuretsu (part of Team Back to the Future, or Team BTTF), with creating it? The second question relates to

LEGO® and Philosophy: Constructing Reality Brick By Brick, First Edition.
Edited by Roy T. Cook and Sondra Bacharach.
© 2017 John Wiley & Sons Ltd. Published 2017 by John Wiley & Sons Ltd.

intellectual property, but it depends on the first question, which is metaphysical. If it's the same model, that explains why the original designers get credit.

Avoiding Mistaken Identity

Philosophers approach the first question as being about the object's identity conditions. Roughly put, under what conditions do we say that object 1 and object 2 are the same object? "Same" doesn't just mean "similar" here. We're concerned with "same" in the sense of *one-and-the-same*. Philosophers distinguish between two uses of "identity"—numerical identity, or being one-and-the-same, and qualitative identity, or having the same qualities or properties as one another.

If we're both following the instructions, my build of set #4842 Hogwarts Castle is qualitatively identical to your build of the same set, but they are not numerically identical (there are two models here, not one). When Emmet Brickowski wonders whether he is the Special, he wonders whether he and the prophesied Special are one-and-the-same (numerically identical), not whether they are two individuals who are similar to one another (only qualitatively identical).

Sometimes we have numerical identity without qualitative identity. Consider the White House (not the LEGO Architecture one, but the one where the president lives). It was initially completed in 1800, but Thomas Jefferson added colonnades in 1801, James Monroe added the Southern portico in 1824, Andrew Jackson added the Northern portico in 1829, William Howard Taft expanded the West Wing and created the first oval office in 1909, just to name a few architectural changes to the mansion. We can say that it's been the (numerically identical) White House all along, yet comparing the 1800 building to the one in 2016, there are many qualitative differences. So we can have numerical identity without qualitative identity. In the same way we can ask whether the original Cuusoo DeLorean is the same model as, or numerically identical to, set #21103, even if they're not qualitatively identical. If they are the same model, that would explain why Team BTTF deserves creative credit. So are they numerically identical?

Defending Your Rights

Before launching into the question of numerical identity, let's take a brief detour to consider the question of why a creator deserves credit, including public recognition and royalties. John Locke (1632–1704) maintained that property rights are natural rights. The way we acquire a property right is through labor. As Locke said, since we own our own bodies, and our bodies do the labor, we mix our labor with raw material (he had in mind nature, since he was thinking about land mostly). In this way, what we produce becomes our property.

Some have extended Locke's view to include intellectual property, including industrial design. The creator of a new design mixes her labor with materials, therefore acquiring a right to what she's produced. By mixing their labor with 403 LEGO bricks, Sakuretsu and Masashi Togami would acquire property rights to what they produce. So is what they produce a model made of plastic bricks?

Does Matter Matter?

Consider a relatively simple case. When I was around twelve years old, I designed and built my own LEGO spaceship, mostly from circa-1979 parts from LEGO sets 487, 493, and 891. When I put my LEGO bricks away during my dark age, the model went into a cardboard box, on top of a pile of loose bricks. Twenty-five years later, I retrieved the box from my parents' attic to present the contents to my then-five-year-old son, only to discover the intact spaceship sitting within. Now, how do I know that the spaceship I uncovered in 2007 is the same spaceship I built in 1982?

One answer is that it's made of the same pieces. I know they're the same pieces, because the box remained unopened for twenty-five years (unless, surprisingly, my parents secretly snuck up to the attic to play with my old LEGO bricks). This is the same answer one could give for a dining room table that's been in your family for generations: it's made of the same wood.

Aristotle (384–322 BCE) was one of the first philosophers to pay close attention to the identity of objects. For him, the individual physical object is a substance, which is distinct from, say, a quality. A particular dark bley 1 × 2 brick lying on the floor is a substance, but dark bley (by itself) isn't a substance, it's a quality. So when we're dealing with inanimate objects like LEGO spaceships, they are substances. Aristotle called the stuff that makes up the physical object its "matter." For our purposes, the matter of LEGO substance is plastic ABS bricks. So what makes my circa 1982 spaceship the same substance as the one I discovered in a box in 2007 is that it's made of the same matter, correct?

Not so fast: there are a few problems that complicate the picture somewhat. It seems that material composition comes in degrees. What if I take the spaceship out of the box in 2007 and replace one or two pieces, perhaps with new blocks that are of the same type, but shinier? Now the spaceship I'm holding is made of slightly different matter; so am I holding a new spaceship? Probably not. One or two changed pieces doesn't change the identity of the ship. But if I replace many bricks, or even all of them, one by one, might I be holding a new ship? It seems as if the amount of matter I change might make a difference at some point. This possibility becomes more distinct if I imagine my five-year-old son (a LEGO prodigy in this hypothetical scenario), carefully taking the worn 1982-ship pieces one by one as I set them aside and meticulously joining them together to construct a spaceship that is built precisely to the specifications of the 1982 ship. At the end of the process he and I would be holding identical-looking ships, except mine would be shinier. Which is the original 1982 spaceship? If it's the one he's holding, when did mine stop being the original 1982 spaceship?

A Formative Account

This puzzle about the 1982 spaceship derives from an ancient philosophical problem known as the "Ship of Theseus" and a seventeenth-century variation introduced by Thomas Hobbes (1588–1679). Fortunately, with a little help from Aristotle, we can begin to solve the puzzle, at least as it applies to our question about the DeLorean(s). According to Aristotle, it's not just the matter that makes up a substance; the substance also has a form. A lump of clay is not a statue until a sculptor gives it shape, and it is in that shaping that the statue comes into being. The statue is a combination of matter (clay) and form (the shape and arrangement). Every non-living physical substance comes into being when matter is given form, whether it's a dining room table or a LEGO spaceship. LEGO bricks are a particularly good illustration of the matter vs. form distinction, because the same matter (set of bricks) can be arranged in numerous forms. The DeLorean Time Machine, set #21103, consists of 403 pieces, and the same set can be used to build three different DeLoreans, corresponding to the way the car appeared in the three *Back to the Future* movies. Indeed, part of the joy of LEGO is that the same matter can be recombined into so many different forms.

In some way, form is what's relevant to crediting the invention to the original Cuusoo designers. After all, when someone submits a LEGO Idea, they are not submitting the matter of a model, but its structure, design, and arrangement of parts. As the LEGO Ideas Guidelines and House Rules specify, a submitted project "includes photos of a LEGO model you create as well as a written description that becomes your proposal for a potential LEGO product."[1] No one, Masashi Togami and Sakuretsu included, has to send a physical model to submit a project to LEGO Ideas. Furthermore, the instructions included in LEGO sets (and the instructions often accompanying LEGO Ideas submissions) provide a way to identify the form of the set. Each person who buys a set purchases matter and the recipe to arrange that matter in the intended form. Once built, the model is a particular substance, in Aristotle's view.

A Tale of Two Time Machines?

So if form is what makes a LEGO model what it is, that settles the question of the DeLorean Time Machine, doesn't it? After all, Team BTTF's original design has a different form from the final set #21103. Different forms, different objects, right? If we come to this conclusion, perhaps the most we can say is that LEGO set #21103, The DeLorean Time Machine, was inspired by Team BTTF's Cuusoo project, or originated in the Cuusoo project, but is a distinct model.

There are reasons to resist this conclusion. For one thing, both the LEGO Group and Masashi Togami seem to treat the final product as the work of the original designers. In the booklet that came with set #21103, Masashi said "I was able to see my dream become an official LEGO product." In describing the Cuusoo/LEGO Ideas process in general, the LEGO Group states later in that same booklet, "If your project makes it through the review, then it will become an official LEGO product," and the ad copy for set #21103 describes the final model as being "selected by LEGO Cuusoo members," suggesting that the final set is the one that received over 10,000 supporters. All of these descriptions suggest that the initial design is *numerically* identical to the one that was commercially released, albeit with some modifications.

A second reason to doubt whether they're two distinct models is that identity of form appears to be a question of degree of change, just as material identity is. Imagine someone took Team BTTF's original design and made one small change, such as mounting a license plate on the rear. Now we have a different form, but intuitively isn't it simply Team BTTF's design, just mildly tweaked? The point here is that it seems we recognize some flexibility in form, while the model remains the same model. The form can change *some*, just not *too much*. So we still don't have a final decision about whether set #21103 is numerically identical to the original Cuusoo model. Things are still just about as clear as Fabuland Brown-colored mud.

If you listen to many of the FOLs' (Fans of LEGO) reactions to the final, released set, their collective response might be summed up as "they changed too much—it's not the same." This might be what philosophers term an aesthetic response rather than a metaphysical one. Perhaps our LEGO Ideas Guidelines can shed some light on the question of whether the Cuusoo-submitted model is the same model as the final set.

Consider again the possibility of someone copying Team BTTF's design and making only one minor change. If submitted as a project, this would violate project guidelines, which state that anyone who submits a project "must be the original creator of all creative work."[2] We could imagine, however, that two people, quite improbably, submit nearly the same design for a model. This may not be entirely far-fetched. LEGO Ideas distinguishes two kinds of project: generic and unique. The Ideas Guidelines describe generic ideas as those that "already exist in the world."[3] Examples include "everyday objects like a fire truck, a historical landmark, or a Boeing 737 airplane. It even includes buildings, vehicles, or characters from TV shows, movies and video games."[4] A unique project, on the other hand, is one "that you conceived entirely yourself." The guidelines elaborate by saying it's "something you make up yourself, for example a fictitious vehicle, building or storyline."[5] Looking at the history of LEGO Ideas submissions as of 2016, most projects fall under the "generic" heading. Of those that have been produced, arguably only the Research Institute, Birds, and the Exo Suit are unique. The others, from the DeLorean Time Machine to *The Big Bang Theory*, are generic.

The Guidelines warn us that generic ideas "are fair game to anyone, so if you submit something like this others are also free to submit their own versions."[6] Indeed, the DeLorean Time Machine is fair game, and while others didn't submit it to LEGO Cuusoo, it would be surprising if no one had tried to build one before. When two members submit projects with models that represent the same object, the project guidelines call this kind of circumstance "overlapping ideas."

Since "the value of a generic project is not just in your model, it's also in the concept (the way you present it)," overlapping ideas will almost always be distinguishable.[7] In fact, the guidelines specify that if two overlapping ideas both make it to 10,000 supporters, the LEGO Review Board "will evaluate the projects separately and make the final decision on which project to produce."[8] Note that each of the two overlapping ideas had to be created independently in order for things to get this far. This requirement that all one's creative work be original is our first step toward answering both the question of whether Team BTTF's design is numerically identical to the final set and why Team BTTF deserves recognition and compensation for its work.

The second step can be found in the description of what happens when someone's LEGO Ideas project is approved by the Review Board and enters the production stage. The Ideas Guidelines state that at this point, "LEGO set designers take the original submission and refine it into a LEGO product that's ready for release ... *the LEGO Group makes all final decisions on how a project becomes a LEGO set, including the final model design.*"[9] (emphasis in the original) The language of "refine" here skates over our question of the relation between the original design and the final model, but it does give us some insight into the process.

Regarding our DeLorean Time Machine(s), the accompanying booklet usefully details some of the process that preceded the release of set #21103. The LEGO designer assigned to the project was Steen Sig Andersen, and, as the booklet describes, "it was his task to transform Togami and Sakuretsu's model into a true LEGO construction set." Andersen says, "the original model was a great starting point and many of the ideas and details could be used in the final construction." He talks about the wheels, which have to both roll and fold into hover mode, as a particular engineering challenge, but he doesn't talk about the hood, roof, doors, or other components that changed. The language of "transform" and "refine" points to another relevant feature of the relation between the models: the initial model was the basis for the creation of the final one.

History Matters!

This points us to another theory of identity—the causal/historical view. According to this view, individuals can change over time, and what is important to their identity is that the changes are fluid and continuous. As long as the parts are changed one at a time, we can see that a single individual persists throughout the changes.

One might look at human beings in this way—while in many respects I am very different from the boy who built that spaceship in 1982, it's correct to say that it was me who built that ship. That boy and I are identical in the sense we're using here. This is because I came from him, through a series of gradual and continuous changes that brought me to this point. Perhaps words like "transform" and "refine" are even appropriate here (though "refine" might give the wrong impression!). What's important is that my history includes that boy in 1982, and through a series of causes and effects involving eating a lot of ice cream, reading a bunch of books, falling in love, and having children, that boy has become me. This is what the causal/historical view of identity says about what makes me and that boy the same person.

We could say something similar about the DeLorean. Surely it changes, but Andersen changed bits gradually, transforming the original Cuusoo model into a model with a somewhat different form. The released set has its causal and historical origins in the Cuusoo project, which is why Team BTTF deserves credit for the design. This also explains why any LEGO Ideas project has to contain only the original creative work of the submitting member. The LEGO Ideas Review Board has to ensure that the submitting member is responsible for the historical origin of the project. Otherwise, that person wouldn't deserve credit for the final result. So if the final set results from the work of both Team BTTF and the LEGO Group, do they deserve equal credit?

Probably not. An analogy to music can help. Imagine a musician who writes some songs, then sings them accompanying herself on guitar, recording a few home demos on a laptop. These demos, whatever their virtues, are usually not ready for public release. If a record company is interested, it might hire a producer, sound engineer, mixer, and studio to record the songs in a manner that will make them ready for commercial release. In the course of this, the producer, in particular, can have creative input into the final product. The producer might bring in additional musicians or add effects to flesh out the sound, all of which hopefully adds to the aesthetics of the songs themselves and makes them ready for the marketplace. The original musician is still considered the creator of the music, but the final product can be significantly different from the original home-recorded demos. Though the producer and other recording professionals deserve some credit, the majority of credit goes to the original creator. Likewise, Team BTTF deserves the majority of credit for creating the DeLorean Time Machine.

So in the end, to say that Team BTTF created a model that was eventually released as a LEGO set means that we can't identify their work with either the physical matter or the form, because their original DeLorean and the final LEGO set differ in both matter and form. Instead, the causal/historical view explains how the DeLorean changed from its origin to its eventual release. This view also explains why Team BTTF deserves recognition (and royalties) for their design. In an important sense, the final set #21103 would not have existed without the work of Sakuretsu and Togami. In Lockean fashion, they mixed their creative labor with LEGO bricks. The causal/historical view recognizes their original idea as the seed that became the final set, reflected by the LEGO Ideas Guidelines' originality requirement. And isn't originality what we value most about LEGO building? Like Emmet, you too can exercise your imagination and have original ideas.

Notes

1. Ideas Guidelines and House Rules, The LEGO Group, available at https://ideas.lego.com/guidelines (accessed November 20, 2015).
2. Ibid.
3. Ibid.
4. Ibid.
5. The terms "generic" and "unique" are a bit misleading. Fire trucks are quite generic, but a historical landmark is not, at least in the real world. A historical landmark actually appears to be a unique site, part of what makes it significant. Yet LEGO Ideas put both in the "generic" category. I can imagine many projects for fire trucks that LEGO Ideas would probably accept as unique, rather than generic. A project for a fire truck model that has rockets strapped to the sides and eight elephants on top ready to shoot water out of their trunks is not "something that already exists in the world," whereas a model of a 1980 Ford Pierce C-900 would satisfy that description. It seems that the category "fire truck" could be either generic or unique. The other confusion is about unique projects being "fictitious." Presumably AT-AT Walkers, X-Wing fighters, and the Batmobile are fictitious, though not in the sense meant here to qualify as "unique." The Ideas Guidelines must mean by "fictitious" "the fictional creation of

the member who submits the project," or something like that. Join LEGO Ideas, George Lucas, and you can submit your unique projects!
6. "Ideas Guidelines and House Rules."
7. Ibid.
8. Ibid.
9. Ibid.

Part II
LEGO®, ETHICS, AND RULES

5

"You Know the Rules!" What's Wrong with The Man Upstairs?

Jon Robson

It doesn't take Batman®'s detective skills to discern that—at least until his last-minute change of heart—*The Lego® Movie*'s Lord Business is the bad guy. The use of laser sharks and the phrase "now my evil power will be unlimited" are pretty clear indications that the audience isn't supposed to be rooting for you. And as for his accomplice Bad Cop, well his name speaks for itself. Yet, when we consider the "real world" inspiration for Lord Business, The Man Upstairs, things become much less straightforward. The Man certainly isn't a moustache-twirling villain, and he lacks Business's most obvious indications of moral turpitude such as plans for world domination and a desire to neutralize all possible sources of opposition. Still, we are clearly meant to think that—again, prior to his own last-minute change of heart—he embodies some significant moral flaw. Yet, it is no easy matter to specify precisely what it is about The Man's character and behavior that we are intended to regard as so objectionable. Nonetheless, the flaw in question is very real and commonly encountered in our everyday lives.

"All of This That You See Before You is All Your Father's"

So, what is wrong with The Man Upstairs? Some initially promising suggestions concerning the flaws in The Man's character quickly

LEGO® and Philosophy: Constructing Reality Brick By Brick, First Edition.
Edited by Roy T. Cook and Sondra Bacharach.
© 2017 John Wiley & Sons Ltd. Published 2017 by John Wiley & Sons Ltd.

turn out to be inadequate. Consider, for example, the possibility that The Man's flaw is his lack of generosity toward his offspring. The Man's unwillingness to allow Finn to play with his toys (or should it be "highly sophisticated inter-locking brick system"?) is, after all, a major source of consternation for his son. Further, his unwillingness to let Finn's sister interact with his LEGO world, while considerably less upsetting for Finn, might be seen to only compound this lack of generosity.

Yet, such a criticism hardly seems fair. To see why, compare this behavior with the way in which the LEGO version of Green Lantern® is treated by the other minifig superheroes in the movie. Throughout the movie, DC's Trinity of heroes—Batman®, Superman®, and Wonder Woman®—have little interest in sharing anything, even common courtesy, with the ring-wielding hero. So much so that Superman expresses a preference for a Kryptonite-induced demise over spending time in the Lantern's company. Of course this is all played for laughs, and we are clearly intended to regard the lack of respect that Green Lantern receives from his peers as a source of amusement rather than pity. Yet, a contrast with The Man's relationship to Finn is still instructive. There is no indication that The Man views Finn with anything remotely equivalent to the disdain with which the other heroes view poor Hal Jordan. On the contrary, he gives every indication of being a loving father who is deeply concerned with his son's welfare. Nor are we given any reason to believe that he isn't extremely generous toward his children in other aspects of his life.

Given this, it seems difficult to maintain that The Man is blameworthy in terms of his lack of generosity. It is not, after all, required that parents share all aspects of their lives, or all of their hobbies and interests, with their children. Doubtless many AFOLs (Adult Fans of Lego) will be keen to share their love of LEGO products with their offspring, but those who choose to pursue their hobby in private, perhaps as a respite from the hustle and bustle of family life, are hardly blameworthy for doing so. Indeed, we often treat it as a sign of a happy and well-adjusted family that its members have individual, as well as shared, interests. Further, it is not even the case that Finn is totally deprived of access to LEGO bricks (a sad fate indeed): he has a whole box of them over by the Christmas decorations to do with as he pleases. The Man's moral failing, then, is not to be found in his unwillingness to allow his children to share in his hobby. Rather, his fatal flaw lies in the way in which he himself engages in this hobby.

"Let's Take Extra Care to Follow the Instructions"

The key to understanding what is problematic about The Man's behavior lies in considering his inflexible attitude toward following a particular kind of rule: the construction instructions accompanying his various LEGO sets.

Of course, merely following these instructions is not, in itself, morally problematic, and it is clear that the makers of *The LEGO Movie* don't intend us to believe anything of the kind. After all, the film itself spawned a range of LEGO sets complete with detailed construction instructions that LEGO enthusiasts are, presumably, encouraged to follow. Further, even within the movie itself, unexpectedly, and somewhat reluctantly, following a set of construction instructions plays a vital part in Emmet's friends' eventual victory. One difference, of course, is that for the Master Builders, acting in this way is the exception rather than, as in The Man's case, the rule. Yet, even consistently following the instructions which come with your LEGO sets need not imply any problematic character traits. Many happy LEGO fans of all ages confine themselves exclusively, or almost exclusively, to builds that follow the construction instructions to the letter. While I personally have never seen the appeal of such an approach, it doesn't constitute a moral failing. The problem, then, is not the fact that The Man follows the rules nor even the extent to which he does so. Rather, I suggest, The Man's central flaw lies in his instantiating a problematic kind of rule worship.

"You Know the Rules!"

The instructions found in your typical LEGO set are not intended to function as absolute and inviolable commandments but merely as suggestions for possible, and hopefully entertaining, strategies for engaging with the available bricks. Yet, The Man treats these instructions as sacrosanct. He is unwilling to countenance any departure from these rules, even when such departures would clearly better serve the purposes for which LEGO products exist in the first place (such as encouraging children to "just imagine"). The problem, then, is not that The Man follows these rules but that he venerates them in a way that is completely inappropriate with respect to rules of this kind.

I say "rules of this kind" because I do not mean to suggest that it is inappropriate to view any class of rules or instructions as if they were never to be violated. Certainly, a number of philosophers, most notably Immanuel Kant (1724–1804), have maintained that certain central moral principles have such a status. For example, Kant notoriously maintained that the moral prohibition against lying is an absolute one which should never be violated, irrespective of the circumstances. Unsurprisingly, though, this view has proven to be controversial and many other philosophers have maintained that there are certain cases (such as the famous example of lying to a prospective murderer about the location of his intended victim) where lying is not merely permitted but morally required. Still, whether or not we take the status of moral rules, such as the prohibition against lying, to be absolute, most of us can readily perceive an important distinction between moral rules and rules of other kinds. A distinction which, it seems, The Man is unable (or unwilling) to grasp.

"First Law of the Sea: Never Place Yer Rear End on a Pirate's Face"

There are various rules which many of us follow in our everyday lives: moral rules, rules for playing chess, rules of etiquette, rules for cooking that Sunday roast just right, and (at least if Metalbeard has his way) rules against sitting on a pirate's face. We also typically recognize that there are important differences between these different kinds of rules. As the philosopher Daniel Kelly and his coauthors put it, most of us

> ... recognize a distinction between two quite different sorts of rules governing behavior, namely moral rules and conventional rules. Prototypical examples of moral rules include those prohibiting killing or injuring other people, stealing their property, or breaking promises. Prototypical examples of conventional rules include those prohibiting wearing gender-inappropriate clothing (e.g., men wearing dresses), licking one's plate at the dinner table, and talking in a classroom when one has not been called on by the teacher.[1]

Indeed, the ability to appreciate this distinction between moral rules and these other kinds of rules (those concerning etiquette, local conventions, and the like) is often taken by psychologists to be a key part of children's moral development. It is, however, a controversial matter among philosophers as to what exactly differentiates moral requirements and rules from instructions of these other kinds. It has been suggested, for example, that only moral rules are absolute in the sense outlined above, or that they are the only imperatives that apply to everyone irrespective of their needs and desires, or that moral requirements trump or overrule all other requirements or … Unsurprisingly, then, I do not intend to say anything definitive about precisely what it is that makes moral requirements special. What we can see, though, is that whatever this distinction amounts to it is one which The Man fails to recognize.

The Man treats the LEGO instructions he is following—which clearly have, at best, the status of conventional, rather than moral, rules—in a manner fitting only for moral requirements. This can be seen in two main ways. First, he refuses to make any exceptions to the requirement to follow these instructions and he is willing to treat his other desires and projects—even things he values very deeply such as his children's happiness—as less important than following these requirements. Second, he treats these rules as if they were important for their own sake rather than, as all sensible LEGO aficionados do, as a means to obtaining some other desirable end. It is a combination of these two errors which, ultimately, makes The Man's behavior so problematic.

"Instructions to Fit In, Have Everybody Like You, and Always Be Happy"

To understand the severity of The Man's mistake here we need only contrast his attitude with that of Emmet at the start of *The LEGO Movie*. As the film opens, Emmet clearly shares one aspect of The Man's attitude toward following the rules. He, along with most other citizens of Bricksburg, has been conditioned to happily (and relentlessly) follow a specific set of pre-approved rules for achieving President Business's vision of the good life. Yet, none of these rules seem to conform to our prototypical idea of a moral rule. Some of them (such as the instruction to "always return a compliment") deal with matters of etiquette, others (such as the reminder to "breathe") with straightforward self-preservation, and still others (such as the injunctions to "watch TV" and "drink overpriced coffee") are clearly aimed at promoting the interests of Business's Octan Corporation.

Importantly, Emmet's devotion to these rules was, if anything, even greater than that of his fellows. Yet, Emmet was not obsessed—as The Man was—with following the rules for their own sake but, rather, with following them as a means for achieving his other goals such as social acceptance and fulfilment (to fit in, have everybody like him, and always be happy). Predictably, though, following the rules so diligently didn't provide Emmet with any of the goods he was chasing after. Indeed, Emmet's obsessive devotion to following the rules made him too much of a conformist even for a society of conformists. He was, as one of his erstwhile coworkers put things, an "average normal kinda guy" but "not normal like us."

Yet, while Emmet's attempts at achieving his goals were lamentably flawed, the goals he was pursuing were, at least for the most part, worthy. As such, Emmet is largely to be pitied rather than blamed for his inflexible rule-following behavior. By contrast, there is no indication that The Man's rule-following behavior is in any way aimed, even unsuccessfully, at attaining some genuine good. Rather, The Man follows the rules merely because they are, well, the rules.

"That's a Suggestion!"

Having said all of this, it could easily be objected that The Man's inflexible attitude toward rule-following for its own sake, while certainly problematic in some respects, hardly makes him worthy of the title villain. After all, it seems to be a fairly minor flaw even in comparison to the various deficiencies exhibited by some of *The LEGO Movie*'s putative heroes (analyzing Batman's character alone would keep an army of therapists in work for years) and certainly when compared to those of a supervillain such as Lord Business.

One possible response to this is to maintain that, though central to his failings as a moral agent, the kind of rule worship I have highlighted is not the only flaw The Man displays. We could, for example, point out that The Man demonstrates a problematic kind of inconsistency when it comes to rule-following. He is slavishly devoted to one kind of non-binding rule—concerning the proper construction of LEGO sets—but, when it suits him, treats equivalent prescriptions as if they had no force whatsoever. Consider the following exchange between The Man and his son prompted by The Man's insistence that his LEGO world is not a mere toy but rather a "highly sophisticated inter-locking brick system":

FINN: But we bought it at the toy store.
THE MAN: We did, but the way I'm using it makes it an adult thing.
FINN: The box for this one said "Ages 8 to 14."
THE MAN: That's a suggestion! They have to put that on there.

In one respect The Man is, of course, correct. It is highly doubtful that anyone in the LEGO Group would be upset to learn that sets primarily designed with those aged 8 to 14 in mind were being used by AFOLs—far from it—but this attitude is clearly in tension with The Man's slavish devotion to following equivalent rules that originate from the same source.

We might well conclude, then, that The Man is acting hypocritically here; treating the LEGO Group's instructions as sacrosanct when it suits him but as mere suggestions when it doesn't. Though I think this is right, and that The Man is certainly open to a charge of hypocrisy, I don't think this will really help us with the charge that The Man is not villainous enough. The various flaws I have highlighted, while genuine, are of little consequence when, as in The Man's case, they are confined to the world of LEGO construction. The real problem arises, though, when the flaws I have highlighted are not limited to such a narrow and relatively inconsequential aspect of someone's life.

"Would You Like to Make an Appointment, or Shall I Summon the Micromanagers?"

In order to see what is so problematic about The Man's rule worship it is important to consider two points. First, the kind of flaw The Man exhibits is, unlike the pantomime evil of a supervillain like Business, not confined merely to works of fiction. Far from it. While few of us will ever encounter sharks or lasers (and still fewer of us laser sharks), we will most likely all have experience of dealing with one of Lord Business's other security measures: overbearing assistants like Velma Staplebot. Every large company or organization has its share of those who are obsessed with following certain rules—about making appointments, about filling in just the right forms in just the right way, about who gets to park where, and so forth—to the letter, irrespective of whether these rules serve any wider purpose.

Secondly, it is important to consider that, while the examples I have described above merely have the status of annoyances, when taken to extremes this kind of rule worship can have some truly horrific consequences. Consider, for example, the dutiful mafioso who treats the mob's code of conduct as taking priority over moral commandments not to kill or maim. Or the heartless official who, like Inspector Javert from Victor Hugo's novel *Les Misérables*, lets an obsession with the letter of the law trump any considerations of justice or mercy. It is characters such as these who show us how an inability to recognize the distinction between moral rules and injunctions of other kinds can sometimes have grave consequences for those who are victims of such misdirected rule worship.

Of course, The Man Upstairs is hardly a mafioso nor even a Javert. The flaw he displays, like most of our human failings, comes in varying degrees, and The Man's—confined as it is to the world of LEGO construction—is a mere peccadillo. Still, it is important to remember that our human capacity to become special—to go far beyond the limits of what is ordinary, normal, or expected—is not confined to our virtues but applies also to our vices.[2]

Notes

1. Daniel Kelly, Stephen Stich, Kevin J. Haley, Serena J. Eng, and Daniel M. Fessler, "Harm, Affect, and the Moral/Conventional Distinction," *Mind & Language* 22 (2007): 117.
2. I would like to thank Sarah Adams and the editors of this volume for useful comments on earlier versions of this chapter.

6

Searching for "The Special"

The LEGO® Movie and the Value of (LEGO®) Persons

Alexander Quanbeck

As the evil President Business and his army of robots storm LEGO® Mountain to seize the Kragle, the blinded guardian Vitruvius prophesies:

> One day a talented lass or fellow;
> A Special one with face of yellow,
> Will make the Piece of Resistance found,
> From its hiding refuge underground.
> And with a noble army at the helm,
> This Master Builder will thwart the Kragle and save the realm,
> And be the greatest, most interesting, most important person of all times.
> All this is true, because it rhymes.

Despite the comedic rhyming, Vitruvius's notion of the "The Special" introduces what will be a central motif for the rest of the film.

As it turns out, the one who finds this "Piece of Resistance" is not quite the hero he was expected to be. Emmet, a construction worker with no close friends, no special talents, and no good ideas, describes himself as "not all that smart. And I'm not what you'd call the creative type. Plus, generally unskilled. Also, scared and cowardly." His low opinion of himself reflects the attitude that others take toward him. Throughout the film, others suggest to Emmet both implicitly and explicitly that he brings nothing of value to any particular individual or to society, and that consequently he himself has no value.

LEGO® and Philosophy: Constructing Reality Brick By Brick, First Edition.
Edited by Roy T. Cook and Sondra Bacharach.
© 2017 John Wiley & Sons Ltd. Published 2017 by John Wiley & Sons Ltd.

Mindlessly accepting President Business's norms of value, Emmet initially views his value as something *extrinsically conferred* by the value judgments of others. Unvalued by others and convinced that he is lacking in all of the qualities befitting "The Special," Emmet fears that he is really a worthless person. Only when he finally discovers that value is an *intrinsic reality* that does not depend upon others' beliefs, attitudes, or actions does Emmet find that he is indeed "The Special."

"You're Not The Special!": President Business's Theory of Extrinsic Value

In President Business's Bricksburg, we see a world in which the value of its citizens is socially determined. On this understanding of value, a person's worth is not something she possesses intrinsically, butit is extrinsically conferred in a variety of ways by the judgments of others. The song "Everything is Awesome," whose message President Business ensures everyone in Bricksburg has internalized, captures the conditional nature of President Business's understanding of value (or "awesomeness," as he calls it here). "Everything is awesome," President Business's pop music propaganda tells us, and on two conditions: "when you're part of a team" and "when we're living our dream." In this catchy tune, President Business proposes that awesomeness depends both on belonging to a "team" through relationships with others and participating in the Bricksburg "dream" that he systematically propagates. As we discover over the course of the film, President Business views the value of individual people as similarly dependent on such social conditions.

We witness one expression of this model of value early in the film during a commercial that encourages its viewers to "eat a complete breakfast with all the special people in your life." The term "special" in this sentence surely is not suggesting that those with whom you eat breakfast are special because of any particular intrinsic characteristic they possess. Rather, they are special by virtue of being of great significance or importance *to you*. The commercial demonstrates an extrinsic account of value, in which a person's value does not depend on any intrinsic quality he possesses but instead is socially conferred by others' valuing him.

This extrinsic account of value reflects the theory of value articulated by the American philosopher Harry Frankfurt in his book *The Reasons of Love*. Nothing in the world is truly valuable in its own right, he says. Instead, "it is by caring about things that we infuse the world with importance."[1] Frankfurt explains this in terms of love:

> As I am construing it, love is not necessarily a response grounded in awareness of the inherent value of its object. It may sometimes arise like that, but it need not do so .... It is not necessarily as a result of recognizing their value and of being captivated by it that we love things. Rather, what we love necessarily acquires value for us because we love it. The lover does invariably and necessarily perceive the beloved as valuable, but the value he sees it to possess is a value that derives from and that depends upon his love.[2]

Frankfurt considers his love for his children to illustrate his point:

> The particular value that I attribute to my children is not inherent in them but depends upon my love for them. The reason they are so precious to me is simply that I love them so much ... In any case, it is plainly on account of my love for them that they have acquired in my eyes a value that otherwise they would not certainly possess."[3]

For Emmet, whose plant is the closest thing to a special "person" in his life to eat breakfast with, the dependence of his value on others' evaluations is problematic. Nobody really values him. Clearly influenced by the account of value that President Business propagates in his television commercials, Emmet tries desperately to fit in with his coworkers and win their approval. A surprised yet forlorn expression comes across his face, however, when Bad Cop reveals to him that his acquaintances do not actually value him or think that he is special. At this moment, Emmet begins to realize just how unspecial and worthless he is according to an extrinsic account of value.

The scene in which Bad Cop interrogates Emmet shows that particular qualities—such as being perky, liking sausage, or simply having a penchant for nearly collapsing in laughter at the mention of your name—can elicit positive value judgments from others. Unfortunately, in Emmet's case, it is the lack of interesting qualities that renders him boring and worthless. "He's just sort of a little bit of a blank slate, I guess," Larry the Barista notes on Bad Cop's recording.

In a similar vein, Emmet is not deemed worthless merely because no particular person values him but because others consider his contribution to society to be negligible. Let's call this an *economic account of value*. According to this model, a person's worth derives from her "market value," or the value of the services she provides to society.

This can be considered another extrinsic account of value because it is socially conferred. Unlike the Frankfurtian account, however, a person's value does not depend on a particular individual valuing him. Instead, a person's worth is determined by the value that the members of society collectively place on the goods or services he produces. We value certain knowledge and skills, such as the experience and technical expertise of a surgeon, because they are not easily replaceable and because we value the restoration of health that the surgeon provides.

Though this value could be partly expressed in monetary terms, we can understand it as a broader expression of the overall value a person brings to others. In President Business's Bricksburg, others' assessments of a person's contribution to society (in addition to her specialness to particular individuals) constitute the principal measure of her value as a human being. Implicit throughout the film is the notion that Emmet's status as a construction worker, holding an unskilled job in which he could easily be replaced, contributes to his unspecialness. More importantly, we are constantly reminded that Emmet's ideas are, as MetalBeard describes them, "so dumb and bad that no one would ever think that they could possibly be useful." Emmet's sole original idea—a double-decker couch—seems so useless that nobody finds it interesting or worthwhile. The general consensus is that Emmet offers nothing unique to society, and he is thus deemed to be a completely useless figure.

Emmet's Vacillating Value

This notion of value as socially and extrinsically conferred deeply informs Emmet's understanding of his worth throughout the film. Both varieties of the extrinsic account of value—the Frankfurtian version, in which his value is conferred by particular individuals, and the economic version, in which his value is derived from the value he brings to society—inform Emmet's thinking at different points in the film. Emmet's self-esteem depends directly on others' widely vacillating assessment of his worth, leaving him with a highly unstable and fluctuating understanding of his value.

Early in the film Emmet sees himself as worthless according to the extrinsic theory of value because he holds no value either to individuals or to society as a whole. After he meets Vitruvius and Wyldstyle, however, Emmet begins to believe that he might possess some value both to them and to Bricksburg. When Emmet finds the Piece of

Resistance and deftly navigates Wyldstyle's car through a host of enemies, Wyldstyle comes to believe that Emmet is "The Special." She tells him not only that he might be the "most important, most talented, most interesting, and most extraordinary person in the universe," but that he will save the universe from President Business.

For once, a particular group of people—Wyldstyle and the Master Builders—value him. Just as importantly, because of his unique ability to stop President Business from freezing the world, Emmet has a great deal to offer Bricksburg. Of course, in light of his new knowledge about President Business's evil plot, Emmet's conception of what it would mean to contribute to society is different than before. His ability to save the ignorant citizens of Bricksburg is not in fact something they presently value. Nonetheless, he offers something they would later value. And his newly acquired belief in his value is not merely of personal psychological significance. Emmet later admits to Wyldstyle that when she told him that night that he was "talented, and important … That was the first time anyone had ever really told me that. And it made me want to do everything I could to be the guy you were talking about." Wyldstyle's statement of his importance gives Emmet the confidence to act and attempt to fulfill the hopes and expectations the Master Builders have for him.

Unfortunately, Emmet's feelings of value do not last long. Once Emmet reveals that all of his opinions and preferences conform to President Business's propaganda, Wyldstyle quickly reverses her judgment and concludes that Emmet is a nobody and a great disappointment. His apparent inability to come up with any ideas more creative than a double-decker couch causes Wyldstyle and Vitruvius to question whether Emmet has anything worthwhile to contribute. Emmet seems to internalize their view that he has nothing productive to offer, conceding to Wyldstyle that "I never have any ideas." Emmet thereby again comes to believe that he is worthless. For not only do no individuals value him anymore but he contributes no value to saving Bricksburg.

Emmet's perception of his value continues to ebb and flow in the scenes that follow. The Master Builders realize that Emmet's seemingly asinine ideas are not useless after all when he saves them from the sinking submarine. Thus their faith in him—and accordingly Emmet's confidence—grows. While Emmet may not properly be "The Special," the Master Builders begin to follow and value him because they believe he might be able to generate and orchestrate a plan to infiltrate the "infinitieth floor" of President Business's office. Emmet likewise has the confidence that his seemingly ordinary plan of simply following instructions might actually work.

But despite overcoming President Business's "security forces of every kind imaginable: lasers, sharks, laser sharks, overbearing assistants, and strange dangerous relics that entrap, snap and zap," Emmet and his friends are ultimately no match for President Business's robot army and penny boomerang. President Business decapitates Vitruvius, and Emmet's efforts to save the world have apparently failed. As a result, Emmet's potential contribution to society has been negated and he is again reduced to a lowly construction worker. President Business quips, "Hey, not so special anymore, huh? Well, guess what? No one ever told me I was special. I never got a trophy just for showing up! I'm not some special little snowflake, no! But as unspecial as I am, you are a thousand billion times more unspecial than me!"

Devastated that he has failed to defeat President Business, Emmet makes it clear that he still understands himself according to President Business's extrinsic account of value. "Didn't you hear him? The prophecy's made up. I'm not the Special. To think for a moment I thought I might be...." At this moment when Emmet despairs because he has nothing worthwhile to offer to anyone, he fully grasps how unstable his value has been. His hopes that he would be special have vanished, and Emmet is left feeling just as worthless as he ever has been.

Intrinsic Value and Emmet's Enlightenment

If we interpret *The LEGO Movie* as being driven by Emmet's quest for discovering his value, the real philosophical turning point in the film is not when Emmet's double-decker couch permits the Master Builders to escape from the sinking submarine and they realize that Emmet's ideas actually are useful. Rather, it is when Emmet realizes their approval is irrelevant to his value. While Emmet despairingly laments that he has failed and that he is not "The Special," Vitruvius's ghost appears to him with the message that he simply needs to believe that he is "The Special." Seeming to undergo a major internal transformation, Emmet sees through the illusion of value that President Business has constructed. The judgments of others cannot determine his value as a person, nor anyone else's value. Emmet places himself within a philosophical tradition that affirms the mind-independent, intrinsic reality of human value, of which the great German philosopher Immanuel Kant (1724–1804) is one of the most notable proponents.

According to Kant's account of the value or worth of human persons, our value cannot derive from anything external, as it does for Frankfurt. In his *Groundwork of the Metaphysics of Morals*, Kant makes it clear that simply being valued or desired by someone is not sufficient to establish any unconditional value.[4] Our value is something intrinsic that derives from our very nature.[5] For Kant, it is human rationality that makes us "ends in ourselves" of absolute, unconditioned worth, for "rational nature is distinguished from others in that it proposes an end to itself."[6] Having the characteristic of rationality is not merely instrumentally valuable because others deem it to be so, but it is valuable in itself, independently of anyone's opinion. Since rationality is something fundamental to human nature, all rational humans are valuable by their very nature, and nobody's opinions can add to or detract from this value.

This sort of principle—that everyone has real, stable, and inherent value—seems to be what Emmet has in mind when he tells President Business, "You are the most talented, most interesting, and most extraordinary person in the universe. And you are capable of amazing things. Because you are 'The Special.' And so am I. And so is everyone. The prophecy is made up, but it's also true. It's about all of us." Of course, unlike Kant, Emmet does not seem to ground the value of persons in their rationality, and it is not entirely clear what he proposes as an alternative source of value. It seems likely, though, that Emmet thinks that each individual's unique capacity for creativity may be what grounds her value. However, Emmet's main point is to emphasize that no matter what others believe about him or tell him, he is still a special and valuable person. Emmet thereby places himself in the philosophical tradition of Kant and those who think that people have intrinsic value independent of anyone's value judgments.

"You Still Can Change Everything": The Implications of Emmet's Belief in Intrinsic Value

The clash between these two competing views of value does not lie at the periphery of *The LEGO Movie*'s plot but is embedded at the center of the conflict between Emmet and President Business. The predominance of extrinsic models of value in the film seems to reflect President Business's own attitudes, disseminated through the media, advertisements, and through the consumerist culture of Bricksburg itself. To some extent, they are attributed to President Business's own psychology. As he taunts Emmet and tells him that he is completely unspecial, we begin to see how President Business's doubts about his personal value inform his attempts to assert his own value above that of others. President Business seems to be the paradigmatic bully, demonstrating his insecurities about his own worth in his treatment of others.

There is also a more sinister element in President Business's endorsement of these extrinsic theories of value, particularly with regard to the economic theory of value. Though the ending of the movie may cause us to wonder whether President Business is truly evil or just misunderstood and misguided, the value theory he endorses and imposes upon others might constitute a great deal of his "evilness."[7] This seems to be an important component of his larger scheme of maintaining his control over the people of Bricksburg and a way to make himself appear more valuable at the expense of others. President Business plays an influential and indispensable role in society, so suggesting that value is extrinsic and socially conferred augments his own value. Even more importantly, by shaping the desires of the citizens of Bricksburg and accordingly what they value, President Business can control the entire notion of value. If President Business can lead others to value what he wants them to, those who contribute to these ends are valuable. On the other hand, anyone who does not provide what President Business considers valuable is worthless. As Emmet learns, the ability to shape value in this way grants President Business tremendous power.

In contrast to the destructive way that President Business utilizes his theory of value as propaganda, Emmet demonstrates how a change in his philosophical views can have a positive effect on his character and actions. It becomes clear at the end of the film that Emmet is not only a political rebel but also a philosophical insurgent, and his successful defeat of President Business's plot to freeze the world is a direct result of the change in his philosophical views. One of Emmet's major discoveries is that there are different ways that value can be understood. His statement of the contingency of President Business's model of value lies at the heart of his ultimately persuasive argument against it. Telling President Business, "You don't have to be the bad guy," Emmet suggests that the very existence of different ways to understand value offers the possibility for radical change. Freed to conceive of a different world, Emmet envisions a society in which we do not become more valuable by becoming more influential or better liked by others. Instead, knowing that our value is inherent, we are ourselves empowered to truly utilize our creativity and to thereby empower others as well.

Although the ghost of Vitruvius's exhortation to believe that he is truly special might "sound like a cat poster," this realization transforms Emmet's understanding of his self-worth and his capabilities. Emmet takes Vitruvius's words to heart and realizes not only that he is special but that he can indeed save the world, sacrificing his life by jumping into the Infinite Abyss of Nothingness. Just as importantly, equipped with an egalitarian conception of value, Emmet is enabled to see the worth in everyone, even President Business. Inspired by Emmet's example, Wyldstyle also accepts Emmet's vision of intrinsic value and capability. Even those who seemingly have nothing to offer society actually possess an invaluable capacity for making a difference, she discovers. Wyldstyle hijacks the television station to empower all the other citizens by informing them of this fact: "All of you have the ability inside of you to be a ground breaker. And I mean literally, break the ground! Peel off the pieces, tear apart your walls! Build things only you could build, defend yourselves! We need to fight back against President Business's plans to freeze us!" Emmet and Wyldstyle are able to turn the tide in the struggle against President Business in large part simply by altering their views on value and acting accordingly, demonstrating the importance of our beliefs regarding the source and nature of the value of individual human, or LEGO, persons.

By contrasting President Business and the Enlightened Emmet, we can see not only that they subscribe to two fundamentally different theories of value but also that they use the content of the theories to great effect on both an individual and societal level. For President Business, everything is awesome on two conditions: "when you're part of a team," and "when we're living our dream." Perhaps Emmet could rephrase President Business's theme song without conditions to read "*Everyone* is awesome. Period."

Notes

1. Harry Frankfurt, *The Reasons of Love* (Princeton, NJ: Princeton University Press, 2004), 23. For another account of value with some similarities to Frankfurt's, see Ronald Dworkin's investment theory of value articulated in *Life's Dominion: An Argument about Abortion, Euthanasia, and Individual Freedom* (New York: Vintage Books, 1994).
2. Ibid., 38–9.
3. Ibid., 40.
4. Immanuel Kant, *Groundwork of the Metaphysics of Morals*, trans. Lewis White Beck (Library of Liberal Arts, 1959), 428.

5. Kant can be construed as arguing that most things we value are indeed conditioned goods, dependent on their use as a means to our rational ends. However, my concern here is only with the objective, intrinsic value of humans, which Kant seems to clearly affirm due to our rational nature and our capacity for valuing other things.

6. Kant, *Groundwork of the Metaphysics of Morals*, 437.

7. I do not wish to suggest that President Business's arbitrary, tyrannical rule is the necessary consequence of the application of Harry Frankfurt's views on value, which are much more subtle and humane than can be shown here. I am merely pointing out that President Business's understanding of value seem to share some basic features with Frankfurt's theory of value.

LEGO® and the Social Blocks of Autonomy

Eric Chelstrom

Think back to your earliest days playing with LEGO® bricks. Building LEGO sets was difficult at first. You had to learn to read the pictorial instructions provided, and most likely you had someone else's guidance through this initial phase of your building. Soon, you no longer needed the additional guidance, however—the instructions provided were sufficient. Later on, you were able to build more and more advanced sets. Eventually, you might have surpassed even the instructions themselves, not just learning to anticipate steps in a build, but perhaps even learning to design and build freely on your own.

Builders who rely on instructions are less autonomous, less able to self-direct their actions and choices—they are still dependent on others in a potentially problematic way. Of course, it was only through the guidance of others that you were even able to begin to act autonomously in the first place—other people helped provide building blocks for your development. But you can also imagine that some nefarious person—Lord Business perhaps—might prefer to block your development, and keep you dependent on their guidance. If the aim is to develop your capacity to choose and act on your own, then how are others involved in your coming to be an independent person?

What Is Autonomy?

Contemporary philosopher Christine Korsgaard provides a helpful basic account of autonomy, "An agent is *autonomous* when her

LEGO® and Philosophy: Constructing Reality Brick By Brick, First Edition.
Edited by Roy T. Cook and Sondra Bacharach.
© 2017 John Wiley & Sons Ltd. Published 2017 by John Wiley & Sons Ltd.

movements are in some clear sense self-determined or her own."[1] If your actions are not determined by yourself, then you're not acting autonomously. If there's some form of external constraint or inner compulsion, then your actions may not be self-determined. In order to be autonomous you also have to be competent and be choosing for yourself; this can mean that you are able to reflect upon and exercise choices based on what you value.[2] If you're being told what to like, value, or do, and that's the only reason you do it, it's not obvious that your actions are really up to you, or that you've decided to do things yourself. To act autonomously is to act in such a way that your choices are free from compulsion or coercion from others.

Thinking about how we come to get better at building with LEGO bricks, it's reasonable to believe that autonomy develops in degrees. As an AFOL who has a son who is a KFOL, this is something I know all too well. The first sets that my son got were basically an excuse for me to end my Dark Age and to share something I love with him. But as he began to build sets without my help, I was left watching. As a parent, seeing my son's newly developed skill and ability to build on his own was great. As an AFOL, I lost an easy LEGO fix. Thankfully, some of the more difficult building techniques still require my assistance. I also have a younger daughter who's very happy to build with DUPLO® bricks—a gateway drug if anything is. Of course my son's developing LEGO autonomy doesn't mean that he's autonomous in all other respects.

Emmet

The LEGO Movie provides even more ways to help us think about the nature of autonomy and how others can either help or hinder our development. At the beginning of *The LEGO Movie*, Emmet is an extreme case of someone who's not autonomous. In spite of being an adult of sorts, he's completely dependent on others. Emmet uses instruction books to live his life. The instructions cover everything from hygiene to making and keeping friends, and Emmet appears completely unable to think for himself. He is especially dependent on whoever put together his instruction books for life. Other people in the LEGO world refer to Emmet's lack of individuality and ability to choose for himself negatively when interviewed by Bad Cop. This is humorously illustrated when Vitruvius, Wyldstyle, and Emmet enter Emmet's mind only to find a vast emptiness.

It's also worth thinking about whether whoever wrote the instruction booklets—presumably Lord Business's Octan Corporation—intends to help or harm people. Since Emmet is presumably not the only one using these instructions, even if he is more dependent on them than others, this represents a scary possibility: we could be subtly made to serve someone else's interests.

In *The LEGO Movie*, Emmet is presented as a likeable, sympathetic figure, but also as someone whose dependence on the instruction booklet goes too far. Others don't seem to be quite so dependent, and we're given the impression that they are more genuinely individual than Emmet. They measure their judgments and pursue their interests. Even if they don't always make the best choices, they appear better off than Emmet. Our sympathy for Emmet resembles something more like our affection for a child.

Emmet's goals and aspirations are shared by most of us: doing well at our jobs, living good lives, having friendships, and so on. Emmet's struggle is familiar, as is his occasional impulse to let others do things for him. Otherwise it'd be hard to imagine why so much attention is paid to horoscopes, advice columns, talk shows, self-help books, and internet comment threads. It's not as if most of us have a genuine moral high ground from which to judge Emmet, even if our own cases are less extreme. Emmet's inability to think for himself is not unique.

Immanuel Kant (1724–1804), whose ethical philosophy centered on the concept of autonomy, believed that to be autonomous is to be capable of using one's reason for oneself and from that, to be able to self-direct one's actions in morally appropriate ways. This doesn't mean that we can't seek advice from others. Of course, it's sometimes best to rely on testimony from experts before making a responsible judgment. That's much different from letting others do our thinking for us.

Kant describes the attitude of the deferential individual who refuses to develop their autonomy thusly: "I need not think, if I can only pay others; others will readily undertake the irksome business for me."[3] Letting others think for us represents a personal failure insofar as we don't develop our own judgment. Kant points out that our attitude of deference to others plays into the hands of those waiting to exploit us; hence it is potentially dangerous.

Of course, mistakes will happen. We shouldn't expect to go from unformed judgments to perfection, and we shouldn't hold ourselves up against some impossible expectation. No one's first LEGO build is mistake free, but it still gets completed. And each subsequent build gets easier. Emmet's development in the movie is like this. We watch him go from rough and deferential, a veritable babe, to a self-confident autonomous agent. We also see clearly how Lord Business profits, both economically and politically, from the deferential attitudes of his subjects. Lord Business benefits from keeping others in a state of ignorant or fearful dependency.

Kant also has something to say about our, or Emmet's, dependence on instructions. He argues against strict dependence on instructions, formulas, or simple precepts. "Precepts and formulas, those mechanical instruments of a rational use, or rather misuse, of his natural endowments, are the ball and chain of an everlasting [immaturity]."[4] Kant's point is that these sorts of things—manuals, self-help books, etc.—can be ways to avoid thinking for ourselves. The autonomous individual will judge rightly for herself. By using her own judgment, she will adopt the principle that is morally best. Even if we have the capacity to act autonomously, a dependence on instructions, formulas, or precepts represents a personal failure, even if they can also aid our development. They are things we should outgrow at some point.

The LEGO Movie doesn't just point to a lack of autonomy in Emmet; different degrees of autonomy also explain the difference between Finn and his father, The Man Upstairs. Finn's father is the LEGO devotee who can't diverge from a rigidly patterned creation. He abhors the mixing of unlike bricks and sets. Finn, by contrast, freely uses his capacities in ways that go beyond the limited, instructed given. While instructions are helpful as guides to help us develop skills in the first place, they become crutches that hold us back once we've developed those capacities for ourselves, and they can shackle us to others' judgments in ways that prevent our own judgments from taking charge.

Emmet is also contrasted with the Master Builders, who are autonomous, making decisions for themselves with confidence and gusto. But, as the film progresses, we begin to see the limitations of the Master Builders. They all have their own ideas about what to do or build and they don't work well together. Batman® wants everything cool and in black (and sometimes very very dark grey). Princess Unikitty has her own manic style. Benny wants only to build a spaceship in the Classic Space style from the 1980s' LEGO space sets. Though autonomous, the Master Builders are still limited. By themselves, they cannot defeat Lord Business, as MetalBeard's disastrous attempt to do so demonstrates. The individualist conception of autonomy found in Kant and represented by the Master Builders may not be enough; it certainly wasn't going to defeat Lord Business. How can fully autonomous persons fail to be able to meaningfully cooperate? Their autonomy, in the individualist sense, isn't disrupted and they're not being coerced. So what more might there be to autonomy?

Wyldstyle

Wyldstyle's case allows us to examine what might be missing in the Master Builders. When we first meet her, she's amazingly capable and confident. However, we later learn from Vitruvius that "Wyldstyle" is only the latest in a string of names and identities that she's adopted. Her given name is Lucy, and she molds her personality to others' expectations. We see in Wyldstyle an individual with many of the qualities of other autonomous individuals, but she nonetheless suffers from a deference to others' expectations. Lucy became Wyldstyle only after wanting to be seen by others in different ways.

Jean-Paul Sartre (1905–1980) argued that we experience ourselves through the look of others. Sartre's point is that you experience yourself partly in terms of how others see you and react to you. Sartre argues that "I am responsible for my being-for-others, but I am not the foundation of it."[5] In other words, you can never fully determine how others see you or think about you. The categories and meanings according to which we understand each other and ourselves are the result of an ongoing negotiation between ourselves and others. Nonetheless, my choices in relation to those categories and meanings make me responsible for how I experience how I am seen by others.

Simone de Beauvoir (1908–1986) further develops this idea, especially with respect to the ways that women's experiences are shaped and limited by how they learn to see themselves and their possibilities. Beauvoir argues that women's experiences are so affected by others, and that their choices are foreclosed so much, that women's autonomy is disrupted. She writes, "what singularly defines the situation of woman is that being, like all human beings, an autonomous freedom, she discovers and chooses herself in a world where men force her to assume herself as Other."[6] Beauvoir doesn't just claim that the choices women make are forced in some way, and therefore not genuinely autonomous. She also stresses that choosing to be identified as fully capable of autonomy—a choice generally available to men—isn't available to women. How others see us determines how we see ourselves, which in turn determines whether or not we can develop autonomy.

If I'm the sort of person who is traditionally seen as being capable of achieving autonomy, then I'm advantaged in at least two ways compared to one who isn't seen this way. First, I'm not impeded by others' expectations, I haven't internalized those expectations, and so I don't have to deal with these sorts of obstacles to developing my autonomy.[7] Second, even if I can work around those blocks and develop my autonomy, it will not be undercut by how others receive my actions. To see how this works, think about how Wyldstyle expresses her discomfort with her identity, and how she doubts her abilities during moments of weakness. Think also about how her ideas aren't given equal consideration, especially by her partner Batman. More generally, consider the gender imbalance of the Master Builders. Apart from brief appearances by Wonder Woman, Cleopatra, a mermaid, and the Statue of Liberty, the only women Master Builders are Unikitty—who is manic and childish—and Wyldstyle. The rest form a literal "boy's club."[8]

Contemporary philosophers have explored how other people might be crucial to the development and maintenance of an individual's autonomy through discussions of relational autonomy. Their point is not that the individualist conception of autonomy is itself wrong; rather, it's incomplete in exactly the sorts of ways demonstrated by the Master Builders and Wyldstyle.

Catriona Mackenzie provides three points in favor of relational conceptions of autonomy. First, a relational account is consistent with the facts of human vulnerability and dependency, in contrast to individualist conceptions where individuals are completely self-sufficient.[9] Second, unlike the individualist conception, relational conceptions are premised on the recognition of how social practices, group identities, and historical contingencies shape the formation of individual persons.[10] Third, a relational account recognizes that unjust social conditions restrict some individuals' capacity for self-determination.[11]

Mackenzie stresses that the individual conception of autonomy is generally structured as an ideal theory: a theory that starts from the perfect ideal and then judges actuality in relation to how far it falls short. By contrast, a non-ideal approach starts from actuality and theorizes what possibilities we have within our actual state of affairs. Compare Lord Business's plan to use the Kragle. He cannot stand the non-ideal, so he seeks to "perfect" everything by freezing it forever into an ideal state. This sort of ideal state is attainable only at the expense of everyone's autonomy via the Kragle. By contrast, Emmet and friends seek to make the actual world a better place. In Wyldstyle's case, we see that she measures herself against an impossible standard, never accepts herself as good enough, and thus always second guesses and reinvents herself. It is better for her to recognize the exceptional person she is, get comfortable in her own skin, and accept being Lucy.

Relational accounts of autonomy help us understand and appreciate how others play constructive roles in developing and maintaining our autonomy. It's not just that others can help us develop our individual skills, but that others help structure the social contexts in which we operate. Cultural and social norms are products of human actions. If everyone thinks that people with a certain characteristic are a certain way, it's hard for someone with that characteristic *not* to see herself that way. If Lucy is always around individuals who don't respect her or her capabilities, she will likely internalize their expectations and attitudes and seek to make herself into something she thinks others would prefer. Her autonomy is thus undermined by others' expectations of her. Likewise, if young women are repeatedly told that LEGO sets and bricks are for boys, then they won't feel that they should play with LEGO sets and bricks. They'll then also lose out on the opportunity to be first guided through complex builds, to then surpass that guidance in a community of peers.

Becoming The Special, "Everything is Awesome"

When Emmet finally comes into his own as The Special, it is only with the help of others. Emmet begins his development by convincing the Master Builders to follow his plan. Among them, only he has the capacity to really understand others' expectations in a way that will result in a successful plan to stop Lord Business's plot. It is also only after he gets praise from the others, and because of his desire to save them, that Emmet finally musters the confidence and strength necessary to complete his development.

Wyldstyle experiences a development similar to Emmet's. True, she starts the film far ahead of him, but she too grows and becomes more autonomous. Consider Wyldstyle's comfort, finally, at being Lucy at the end of the film. This isn't something she developed on her own. The other people in her life tended to prevent her from taking that extra step necessary to acquire confidence in herself and her abilities. In large part, Wyldstyle's growth seems to be thanks to Emmet's friendship. It isn't because Emmet is a man that Wyldstyle is so affected. Rather,

Emmet clearly and strongly establishes alternative expectations for Lucy that allow her to be okay with herself. Emmet does what any of us should do in supporting a friend—promote his or her autonomy and its development. Friends should also hold each other accountable for errors of judgment, especially when our actions or beliefs undermine or limit the autonomy of others. Our parents weren't wrong in insisting that who our friends are significantly impacts who we become. Someone who acts against our autonomy may seem like a friend, but they demean us by their actions and we harm ourselves through our complicity.

Others can provide us with building blocks for autonomy when they offer guidance in developing our abilities. But they can also create obstacles when they impede our development or create a context in which our capacities aren't recognized or a context which establishes a dangerous deference to those in power. This is why it's so great that at the end of *The LEGO Movie*, The Man Upstairs includes Finn's sister in the joy of playing with LEGO bricks. The hardest part for others, and us, is probably recognizing when to shift from offering concrete building blocks of guidance toward offering supportive blocks of recognition, as The Man Upstairs had to realize in relation to Finn. We have to recognize that the goal isn't to just become a self-sufficient individual in the mold of the Master Builders or Lord Business, seeing others only as outside their autonomy and as potential impediments to one's individual success. Instead, being able to work with others is also a legitimate mark of autonomy. As Paulo Freire put it: "The pursuit of full humanity … cannot be carried out in isolation or individualism, but only in fellowship and solidarity."[12]

It is worth thinking about the song of *The LEGO Movie*, "Everything is Awesome." From the standpoint of individual autonomy its lyrics could be interpreted as endorsing a chilling sort of dependency on others. When we first encounter the song, its reception within the LEGO world suggests a herd-like mentality. Its principal message appears to be how awesomeness comes only through conformity—everything's better if one doesn't think for oneself. "Let's take extra care to follow the instructions or you'll be put to sleep," smirks Lord Business. A cutaway scene shows that Lord Business's corporation specifically crafted this song, and they even released separate versions of it to appeal to distinctive parts of the LEGO world. His robots churn out these hits to keep people in a state of unquestioning complicity, a state of deference to him: genuinely soulless corporate pop.

Wyldstyle has a strong disdain for the song's endorsement of conformism—the song enshrines the failure of individual autonomy within the LEGO world. However, from the standpoint of relational autonomy, the song expresses something positive. It is only through others that we can achieve robust autonomy. It's one thing to be an individual; another to be an individual among others whose very being is acknowledged and given recognition. Everything really is better when you're part of a team—not as a mere member, but as a peer among other autonomous persons.

Notes

1. Christine M. Korsgaard, *The Constitution of Agency* (Oxford: Oxford University Press, 2008), 83.
2. John Christman, "Autonomy in Moral and Political Philosophy," in Edward N. Zalta, ed., *The Stanford Encyclopedia of Philosophy* (Spring 2015 edition). Available at http://plato.stanford.edu/archives/spr2015/entries/autonomy-moral/: Section 1.1–2 (accessed February 24, 2017).
3. Immanuel Kant, "An Answer to the Question: What is Enlightenment?" in *Practical Philosophy*, trans. and ed. Mary J. Gregor (Cambridge: Cambridge University Press, 1996), 17/8: 35.
4. Ibid., 17/8: 36.
5. Jean-Paul Sartre, *Being and Nothingness*, trans. Hazel E. Barnes (New York: Washington Square Press, 1984), 475.
6. Simone de Beauvoir, *The Second Sex*, trans. Constance Borde and Sheila Malovany-Chevallier (New York: Vintage Books, 2011), 17.
7. See also Frantz Fanon's *Black Skin, White Masks*, trans. Richard Philcox (New York: Grove Press, 2008).
8. While *The LEGO Movie* is given a technical pass on the Bechdel test (two female characters who talk to one another about more than a man) due to a one-line exchange between Unikitty and Wyldstyle, the sequel's director, Chris McKay, is on record doubting it passes, and fully supporting doing better in the sequel. See http://www.dailymail.co.uk/tvshowbiz/article-2597511/The-Lego-Movie-filmmaker-Chris-McKay-promises-strong-females-sequel.html (accessed February 24, 2017).
9. Catriona Mackenzie, "Three Dimensions of Autonomy: A Relational Analysis," in Andrea Veltman and Mark Piper, eds., *Autonomy, Oppression, and Gender* (Oxford: Oxford University Press, 2014), 21.
10. Ibid.
11. Ibid., 22.
12. Paulo Freire, *Pedagogy of the Oppressed*, trans. Myra Bergman Ramos (New York: Continuum, 2000), 85.

Building and Dwelling with Heidegger and LEGO® Toys

Ellen Miller

From their beginning in 1932, LEGO® toys have expressed and were designed with an *ethos* grounded in simplicity, care, fun, and sustainability. The name LEGO—an abbreviation of the Danish "leg godt," meaning *play well*—includes an ethical and social mandate. This *ethos* can also be found in contemporary LEGO organizations such as LEGO Serious Play®, a community-based business model where participants use LEGO materials for professional development. This organization—the only one of its kind officially approved by the LEGO Group—extends LEGO values into the adult business world. Interestingly, the LEGO Group and LEGO Serious Play articulate an explicit systemization, yet they also endorse openness, flexibility, and creativity. The LEGO corporation's emphasis on openness parallels the philosopher Martin Heidegger's (1889–1976) emphasis on openness, releasement, and working creatively within the structures and limitations of history and culture.

Emmet as Existentialist: No More Mr. Conformist

Even though Heidegger's writings are not easily categorized, his themes resonate with those explored by existentialists: authenticity, the connectedness between self and world, the importance of our first-person experiences, and the limitations of traditional philosophy.[1]

For Heidegger, each person must define what it means to be human by choosing how to act. We must make our lives meaningful since

LEGO® and Philosophy: Constructing Reality Brick By Brick, First Edition.
Edited by Roy T. Cook and Sondra Bacharach.
© 2017 John Wiley & Sons Ltd. Published 2017 by John Wiley & Sons Ltd.

life does not come with pre-packaged meanings. When Vitruvius tells Emmet, "Don't worry about what others are doing. You must embrace what is special about you," his pronouncement parallels this existentialist theme. We must make our lives awesome through our efforts and actions. Emmet's journey alongside the Master Builders—those able to build without instructions—shows some of the difficulties involved in stepping outside the norms of one's society.

The existentialist self is in the world with others but must learn to make choices that are not determined by group values alone. For Heidegger, we are often too comfortably absorbed in the values and ideas that stem from those around us.[2] We find ourselves in a world filled with others where we learn what "One does not do and what one must do." For example, in North American societies, "One does not throw LEGO bricks at the dinner table." This simply is not the way "one acts."

In *The LEGO Movie*, the awesomeness of teamwork makes it comfortable and easy to conform and not stand out as unique. The movie's opening sequence offers us a laundry list of items one must and must not do, from making breakfast to getting one's $37.00 cup of coffee. Initially, Emmet loves being lost in this sea of conformity: "Tell me what to do, and I'll do it!" Hearing, listening, and being open to others are part of how we understand the world. Yet, following these voices can limit our ability to speak with an authentic voice. Emmet's journey exemplifies the existentialist journey toward such authenticity. And, importantly, the movie ends with the revelation that creativity is available to everyone, not just one special individual.

Moods and Play

One way we make sense of ourselves and our worlds is through what Heidegger calls our moods.[3] Moods—joy, boredom, anxiety, bliss, anger—influence and determine how things matter to us. The way we act, listen to others, and reflect on our actions influences our world, and our world in turn influences the ways we act and respond to other people. We are not separate from the world; rather we are always what Heidegger calls being-in-the-world. We do not just find ourselves in situations that we then work to understand; our actions influence the situations in which we find ourselves. For example, suppose we care about animals and children. When we look at a pile of LEGO bricks, we might create an animal hospital and a school. Our concerns and ways of attuning ourselves to the world allow us to see and experience the world.

We do not look at the world neutrally. Rather, the same object appears differently depending on our practical situations and the contexts in which we find ourselves. Whether our building arises through solitary play or building alongside Batman® and Unikitty, moods help determine our sense of what is possible for us and others.

According to Heidegger, humans always look ahead into the future, projecting forward. Yet our past encounters leave their mark on our present experiences and our expectations for the future. Childhood play and being playful link together our present situations, past encounters, and our future horizons. For many of us, our first LEGO building happened at home. Our future creating might arise in different settings with friends or the organized building of a LEGO First league. And yet, these early building experiences—including our emotional connections to past building experiences—remain part of our LEGO memories.

When we are most engaged in building and creating, past, present, and future are connected. Constructing and creating with LEGO toys helps us understand how we are always creating and re-creating, building and constructing our own identities and possibilities. This is especially important for the adult LEGO creator who maintains what one LEGO artist calls "a sense of youthfulness" through creating with childhood toys.[4]

Engaged Play with Modular Bricks

When we play with LEGO toys, we eventually realize our creations can be taken apart or knocked down. Heidegger explains that these moments of destruction are opportunities for understanding. When a tool or piece of equipment no longer works, we begin to observe the object in a more detached and objective manner. Heidegger names our relationship with tools when we are engaged and using them as experiencing them as "ready-to-hand." If we stand back and view the tool at a distance, outside our engaged use, we are analyzing the tool as something that is what he calls "present-at-hand." Even though our age privileges the knowledge and understanding produced by the detached techniques that turn nature and things into present-at-hand entities, Heidegger thinks the connectedness with things we feel through actively engaging with them is more basic and primordial than the detached mode we adopt in scientific investigations. For Heidegger, our engaged, lived experiences with things tell us about what it means to be human. Thus, it makes sense that we learn more by playing with LEGO bricks than by merely contemplating them. For Heidegger, play is especially important because it reconnects us with the awe and wonder that are foundational to what it means to be human. Indeed, play—especially a capability to remain open and creative—helps us to live authentically.

The open structure of LEGO toys invites openness from creators. Other toys—board games, for example—might create, require, and sustain different moods and modes of play. However, LEGO play reveals moods and desires in a unique way. LEGO play often extends over a sustained period of time, inviting play with the same bricks in diverse environments with different emotional settings.

Unfortunately, the master narratives and Master Builders often cover up our playful moods in favor of what Heidegger calls "calculative thinking." Calculative thinking values efficiency and flexibility; it demands that nature and humans be on-call, available, ready to respond to our need for maximum efficiency and flexibility, and adopts an attitude of mastery toward things.[5] We assume we can use things, use them up, in any way we see fit. Everything shows up as a resource that can be manipulated, mastered, and controlled by humans.[6] Play—perhaps especially when our creation needs to be built again and again—can awaken us to ways of relating to things without seeking mastery over them. Such play is marked by an openness, where we do not need to completely understand and control things, though admittedly play can also fall back into more inauthentic, mastering attitudes.

Existence is fundamentally for Heidegger "without why," without a definite purpose, meaning, or ground. Even time unfolds in ways that are not completely under our control and mastery. Our everyday play can show traces of this deep sense of play. In engaged play, we let things be and let ourselves be with others in ways that follow Heidegger's call for more meditative thinking.

Instances of boredom—that often arise prior to engaged play— show that contemporary life has become preoccupied with consuming, producing, and mastering things. When things show up for us in only one way, dominated by the rhythms of familiar patterns, our capacity for boredom increases. Our bored moods help awaken us to the dangers within closed-off thinking that does not embrace creativity.

When we attend to our moods during play, we focus on the shared values that arise during LEGO construction. LEGO builders, filled with moods of care and wonder toward nature and our built environments, are in an ideal position to transform LEGO bricks into recyclable pieces.

Too often, we regard play as a break from the more important aspects of our lives marked by work, especially work that conforms with societal norms. It is important to become aware of how our moods and values influence whether our play becomes transformative or merely follows pre-packaged instructions. The modularity of LEGO bricks allows for the expression of multiple values on different occasions.

Heidegger uses the word "play" to describe even the most serious aspects of how history unfolds and how we should respond to those aspects of life beyond our control. Play has a dual structure that can involve everyday playful encounters with others and the more serious play of time and history that is also always just outside our control. Our existence is fundamentally and foundationally characterized by play. For Heidegger, this means that meaning and truth always have mysterious aspects—not unlike our mysterious friend Batman—that remain hidden.

"It's a New Toy Everyday"

Even though we have this fundamental capacity for care and play, Heidegger thinks our careful nature can easily be covered over by a more dominant way of relating with things. Often, we confront things as disposable resources that we can use in any way we wish. Think, for example, about how we use waterways, plastics, natural gas, and other people in ways that maximize our efficiency and productivity. Even our free time and vacations are designed to maximize our productivity once we return to work. One of Heidegger's main tasks was to explore the problems of this technological worldview and the calculative thinking that results from it. The potential for commodification and systematization during our building with LEGO bricks parallels this potential in our broader relationships with nature, artworks, and people.

Humans are the great calculators (like Lord Business) who strive for productivity. In *The LEGO Movie*, teamwork and rule-following lead, at least initially, to productivity and happiness. Lord Business proclaims "Let's take extra care to follow the instructions or you'll be put to sleep!," emphasizing the drive to follow the rules that have been created by those in power. Teamwork is so awesome that you will not want to stand out, challenge the rules, or work in isolation from your team members. The resulting contrast between Lord Business and the Master Builders displays the tensions we experience between wanting to be special and knowing that we often accomplish more when we collaborate and work together, even if that means abandoning what is special about us.

LEGO toys and *The LEGO Movie* highlight these tensions between the mass appeal of products and the desire to feel your creations are special and unique. We play in part because we want to overcome this tension that can never be completely resolved. Even activities that bring us outside dominant and dominating ways of thinking can lead us right back to technological ways of relating.

Although LEGO bricks are made out of non-recyclable plastic, LEGO building holds out the potential for creative and sustainable play. One of the most famous LEGO slogans, "It's a new toy every-day," reveals the toy's demand for constant renewal and creativity. The end of *The LEGO Movie* shows how the durability of LEGO bricks contributes to a kind of recyclability. We can always make something new out of our LEGO toys. This reminds us that our lives are much like our LEGO creations; they can be taken apart at any moment.

The LEGO Movie expresses concern over whether children's play has become commodified to such an extent that open and free play is impossible. But the movie itself is a sustained advertisement cleverly crafted—yet not even hidden—to look like an endorsement of individuality. LEGO's growth into a Disney®-like entity—hotels, amusement parks, playsets that accompany blockbuster films—can leave us yearning for a purer space outside the influence of advertising and Lord Business. It would be nice if there were some possible world without Lord Business and where there was no Good Cop/Bad Cop. However, this place does not exist. Our world and LEGO worlds are filled with dangers and the ever-present threat of destruction. One of the main ways we can guard against these dangers is by becoming mindful, aware, and attuned to our everyday worlds. In this way, we become philosophical LEGO builders. Part of the essence of LEGO work is that we must return to our building each day. Even if we Kragle our creations, new creations will require even more unglued bricks.

Serious Play as Art: The Saving Power in LEGO-building

Heidegger's writings, especially his later works, stress how art can help us break free from the control and manipulation characteristic of calculative thinking. In "The Origin of the Work of Art," Heidegger interprets Van Gogh's depiction of shoes, writing that the shoes show the world of the peasant, the work and toil of a life rooted to the earth. Heidegger claims artworks—not just scientific studies—open and reveal truth.

By art, Heidegger does not just mean Van Gogh's paintings, Mozart's sonatinas, and Rodin's sculptures. Rather, he has a very broad and expansive understanding of art and emphasizes how understanding art can help us approach ourselves, others, and nature in less domineering ways.[7]

Using Heidegger's descriptive approach, we can analyze a more contemporary shoe example. Even commercial ads show up and reveal the values of our culture in the ways Heidegger describes. The famous "Just Do It" Nike sneaker slogan reveals the contemporary values of individual achievement and pushing your body past what you think it can do.

We see another example of how art reveals normally hidden truths in a 2014 LEGO ad by Union Made Creative and director Brigg Bloomquist. Focusing on young girl LEGO builders, the ad emphasizes how girls can solve problems on their own. Because gender impacts our world and makes it especially difficult for girls to keep building into adulthood, the ad urges girls to #KeepBuilding. Thankfully, traditional LEGO pieces allow the construction of differently gendered characters during separate play sessions. Thus, the ability to create and re-create characters also highlights gender's constructedness and fluidity.

Dwelling and Building with LEGO

In one of his meditations and critiques of architecture, Heidegger writes, "Only if we are capable of dwelling, only then can we build."[8] Here he links the quality of our dwelling to the quality of our building. According to Heidegger, authentic dwelling is marked by the virtues of sparing and preserving—environmental virtues. Heidegger would include what is now called interior design—a field currently dominated by female designers—as part of construction and architecture. Unfortunately, these fields have now become separated, with engineering being privileged over both architecture and interior design. Heidegger's emphasis on the interconnections among personal, social, and global building breaks down the boundaries that have developed among these fields. Building and dwelling are ways we make sense of the world and come to understand our existence. For Heidegger, these activities are rooted in a poetic, thoughtful encounter with the world.

LEGO activities help connect adults and children and allow adults to retrieve their more child-like and play-ful natures. In a broad sense, most people have experienced the flow of time and intensity characteristic of childhood. This immediacy and being-in-the-present we feel as children only appears as such to the adult who is able to retrieve the child's perspective.

Heidegger describes children as in a "twilight of existence," and helps us understand how children can be part of the adult world yet separate from it.[9] Building and dwelling with LEGO toys can help adults retrieve the more poetic modes of revealing discussed by Heidegger, especially in his later writings. Dwelling and building in worlds of LEGO toys is one way to sustain the awe and wonder needed for authentic building and philosophizing. Indeed, engaged philosophizing (including philosophical LEGO building), which is attentive to emotionality and mood, is one way to sustain the awe and wonder needed for more meditative playing, building, and dwelling.[10]

Notes

1. Heidegger—like most writers placed into this category—would have resisted such labelling. See *Existentialism: A Beginner's Guide* by Thomas Wartenberg (London: OneWorld Publications, 2008) for a good introduction to existentialist philosophy.
2. Heidegger uses the term *Das Man*, meaning a generic self, the One, the they-self. This indeterminate yet powerful collective guides our actions and thoughts in often unconscious ways. When we pronounce, "One simply does not do that," we can see the influence of this unnamed force.
3. Mood (*Stimmung*) contributes to our understanding and meaning of the world. *Befindlichkeit*, attunement, refers to a fundamental state of existence that grounds our moods.
4. Mark J.P. Wolf, ed., *LEGO Studies: Examining the Building Blocks of a Transmedial Phenomenon* (London: Routledge, 2014), 212.

5. Martin Heidegger, "Question Concerning Technology," in *The Question Concerning Technology and Other Essays* (New York: Harper and Row, 1977).

6. Heidegger's term for this is *Bestand*, often translated as "standing reserve." No longer are entities understood even as objects separate from human subjects. We have transformed them even more into "holdings," "assets" always available for human use and consumption.

7. He does also use art, especially *Dichtung*, in a narrow sense. However, his broader understandings are especially helpful for our encounters with LEGO toys as art.

8. Martin Heidegger, "Building, Dwelling, Thinking," in *Poetry, Language, Thought* (New York: HarperCollins, 1975).

9. Lawrence Hatab, *Ethics and Finitude: Heideggerian Contributions to Moral Philosophy* (Lanham: Rowman & Littlefield Publishers, 2000), 67.

10. I appreciate the helpful suggestions (and Lego creations) I received on earlier versions of this paper from Rowan University faculty and students. I would also like to thank the participants at Towson University's Geo-Aesthetics Conference.

Part III
LEGO® AND IDENTITY

Ninjas, Kobe Bryant, and Yellow Plastic
The LEGO® Minifigure and Race

Roy T. Cook

When the modern version of the LEGO® minifigure was introduced in 1978 its bright yellow color was a conscious choice, meant to be racially and ethnically neutral. Further, all the yellow-skinned minifigures had the exact same printing on their faces—the "smiley"—obscuring any differences between minifigures. Within the original world, any minifigure could be anyone. Race (as well as gender and other differences) was erased via the creation of a uniformly bright-yellow-skinned world where minifigures could not be distinguished or discriminated against based on the color of their ABS plastic skins. Or, at least, that was the intention.

Where's Lando?

We could, of course, argue about the desirability of a uniformly hued fictional world where differences in skin color and physical appearance don't exist, as compared to a more pluralistic vision where such diversity exists but does not provide the foundation for systematic discrimination and marginalization. But the LEGO Group faced a much more practical challenge to their attempt at racial neutrality in 1999, when they acquired the license to produce *Star Wars®* themed sets. The first *Star Wars* sets were based on the original trilogy, but fans soon noticed that none of these sets included a Lando Calrissian minifigure. And how could they? How could or should LEGO represent Billie Dee Williams's iconic character as a minifigure? In short,

LEGO® and Philosophy: Constructing Reality Brick By Brick, First Edition.
Edited by Roy T. Cook and Sondra Bacharach.
© 2017 John Wiley & Sons Ltd. Published 2017 by John Wiley & Sons Ltd.

they faced a simple problem: How do you represent a world like Star
Wars where race exists within a pre-existing framework that explicitly
eliminates race?

LEGO's solution to this dilemma was simple. In 2003 they introduced another licensed theme: a series of minifigures and sets based
on famous players in the National Basketball Association (NBA). The
heads and arms of black NBA players were molded in brown plastic, while the white players' heads and arms were molded in a new,
peachy-colored plastic. Race had now entered the world of the LEGO
minifigure.[1]

Shortly after this controversial move, a brown-skinned Lando
minifigure finally appeared in the Cloud City set (set #10123). Interestingly, other characters in the Cloud City set were molded in yellow, but
eventually all licensed LEGO sets (Star Wars, Harry Potter®, Superheroes, etc.) included minifigures molded in an ever-widening variety
of brown-, pink-, and peach-colored plastic. There are over two dozen
different shades of plastic that have been used for minifigure heads and
hands in licensed LEGO sets! Non-licensed themes, such as the ven-
erable City, Farm, Space, Pirate, and Train themes, still contain the
purportedly racially neutral yellow minifigures.[2]

In one sense this seems like an elegant solution to the problem:
LEGO licensed sets take place in a world (or in a number of distinct
worlds—as many as there are different licenses) where race, indicated
by the color of plastic used to mold their heads and hands, *exists*
and *matters*, since race, and distinctions and discriminations based
on race, matter within the original films, television shows, and other
media on which the licensed sets are based. Non-licensed sets such as
City and Space, however, take place in the original racially idealized
world of the original all-yellow LEGO minifigure, where race, and
hence distinctions based on race, do not exist. More generally, *any*
LEGO builds—official or not—that contain flesh-toned minifigures
represent characters that are white, Asian, black, native American,
or any of a host of other racial identities, while LEGO builds that
contain yellow minifigures represent characters that have no race (or
represent characters whose race is not identifiable, at the very least,
and thus cannot matter to our understanding of the LEGO build in
question).

It's certainly a simple story regarding how race works in the LEGO
world. But it's also one that can't be quite right. Race is not a fixed
category that is inherent to a person and can be represented by one
of a fixed number of colors of plastic, but is instead constituted by

changeable, unstable social and political factors and contexts as much as, if not more than, it is determined by skin color and ancestry. And the concept of race is at least as unstable in the world of the LEGO minifigure as it is in the real world. As a result, we can use the complicated connections between the race of a minifigure and the color of the plastic in which they are molded to help us understand both how race works in the world(s) of the LEGO minifigure and how race works in our own world.

The Building Bricks of Race

Traditionally, people (and peoples) have been divided into races based on three criteria:[3]

1. Ancestry
2. Geographical origin
3. Physical characteristics (skin color, facial structure).

Sorting humankind into races, in and of itself, need not be pernicious, any more than sorting humans into other categories (gender, sexual preference, socioeconomic class, Zodiacal signs) or sorting LEGO bricks by color or shape is inherently immoral. The important question is what we *do* with these categories. And it is hard to imagine a division of people into kinds that has been associated with more immorality than divisions based on race. Historically, race has been used to justify differential treatment based on the idea that one race is more human, or more capable physically or mentally, or religiously chosen, or more pure, or superior in some other way, when compared to another (or all) other races. Fortunately, many of us have moved beyond explicit acceptance of such morally repugnant views.

Here, however, we are less interested in the negative effects of racism, and more interested in how we should understand race itself. Again, this is not to say that the latter is more important than the former. Quite the contrary. But the examination of race in LEGO has more to teach us about the nature of race—what it is, and what it is not—than it has to teach us about the consequences of racism.

The concept of race is relatively new. The ancient Greek and Roman worlds had no notion of race. This is not to say that they were all very nice people who never discriminated. The Greeks and Romans treated people differently based on their gender and based on whether or not they spoke the right language (so-called "barbarians" did not).[4] But they didn't divide people into different races, and the word "race" did not even enter the English language until the early sixteenth century.[5] Thus, it has not always seemed evident to everyone that humanity is naturally divided into distinct races.

Until the mid-twentieth century the traditional, three-part conception of race mentioned above was explained in biological terms: a person was a member of a particular race based on some objective biological property had by that person. This is the *biological essentialist* account of race. One of the first challenges to biological essentialism came from Franz Boaz, a German-American anthropologist, who showed that there was no measurable relationship between race and cranium size (at the time this was a popular essentialist account of the nature of the supposed physical and cognitive differences between different races). Later research demonstrated that race could not be explained in terms of genetics. This research, and research like it, eventually led the United Nations Education, Scientific, and Cultural Organization (UNESCO) to issue a statement denying the existence of any biological foundation for race in 1950. Unfortunately, despite this evidence, the idea that race has some kind of biological underpinning remains widely accepted.

If race, and the categorization of people into distinct races, has no biological foundation, then how do we explain race? One option is to abandon the concept altogether, arguing that there is no such thing as race in the first place. On this view our world is very much like the all-yellow minifigure world of the non-licensed LEGO sets, where there are no races, and hence no need to distinguish races based on the color of plastic or skin. Some philosophers, including Anthony Appiah[6] and Naomi Zach,[7] have defended this *eliminativist* approach, but it comes with several drawbacks. One is that, if race does not exist, then it is hard to explain the systematic oppression of various groups throughout history such as blacks, native Americans, and Asian-Americans. After all, that oppression has often focused on racially identifying its targets. Racial self-identification has also typically been central to the struggles of those who resist that oppression. Thus, if there is no such thing as race, then it is difficult to understand or endorse social and political movements, or legislation, predicated on the notion of race. For example, if there really is no such thing as race, then what effect could or should laws prohibiting discrimination based on race have?

We can solve these problems by adopting a view called *racial constructivism*. According to racial constructivism, race is a real category, and particular people do, or do not, belong to various races. These categories are not determined by biological factors (e.g., particular genes), however, but are instead determined by various activities, conceptions, conventions, behaviors, agreements, and decisions we make with regard to how to categorize people into races. The division of the population of the world into particular races is, on the constructivist view, not something that we *discover* in the world, but rather something that we *build* out of our attitudes and behaviors. In short, we don't treat people differently *because* they are members of different races—rather, they are members of different races *because* we treat them differently!

On this view we don't live in the all-yellow minifigure world of the non-licensed LEGO sets, where there are no races, but not because race was there all along. Rather, our actions and attitudes gradually transformed our world from one that resembled the world of the non-licensed all-yellow minifigure into one that more resembles the racially divided world of licensed LEGO sets.[8]

We can explain the role that geography, heritability, and physical characteristics like skin color play in our understanding of race by noting that the various attitudes and activities we have adopted make these characteristics important ingredients in determining to which race a particular person belongs. In short, ancestry, home, and skin color (among other things) are relevant to determining whether a person is white, black, Asian, or a member of another race solely because we have (often unconsciously) adopted rules for using the concept of race in a way that makes these factors salient.

The constructivist approach has some advantages over the eliminativist approach. For example, because it retains the idea that races are real, albeit socially constructed, categories, it allows us to use the concept of race legitimately in legislation and social programs. But, perhaps more importantly, on the constructivist account we are not forced to claim that a black person's status as black cannot play any legitimate role in explaining and understanding their experiences: this view allows particular members of various racial categories to use race to help them understand themselves and their place within and relationship to a racially categorized world.

There is another aspect of racial constructivism that differentiates it from both biological essentialism and eliminativism: the idea that racial categories can be (and in fact are) dynamic, changing, and at times unstable. Since our beliefs, behaviors, customs, agreements, and laws can change over time, the nature of the racial categories that arise due to these practices can differ over time as well. In addition, such practices vary not only from one time to another, but also from place to place. Philosopher Michael Root notes that the conventions and rules regarding racial classification in Brazil differ from those at work now in the United States, and both differ from the rules at work in the United States in the past. Thus, there exist people who are categorized as black in New Orleans, as white in Brazil, and would have been categorized as octoroon in New Orleans in the nineteenth century.[9] According to essentialism, at least two of these judgments must be wrong (and according to eliminativism they are all wrong), but the constructivist can accept all three judgements as correct with respect to the contexts in which they are made: The person in question really is black in the U,S, and white in Brazil. This both illustrates the flexibility and instability of race (without denying the reality of race) and explains the very different experiences such a person can have when, for example, attempting to flag a taxi in Manhattan versus flagging a taxi in Rio de Janeiro.

Kobe Bryant, Ninjas, and Race

One simple truism of the world of Adult Fans of LEGO (AFOL): If there is a way to use LEGO bricks to subvert, undermine, or circumvent whatever it is that the LEGO Group had in mind when creating particular bricks and elements, an AFOL will eventually find it. Similarly, an AFOL will also eventually find ways to subvert, undermine, or circumvent the role that the distinction between purportedly nonracial yellow minifigs and racially specific flesh-toned minifigs plays in the worlds of official LEGO sets.

Our first example is not actually a LEGO build, but rather a comic: the December 21, 2003 installment of Japanese-American Tak Toyoshima's webcomic *Secret Asian Man*, titled "Old School Secret Asian Man."[10] The first panel of the comic shows a Christmas tree from above, with a caption that reads "One Magical Christmas Eve." In the second panel we see a late 1970s-era yellow-skinned classic castle soldier minifigure (similar to, but dressed slightly differently from, the figure contained in set #6002) conversing with a version of the Kobe Bryant NBA figure released in 2003.[11] Their dialogue is as follows:

SOLDIER: Hark! Art thou not ye **Kobe Bryant** LEGO?
BRYANT: You a **reporter**?
SOLDIER: Nay. I am **Medieval** LEGO. Thy hide is **brown**.
BRYANT: … yeah.

In the next panel the conversation continues in close-up:

SOLDIER: It **matcheth** the hide of your people. Should not **my hide** too match the **alabaster** colour of my kindred?
BRYANT: Well, they only made brown people for us **NBA LEGOS**. Everyone else is yellow. There's only **one group** happy with the way things are now.

In the fourth and final panel we get Toyoshima's racially charged punchline, as two yellow-skinned LEGO ninja figures (similar to those released around 2000) enter the panel from the right, pointing and laughing at the classic castle soldier and Kobe Bryant.

Toyoshima's point couldn't be clearer. The introduction of flesh-toned figures does not merely introduce race into the worlds of LEGO licensed sets (or, perhaps more accurately, reproduce the racial dynamics already present in the stories being licensed), but the appearance of flesh-colored minifigures also forces us to re-construe the older non-licensed minifigures produced in the supposedly racially neutral yellow. In particular, Toyoshima's strip clearly illustrates that the yellow-skinned ninja figures are difficult to read as racially neutral, rather than as yellow-skinned-because-Asian (and possibly offensively so), when juxtaposed against the flesh-colored Kobe Bryant minifigure.[12]

Of course, Toyoshima has a great deal of control over how we interpret the race of the yellow-skinned minifigures in these images—in particular, he encourages us to (actually) identify them as Asian because the figures themselves (fictionally) identify themselves as Asian. With this in mind, I conducted an experiment at Brickworld 2016, the largest annual AFOL gathering in North America. I built a small vignette, titled "Seven Smiley Samurai," that consisted of twenty-one minifigures posed on a cobblestone street. On the far left was a group of casually dressed men, constructed using brown-skinned NBA player heads and hands. On the far right were seven police officers, constructed using Caucasian flesh-toned heads and hands. In the center were seven minifigures built using bodies from LEGO ninja sets and other Asian-influenced martial arts themes (for example, Ninjago®) and yellow "smiley" heads.[13]

At a symposium on race and LEGO that I moderated at Brickworld, I asked participants about the race of the seven minifigures in the middle. After an extended discussion of race and LEGO, everyone in the room agreed that in this context the yellow "smiley" heads were not racially neutral, but were unambiguously Asian. Of course, the yellow plastic of the "smiley" heads used for these figures was not the only factor contributing to this judgment—in addition, the traditional Asian clothing and the fact that the other, flesh-toned minifigures were clearly racially coded were also contributing factors. Nevertheless, in this context at least, the yellow heads and hands of the central minifigures were not taken to be racially neutral.[14]

Thus, just as changes in our own behavior, beliefs, and rules can affect who is and who is not a member of a particular race on the constructivist account, changes in the way that race is currently portrayed within the world of LEGO can have profound effects on how we understand past representations of race (or attempts to erase race altogether) in official LEGO sets. To emphasize the point even further, we need only think about how we are likely to conceptualize the race of a yellow-skinned ninja figure prior to 2003, when we might find it in a child's toy box surrounded by other yellow-skinned minifigures, and how we understand that same figure post-2003, when in the same toy box it might be surrounded by racially specific minifigures molded in various flesh-like shades. It is difficult not to read the yellow as racialized in the latter instance, regardless of the LEGO Group's original intention.

To put the point bluntly: LEGO's introduction of race into their products in 2003 did not just create a space for racially specific licensed sets separate from their idealized racially neutral system of play as exhibited in City, Space, Pirates, and Farm sets. In addition, it in effect erased the "erasure of race" from these non-licensed sets by forcing us to read at least some of these yellow-skinned minifigures, in at least some contexts, as racially specific.

The point, of course, is not to accuse LEGO of moral wrongdoing with respect to their original all-yellow attempt to create a non-racial world of play (one might criticize such an attempt for various reasons, but that isn't my purpose here). The point, instead, is to show how the introduction of new ways of representing race via the introduction of racially specific minifigures can not only change the way that race currently is represented within LEGO, but can also alter our understanding of how race functioned in LEGO all along.

Race in *The LEGO Movie*

The LEGO Movie presents an even odder juxtaposition of the various ways in which LEGO has represented race. In the film, Emmet meets Wyldstyle and her paramour, Batman®. Wyldstyle, like Emmet and the majority of the characters in the film, is molded/rendered in the supposedly racially neutral yellow. But a handful of the characters in the film, including Batman and Shaquille O'Neal, are lifted straight from licensed sets, and these characters, like the real-life minifigures upon which they are based, have flesh-toned heads and hands. Thus, the racially neutral yellow-skinned world of non-licensed sets and the racially specific worlds of licensed sets, which were subversively combined in works like Toyoshima's comic and "Seven Smiley Samurai," collide in the officially sanctioned LEGO movie.

The instability of race in the LEGO world becomes even more apparent if we ask some very simple questions about how race functions within *The LEGO Movie*. Batman is clearly white, and Shaq is clearly black. But what race is Wyldstyle? If she is white, then how are we to understand the difference between the color of her head and hands and those of Batman? If she is not white, then what race is she? Is she Asian, like the ninjas in Toyoshima's comic and the central figures in "Seven Smiley Samurai"? If so, then so are the majority of characters in *The LEGO Movie*—including Emmet, who is also clearly meant to be a counterpart of Finn in the (fictional) "real" world, who is white.

Perhaps Wyldstyle lacks race altogether, in keeping with the original intention of minifigures with yellow heads and hands? If so, does this mean that *The LEGO Movie* takes place in a world where some people belong to races, but some (in fact, most!) do not? If Wyldstyle had (spoiler alert!) stayed with Batman, and they had little LEGO babies, would those babies only have half a race? What color plastic would be used for the babies' heads and hands?

Of course, on one level these questions are silly: presumably the creators of *The LEGO Movie* did not intend to make any kind of deep statement about race with their film, and questions about race in the real world are obviously more important than questions about race in the world of LEGO minifigures. But at another level these questions *are* important, since they help us understand how LEGO's attempt to create a racially neutral, all-yellow-skinned world ultimately failed, and, more importantly, they remind us that race—both in the world of LEGO minifigures and in the real world we live in— is socially constructed and depends on context, customs, convention, and attitudes.[15]

Notes

1. The NBA minifigures were not LEGO's first attempt at representing race via different colors of plastic. The Red Indians set of 1977 (set #215) contains four "Homemaker"-style figures representing native Americans, along with a canoe (Homemaker was an earlier line of larger LEGO figures with brick-built bodies and molded heads, hands, and arms). The four figures in the Red Indians set have heads and hands molded in bright red plastic.

2. Within LEGO fandom, the word "fleshie" has become a technical term for those minifigures molded in the various shades of pink and peach meant to represent Caucasians (and occasionally other non-black races) in the worlds of licensed LEGO sets. This usage is problematic, since minifigures molded in the standard LEGO brown, representing black characters, are equally "flesh-toned." Thus, in what follows, I will use the term "flesh-toned" rather than "fleshie," which should be understood to include not only pink/peach "fleshies" but also figures molded in brown plastic, and meant to represent black characters.

3. For a detailed discussion on the philosophy of race, the reader is encouraged to consult Michael James, "Race," in *The Stanford Encyclopedia of Philosophy*, 2016. Available at http://plato.stanford.edu/entries/race/ (accessed February 26, 2017).

4. Ali Rattansi, *A Very Short Introduction to Race* (Oxford: Oxford University Press, 2007).

5. Ibid.

6. Anthony Appiah, "Race, Culture, Identity: Misunderstood Connections," in Anthony Appiah and Amy Gutmann, eds., *Color Conscious* (Princeton, NJ: Princeton University Press, 1996).

7. Naomi Zach, *Philosophy of Science and Race* (London: Routledge, 2002).

8. It is worth noting that the all-yellow world of non-licensed LEGO sets, where there are no races, is not necessarily a world of boring homogeneity. Rather, by not imposing rigid, pre-constructed racial identities and differences on minifigures (or real people), such a world leaves open the possibility (imaginatively in the case of LEGO minifigures) of unscripted

idiosyncratic difference – the possibility that individuals can craft their own identities and differences.

9. Michael Root, "How We Divide the World," *Philosophy of Science* 67 supplement (2000), S62–S639.

10. Available at http://secretasianmancomics.blogspot.com/2011/12/old-school-wednesday-racial-justice.html (accessed April 15, 2016).

11. Toyoshima takes some liberties with the Kobe Bryant minifigure, combining the purple jersey from the home uniform figure (set #3433) and the yellow legs from the away uniform figure (set #3563). The latter figure also illustrates another practical reason for abandoning the traditional yellow head in licensed sets, since some licensed figures require yellow clothing that might read as 'naked' when combined with yellow hands and head.

12. By the time flesh-colored NBA minifigures were introduced, LEGO had effectively abandoned the idea that yellow minifigures were racially and ethnically neutral, since they had replaced the single iconic "smiley" with a range of different faces, some of which were racially and ethnically stereotyped. At the same time minifigure heads also ceased to be gender neutral, as heads with explicitly feminine features (eye shadow, lipstick) began to appear.

13. Interestingly, "Seven Smiley Samurai" was nominated (but did not win) the Best Humor Category at Brickworld 2016. It was not built with the intention of being humorous, but apparently was inadvertently chuckle-inducing. I am not sure what this means, exactly, with respect to the issues discussed here.

14. It is perhaps worth noting that LEGO does make minifigure heads with explicitly "Asian" facial features, in both yellow (for example, the Blue Shogun in set #6083 Samurai Stronghold) and flesh-toned (for example, Short Round in set #7199 The Temple of Doom).

15. This essay is deeply indebted to participants in the "LEGO and Race" roundtable at Brickworld 2016.

Girl, LEGO® Friends is not your Friend! Does LEGO® Construct Gender Stereotypes?

Rebecca Gutwald

In January 2014, seven-year-old Charlotte Benjamin wrote a letter to LEGO® in which she described a lack of LEGO options for girls. "I don't like that there are more LEGO boy people and barely any LEGO girls. If there are girls," Charlotte wrote, "all the girls did was sit at home, go to the beach, and shop, and they had no jobs, but the boys went on adventures, worked, saved people, and had jobs, even swam with sharks." Charlotte was mainly referring to the LEGO Friends theme, which features female core characters and typically "girly" colors such as pink, red, and purple.[1]

Charlotte's letter has since gone viral. Many critics of the LEGO Friends theme have cited it in articles and blog posts about how this girls theme reinforces negative gender stereotypes. Yet many other young customers and their parents disagreed. In the comment sections of the websites where the letter was shared, some users remarked that Charlotte was overreacting and failed to notice that she can play with other toys. Other commenters flat out accused Charlotte's parents of planting their ideas of gender equality in her head.

The argument went back and forth on web forums, in debates over whether LEGO is guilty of sexism or whether feminist advocates are just hysterical. By creating a seemingly innocuous new theme, LEGO suddenly found itself in the middle of a controversy about the equality of the sexes, which feminist philosophers and their critics have been discussing for years.

LEGO® and Philosophy: Constructing Reality Brick By Brick, First Edition.
Edited by Roy T. Cook and Sondra Bacharach.
© 2017 John Wiley & Sons Ltd. Published 2017 by John Wiley & Sons Ltd.

Girls' Best *Friends* or Worst Toy of the Year?

Browsing the internet, you'll find that LEGO Friends regularly hits
the top ten on lists like "worst LEGO themes" or "worst toy." The
Campaign for a Commercial-Free Childhood (CCFC) nominated the
Butterfly Beauty Shop (set #3187) for a TOADY (Toys Oppressive
And Destructive to Young Children) award in 2012. They claim that
"Voters were especially irked by LEGO's marketing for the Butterfly
Beauty Shop, which encourages girls to 'get primped and pretty and
have some serious salon fun' and 'gossip out on the bench by the scenic
fountain.'"[2]

There is no doubt that LEGO Friends is for girls. LEGO introduced the Friends theme in early 2012 explicitly as the "girls theme"
to replace the unsuccessful LEGO Belville theme. As LEGO's CEO,
Jørgen Vig Knudstorp, put it: "We focused on a play experience centered on the joy of creation, while heeding the way girls naturally
build and play."[3] The company thus aimed at counteracting a problematic trend: since the 1980s LEGO had an image of being mainly
for boys.

Many fans of LEGO found the gender imbalance unfortunate,
because, as studies indicate, playing with blocks, in particular in structural play, can significantly enhance spatial and mathematical skills.[4]
LEGO's solution was to create a theme in which purple and pink
colors dominate the fictional place: Heartlake City. LEGO also introduced a new kind of figure: the mini-doll. The mini-doll is different
from the traditional LEGO minifigures in being less blocky, more
styled and taller; it is also a bit more feminine in appearance. In addition, the LEGO Friends sets de-emphasized the construction aspects
of LEGO to a certain extent (although though not as much as similar
toys like the Barbie Megabloks sets).

Feminists, educators, and parents objected, because LEGO Friends
entered the sexist ground of pinkification.[5] With Friends, LEGO
created a theme populated by conservative female stereotypes. The
Friends' activities included clichéd female occupations such as caring
for animals (the Heartlake Vet, set #3188 or the Heartlake Pet Salon,
set #41007), styling (the infamous Butterfly Beauty Salon, Emma's
Fashion Design Studio, set #3936), and homemaking, baking, and
cooking (Olivia's House, set #3315; Stephanie's Outdoor Bakery, set
#3930; or the Heartlake Juice Bar, set #41035).[6] While there is noth-
ing wrong with these activities as such, the problem with Friends is
that they seem to be presented as the *only* options for girls in this

LEGO world and in the world in general. This becomes clear when the Friends sets are compared to the sets that are usually marketed to boys. As Charlotte observed, boys get a much wider range of characters in themes like Pirates, the Research Institute (set #21110),[7] Speed Champions, or Knights. The mini-dolls are not compatible with these other sets; they do not fit into Lego spaceships, for instance. So, crossover playing with "normal LEGO" becomes difficult.

Rejection of Friends was not unanimous, however. A lot of girls (and their parents) who otherwise might not have been interested in LEGO loved it. From a philosophical point of view, we may wonder: Does "being girly" equal sexism? Why should it be so bad to represent girls more prominently in LEGO? Is there, as Knudstorp suggests, a *natural* difference in the play of boys and girls?

LEGO Friends' Friendly Sexism

Philosophical arguments for feminism originate with Plato (circa 428– 348 BC), who claimed in his *Republic* that women can and should be trained to rule.[8] However, Plato remained an exception. Almost 2000 years passed before philosophers took up the cause again.[9] The first book-length work in feminist philosophy was written by Mary Wollstonecraft (1759–1797), who argued that the upbringing of women, based on a self-image dictated by the typically male perspective, created their limited expectations. Contrary to popular thought at the time, Wollstonecraft claimed that women were as capable of rational thinking as men and therefore should receive proper education in the use of their reason.

Wollstonecraft observed that not all discrimination takes the form of explicit oppression. There is also a kind of "friendly sexism" practiced by men who adore women, but view them as beautiful "playthings" or princesses, whom they revere but do not take seriously. Since LEGO does not seem to intend malevolent discrimination with Friends, the sexism we find in this theme is of this friendly kind. The Friends are, of course, literally play-things. The range of activities that the sets are designed for is something that Wollstonecraft would probably take issue with: what the Friends can do is rather limited, confined to being pretty and playful in a house-bound world without challenge and adventure.[10]

Friendly sexism was not the main concern of historic feminist arguments, for the obvious reason that women did not even have the same rights as men for a long time. The case for equal gender rights came from philosopher John Stuart Mill (1806–1973). Supported by his intellectual companion (later his wife) Harriet Taylor (1807–1958), Mill wrote *The Subjection of Women*. He observed something that is true but highly disappointing, namely that mere argument is not enough to convince people in cases when "there is a mass of feeling to be contended against." If an argument rests "solely on feeling, the worse it fares in the argumentative context, the more persuaded its adherents are that their feeling must have some deeper ground, which the arguments do not reach."[11] Social psychologists today make similar observations, as we shall see.

Thus, the feminist activism at the end of the nineteenth century was necessary to establish basic rights for women such as the rights to vote, study, and work. The conundrum is, however, that women have not closed the gap. They are still underrepresented in many fields: for example, in academia, politics, and STEM jobs. If the coercive barriers are gone, what is keeping women from succeeding in these fields? Maybe girls and boys are just naturally different?

At the bottom of these questions lies the "nature or nurture" debate: determining whether gender differences are inherent (fixed by genes or brain structure) or largely produced and nurtured by the social environment. If you believe in natural differences, you are not alone. Even many modern parents who take themselves to be open-minded and free of sexism think along these lines. They cannot help but observe that girls are drawn to playing with dolls, decorating, and shopping. Boys, on the other hand seem to be more aggressive, outspoken, and adventurous. If this gendering does not come from parenting, it must come from nature, they conclude. However, the "nurturers" object, the fact that something is persistent does not entail that it is rooted in nature. We may need to look in our unconscious—into what Mill called the "deeper ground."

Is LEGO Playing with Stereotypes?

"One is not born, but rather becomes a woman,"[12] writes Simone de Beauvoir (1908–1986) in what has become one of the most influential books in feminist philosophy, *The Second Sex*. She goes on to explain that "representation of the world, like the world itself, is the work of men; they describe it from their own point of view, which they confuse with absolute truth." If gender roles seem deeply entrenched, this is because they are—not by nature, but by society enforcing them since hundreds of years.

Many modern feminists follow Beauvoir's general approach and support their arguments with findings from social psychology. There is strong evidence that two psychological effects that we are largely unaware of—even girls and women themselves—impede women's progress in society. They are called *implicit bias* and *stereotype threat*.[13] Implicit bias often rests on what psychologists call schemas: a simplified representation of a kind or type that unconsciously organizes our beliefs about that kind, and which guides our expectations and predictions. For instance, a child learns how dogs look and behave from a picture book and then applies this dog-schema to the real-life dogs she sees. If there is no contrary information, she will assume that dogs will behave similarly to her dog-schema. Similarly, if your son or daughter has been invited to a birthday party and you don't know more about the birthday child than that she is a girl, you might buy a set from the LEGO Friends theme (or you might not, if you read to the end this chapter).

Using schemas is not always problematic. They are pulled out when certain stimuli require us to react quickly. When it comes to gender, however, schemas may become harmful. Experiments indicate that most people—even those who are sincerely committed to anti-discrimination—unconsciously and unintentionally hold negative biases against various groups including black people, women, and LGBT persons. In the case of gender, these biases manifest by associating certain skills or activities with the male or the female—and by evaluating the female more negatively with respect to certain skills. For instance, the same résumé is rated more highly when it has a male (white) name on it than a female one. This happens in particular when the job requires stereotypically male qualities such as being assertive, having mathematical knowledge, or fulfilling a leadership position.[14]

In her book *The Delusion of Gender*, psychologist Cordelia Fine surveys a large number of studies from social science and neuroscience to illustrate the firm roots of implicit bias in the unconscious.[15] Parents are no less prone to these effects. In an illustrative example, Fine describes a study in which mothers were asked to estimate how far and steep their babies can climb. Even though there was no difference in the crawling abilities of the babies, male babies were rated significantly better than female ones.[16]

When it comes to traditional male activities and skills, stereotype threat is a huge risk. Individuals are stereotyped as poor performers in a domain that is viewed as less suitable for them. The performance of persons subject to this sort of bias may seem to confirm this stereotype, because they adjust to expectations—or their performance is rated differently. For instance, in basketball, white men are often judged to be worse than their black counterparts even when they score the same number of points (this is one of the few occasions where white men face stereotype threat). In the case of girls, this stereotyping may be well hidden or even disguised as praise for ladylikeness.

The LEGO Friends are not an oppressed, miserable bunch. They have a lot of fun, and they run their own businesses. They also have close circles of female friends and some male spouses. Like popular "chick-lit" and fashion magazines for the modern woman, the Friends sets seem to celebrate female qualities and the differences between men and women. They claim that there is a particular female domain in life—and in play. But what they actually do is segregate the female world from the male world: the male world is where the things that really matter in society happen, and where the *real* knowledge and ability is found—like mathematics, construction, and leadership. As Charlotte so well described, the LEGO Friends girls are not the ones who go on adventures, fight dragons, or rescue people from fires.

In the themes that LEGO has introduced during the last two decades, stereotypical male activities and objects prevail. For instance, about twenty years ago, the Star Wars® license deal lead to the introduction of guns and combat machines into the world of LEGO. This is remarkable, because LEGO had always refused to produce any kind of military themes. Arguably, the Star Wars theme itself implies some form of violence and aggression that has been hitherto absent in classic LEGO. Aside from the Star Wars sets, the most popular characters are ninjas, firefighters, and knights.

Even though LEGO still refuses to do anything explicitly militarily related, their toys have become more gender stereotyped, because LEGO has changed the ways to play with their products. LEGO thus also strongly guides boys' ideas on what is typically male. This discriminates against boys who are not interested in these activities (and who are, as it is often said in a derogatory tone, into the "girly" stuff). Boys who learn via playing with LEGO how boys and men should stereotypically behave miss out on exploring other ways to play and learn. For instance, psychologist Christia Spears Brown points out that playing with dolls teaches kids valuable skills like empathy.[17] So, come to think of it, LEGO is not a boy's friend either.

Still, for girls, there is another negative effect. Girls and women cannot bridge the gap by acting more "male." If a woman acts confident and, even worse, is comfortable with power, she runs the risk of being called "cold," "iron," or "dramatic." We speak of "tomboys" or "bitches." Men and boys, on the other hand, are perceived as strong, confident, and assertive if they display the same qualities and attitudes. Hence, social psychology presents us with pretty hard evidence that people still have some simplistic biases lingering in the deep dungeons of their minds.

These unconscious effects are harder to criticize than explicit discrimination, because very often the people involved think that they make judgments on a neutral basis such as competence and performance alone. However, addressing the phenomena of implicit bias and stereotype threat may help us in pointing out that more is going on below the surface of our (allegedly) rational deliberation. It also shows that the social barriers for women have not vanished, but just have become more invisible—like the infamous glass ceiling in the workplace.[18]

If we, as adults, are victims of these effects, how could children, whose minds are highly prone to social learning, elude these biases? Children mimic the behaviors, attitudes, and habits of those around them. Between the ages of three and five, gender becomes very important to children, while before that time they show no gender preferences. When children see clearly divided aisles with gender cues like pink or blue toys, they pay careful attention and thus learn what is expected of them.[19] Their brains are like sponges primed to absorb information from their surroundings, so that they can act like their role models (usually their parents). Brown and Fine argue that this applies especially to body language and the implicit attitudes we display. The proverb "do as I say, not as I do" could not be more inefficient then.

Let's say a girl's parents clothe her in girly colors, talk more about emotions to her than to her brother, and give her LEGO Friends to play with. The girls in the sets are pursuing what we have identified as classic female activities. The contrast is sharp when compared to the more recent LEGO themes, which, even if they are intended for both genders, are primarily marketed to boys. For instance, in LEGO's catalogue the non-Friends themes are usually illustrated with boys. Would a little girl think that her parents and LEGO are wrong? Especially if almost of all of the people around her confirm what she sees?

So, there is some solid evidence that LEGO Friends is supporting and expressing implicit biases and stereotypes associated with gender, and that both boys and girls will take up these attitudes as they play. LEGO Friends is one small, but noticeable building block (or brick) in the construction of society that still has massive inbuilt stereotypes. It's not merely a harmless children's toy. Still, does this mean that LEGO should change their themes? Should we throw away our Friends?

Let the Friends Go to Space! How to Build a More Diverse World with Bricks

Why should LEGO care? After all, it's a private company run for profit and free to do what it wants. The girly bricks sell, and girls like them. So LEGO may be constructing biases out of bricks, but no parent is forced to buy them. Plus, there are way worse sexist toys (Barbie, Monster High, many other things in girls' toy sections).

Though this is all true, the fact that there are worse things is not a good justification for doing something morally reprochable. Just because everybody is a sexist doesn't mean you should be too. LEGO is a company that seeks profit. If it does not violate any laws, LEGO can produce what sells. Legally, this is true. In addition, political action against sexist toys may be too strong a move, constraining the freedom of people in an open society.

Yet we need to consider moral philosophy, which applies to everyday conduct and to everybody regardless of the legal and political context. If we can agree that promoting sexism is morally problematic, we can say that LEGO's actions are morally questionable.

People tend to be especially disappointed in LEGO with respect to the creations of sexist toys. In the past LEGO created a different self-image as, and which was perceived as, being gender neutral and more morally upstanding than other toy companies. That LEGO succumbed to "pinkifying" their toys is thus a letdown for many people, and they justifiably feel betrayed.

LEGO's blatantly gendered toys feel like a huge step back *for them*. In 1981, they launched their famous ad "What it is is beautiful"—a perfect example of how to design and market a toy in a gender neutral way. In the ads, a girl proudly presents a house she has constructed of colorful LEGO bricks. No pink, no mini-dolls, no stereotypes.[20] Images of these kinds are significant, because they raise the hopes and expectations of consumers. We cannot sue LEGO for not fulfilling these expectations, but we may justifiably feel let down.

As feminists, we realize that our world is not perfect yet, and girlifying LEGO may be one way to introduce many girls to a world of creative play with a toy that enhances spatial skills—even if in pink. Friends has the potential to spark interest in construction and creative play, which may then lead to exploring the other themes of LEGO. Or so some might say. In reality, it is hard to shake off the stereotypes that are expressed in gendered toys and their marketing. Even if parents and children try to ignore the gendered marketing, they might be socially pressured to align with the stereotypes. And children who are different from the norm—especially with respect to gender—are often left out in play, thus paying a high social cost.

So, using Friends as a stepping stone (or brick) to broadening girls' *and* boys' options in play is a tricky move. Maybe it could work, if LEGO were to drop the segregation of Friends by making the bricks and mini-dolls compatible with other LEGO themes, so that, for instance, Friends could go to space. Friends and the female LEGO scientists could also be more closely aligned—there was one Friends set, namely Olivia's Invention Workshop (set #3933), which showed the construction of a robot, after all. Why not design more of these settings instead of a tenth popstar set? Finally, the marketing needs to change, or rather return to the point where LEGO once was in 1981. Unless some of these changes are made, however, LEGO Friends are not girls' friends—and not boys' either.

Notes

1. See http://thesocietypages.org/socimages/2014/01/31/this-month-in-socimages-january-2014 (accessed February 27, 2017).
2. See http://commercialfreechildhood.org/blog/toady-2012-fisher-price-laugh-learn-apptivity-monkey (accessed February 27, 2017).
3. See http://feministfrequency.com/2012/01/30/LEGO-gender-part-1-LEGO-friends (accessed February 27, 2017).
4. See http://www.parentingscience.com/LEGO-bricks-construction-toys-and-STEM-skills.html (accessed February 27, 2017).
5. Peggy Orenstein, *Cinderella Ate My Daughter: Dispatches from the Front Lines of the New Girlie-Girl Culture* (New York: Harper Paperbacks, 2012).
6. Visit the website http://www.friendsbricks.com for all the information you may want to have about the theme (accessed February 27, 2017).

7. See Rhiannon Grant and Ruth Wainman, "Representation in Plastic and Marketing: The Significance of the LEGO Women Scientists" in this book, 113–22.
8. Plato, *Republic*, trans. C.D.C. Reeve (Indianapolis: Hackett, 2004).
9. Mary Wollstonecraft, *A Vindication of the Rights of Woman: Abridged with Related Texts* (Indianapolis: Hackett, 2013).
10. See http://feministfrequency.com/2012/01/30/LEGO-gender-part-1-LEGO-friends (accessed February 27, 2017).
11. John Stuart Mill, *The Subjection of Women* (Indianapolis: Hackett, 1988).
12. Simone de Beauvoir, *The Second Sex* (New York: Vintage Books 1973), 301.
13. For a good overview of these effects, see Samantha Brennan, "Feminist Ethics and Everyday Inequalities," *Hypatia* 24 (2009): 141–59 and Sally Haslanger, "Gender and Race: (What) Are They? (What) Do we Want Them to Be?" *Nous* 34 (2000), 31–55.
14. See http://www.cos.gatech.edu/facultyres/Diversity_Studies/Steinpreis_Impact%20of%20gender%20on%20review.pdf (accessed February 27, 2017).
15. Cordelia Fine, *Delusions of Gender: How Our Minds, Society, and Neurosexism Create Difference* (New York: W.W. Norton, 2010).
16. Ibid.
17. Christia Spears Brown, *Parenting Beyond Pink and Blue: How to Raise Your Kids Free of Gender Stereotypes* (Berkeley: Teen Speed Press, 2014).
18. If you doubt the existence of these deeply buried creatures in your own mind, I suggest you take some of the tests developed by Harvard's "project implicit": see https://implicit.harvard.edu/implicit (accessed February 27, 2017).
19. Brown describes the following case: "For example, in one experiment, researchers took toys that kids had not seen before and put them in stereotypical girl boxes or stereotypical boy boxes and gave them to a group of children. Girls played with the toys in the girl boxes and boys gravitated to the toys in the boy boxes. Both genders focused on the toys in the boxes meant for their gender and did not pay much attention to toys marked for the opposite gender," available at http://www.theguardian.com/lifeandstyle/2016/may/28/toys-kids-girls-boys-childhood-development-gender-research?CMP=share_btn_fb (accessed February 27, 2017).
20. http://www.huffingtonpost.com/2014/01/17/LEGO-ad-1981_n_4617704.html (accessed February 27, 2017).

Representation in Plastic and Marketing
The Significance of the LEGO® Women Scientists

Rhiannon Grant and Ruth Wainman

Ellen Kooijman's aim was simple. As a practicing geoscientist and Adult Fan of LEGO® (AFOL), she was keen to promote her own profession and to address the gender imbalance of scientists' representation in LEGO sets. She wrote in a blog post:

> As a female scientist I had noticed two things about the available LEGO sets: a skewed male/female minifigure ratio and a rather stereotypical representation of the available female figures. It seemed logical that I would suggest a small set of female minifigures in interesting professions to make our LEGO city communities more diverse.[1]

In 2014, Kooijman's ideas paid off after the LEGO Group announced the launch of the Research Institute set (set #21110)—the first LEGO set to feature women scientist figurines.

Here's why this matters. Scientists, policy makers, and psychologists have identified the impact that toys have on the uptake of science and the perception of gender roles. Studies have shown how toys reinforce the gender binary, exposing the supposed differences in boys' and girls' interests and attributes.[2] "Boys' toys" as such have tended to be dominated by action and construction, whereas "girls' toys" have focused on caring.[3] These features of toys have certainly started to make their way into more mainstream debates. Among those leading the debates include renowned physicist Athene Donald, who has argued that girls' toys are more likely to encourage passivity instead of the creative skills fostered by boys' toys.[4] Science Studies scholar Sherry Turkle has also

LEGO® and Philosophy: Constructing Reality Brick By Brick, First Edition.
Edited by Roy T. Cook and Sondra Bacharach.
© 2017 John Wiley & Sons Ltd. Published 2017 by John Wiley & Sons Ltd.

written extensively about how objects, such as computers and toys, have influenced people's paths into science.[5] In particular, LEGO sets have been recognized as an important way of developing creativity and imagination during childhood. This makes sense in light of the versatility of LEGO and the ways people have shaped the toy to their own ends. Furthermore, the progress of science itself can be affected by who is doing the work. The alternative perspectives brought to science by women, who are often treated differently in society and hence see it differently, can change the way we understand the world.

On this basis, delving deeper into LEGO's products and marketing provides an important perspective on the development of the Research Institute set and LEGO's attempt to engage women in science. What does it mean for LEGO to finally represent the woman scientist? How exactly does the Research Institute achieve this, and does it succeed?

"Explore the World and Beyond!"

After gaining support from fellow LEGO ideas members (an online community which shares ideas for LEGO sets), Kooijman created a design that could represent a Research Institute, featuring a paleontologist, an astronomer, and a chemist. According to the packaging, there is a chance to "explore the world and beyond!" This is the motto of the women scientists as they each set out to make their own discoveries in the Research Institute. The astronomer gets "to discover new stars and planets with her telescope" while the paleontologist studies "the origin of the dinosaurs" and the chemist undertakes "experiments in the laboratory."[6] The message of the set is clear: "girls can become anything they want."[7] The accompanying booklet provides further background information about the three occupations and a photograph of a real scientist—Ellen Kooijman—in her laboratory at the Swedish Museum of Natural History.

The set relies on role play, reminding us that the three women scientists have their own story to tell. The interchangeable heads providing alternating facial expressions of the scientists also help to facilitate a narrative form of play. On the official LEGO web store, potential customers are reminded that the sets provide a chance to learn that science can also be an occupation for women: "There's a whole world of exciting professions out there to explore—build and role play them to see if they suit you!"[8] The sets must have struck a chord with the public as they sold out in a matter of days.

There is something, then, that is both typical and atypical about the representation of women scientists in the LEGO Research Institute. By launching a set featuring women scientists, LEGO is raising the profile of women in an area where they remain outnumbered. According to the 2012 World Development Report, men outnumber women in science in two-thirds of the world's countries.[9] On closer inspection, though, the women of the LEGO Research Institute are wearing lipstick while some even come replete with drawn-on curves. Wearing makeup in a laboratory—surely not! This did not escape the attention of Kooijman who wrote a blog post reviewing the Research Institute and strongly discouraging the wearing of makeup in labs because of the potential contamination of samples. The sets, however, have also inspired their own Twitter feed set up by archaeologist Dr. Donna Yates from the University of Glasgow—@LegoAcademics— which provides a tongue-in-cheek look at the experiences of being an academic and a woman.

As part of the minifigure range as a whole, women in both scientific and technical occupations are still seldom featured. Instead, stereotypical roles and characterizations of women loom large with the inclusion of figurines such as the Bavarian Pretzel Girl, the Diner Waitress, and the Cheerleader. The gender-differentiated LEGO sets have also served to reinforce such divisions between the sexes. LEGO Friends, introduced in 2012, is just one of the latest themes LEGO has aimed at girls over the years (see also the Homemaker, Paradisa, Scala, and Belville themes).[10] These have mostly been reliant on channeling feminine occupations and interests through settings including the hair salon, the beauty shop, and the shopping mall. The combination of aesthetic appeal and a message of friendship between named characters help to mark these sets as feminine or girls' toys.

LEGO did not originally set out to be a toy that was mostly reliant on role play. From its wooden beginnings in 1932, LEGO has primarily been a construction toy. During the 1990s, the LEGO brand shifted from a toy about construction play to one based on narrative and role play, although this strategy was subsequently overturned to achieve a balance between the classic lines and the more fad-driven products.[11] More recently, users of LEGO (mostly adults) have started to become an increasingly important part of the LEGO marketing strategy with the collaboratively driven development of the robotics kits—Mindstorms®.[12] In this context, the Research Institute can be seen as part of a wider strategy to turn its users into both producers and consumers to dictate the future direction of LEGO.

Although the Research Institute alerts us to the fact that science can be a woman's occupation, its focus on role play may disguise a more problematic issue about how toys such as LEGO attempt to draw girls into the world of science. Where is the creativity in the Research Institute that scientists and policy makers have complained is absent in girls' toys? The LEGO Group argues that girls and boys simply play differently. LEGO's own research shows that boys tend to build in a more linear fashion by replicating what is inside the box whereas girls prefer a more personal approach, to create their own story and to imagine themselves living inside the things they build.[13] Creativity for girls thus derives from the use of their imagination more than it does for boys.

A glance back at older LEGO advertising seems to suggest that the company could also look beyond gendered ideas about its users. Take, for example, the 1981 advertisement of the girl, dressed in jeans and sneakers and holding up her own LEGO model, which seems to be less dictated by gender stereotypes than the LEGO sets of today. The message—"What it is is beautiful"—was simple and drew our attention both to the creation the girl designed and the self-fulfillment she gained from playing with LEGO. In comparison, the Research Institute seems to have taken a backward turn, since it is mostly reliant on the narrative it can create by allowing girls to imagine themselves as one of the scientists that the LEGO women represent. In order to understand this, we need to look more deeply into the socialization process itself and how it has shaped ideas about science among boys and girls.

Girls' Toys, Boys' Toys: The Gendered Bias

Having looked at the marketing LEGO produces and the depictions of women and scientists in LEGO sets, it might be tempting to say "so what?" You might follow this up with the thought that LEGO, as a sensible company, is merely being realistic in marketing different toys to girls and boys—everyone knows that boys and girls play differently. Unfortunately, it isn't that simple. Yes, girls and boys do play differently. But is this because they are innately different, or is it because they are being taught, from birth if not before, that they ought to be different? Let's look at the evidence for the latter, along with some ideas about how LEGO toys might be involved in that process.

Sociologists have looked at every stage of children's development, and found that parents treat babies differently as soon as the sex of the child is known. For example, they describe girls as "sweet" and "pretty" and boys as "athletic" and "tough" from birth.[14] Children learn from this treatment how they ought to be, and are actually shaped to be that way: girls play with more toys that teach caring and literacy, while boys play with more toys that emphasize engineering and fighting.[15] Toys are also frequently color-coded, with girls' toys especially likely to feature shades of pink and pastel colors. When LEGO produces materials for children that assume girls are more interested in characters, stories, and emotions, and boys are more interested in building, cars, and explosions, they are both playing into a dominant cultural narrative that tells children how they should be, and helping to create a world in which children are shaped to fulfil those expectations. One of these key expectations is that boys are more interested in, and better at, science.

Overall, girls are much less likely to study STEM subjects at school or to pursue careers involving science or mathematics. This has changed little over several decades, and studies on the subject reveal that it is partially shaped by children's out-of-school experiences. Girls who feel good about science report that this is partly because they are engaged with science outside school—"doing science at home, reading about science, or watching science-related television shows."[16] Gendered differences persist among children about the image of the scientist. For example, in the "draw-a-scientist-test" only girls drew women scientists.[17] The Research Institute set could help to counteract this. For girls it provides the possibility that science too can be part of their experience, and challenges the perception that science is a male subject.

That said, the Research Institute set continues to support stereotypical ideas of girls' play in other ways. Apart from building the equipment and figures, no engineering or scientific skills are embedded in playing with the set, and the accompanying marketing focuses on stories about these three women scientists and their research. Other sets within the wider LEGO range are coded differently, such as the City theme, which is framed with an emphasis on masculine roles. LEGO attempts to include women in these sets. For example, the Swamp Police Station (set #60069) comes with six minifigures, four police officers and two criminals. One police officer and one criminal are feminine in the usual LEGO style, that is, wearing makeup; one police officer and the other criminal are bearded; two police officers are unmarked and likely to be read as masculine because our society offers that as the default option.

Although we applaud this attempt, we do not think that this overcomes the general masculine coding of the sets involved. Unlike the Research Institute, there is no all-women police station, and in the Spaceport set, the astronauts are unmarked and therefore most likely to be read as men. Most of the City theme has mainly masculine minifigures and includes models with an engineering emphasis—the City theme focuses on modes of transport (rockets, fire engines, trains, police cars, and so on) in particular. Boys are thus directed toward these toys, and girls away from them, giving boys a practical advantage in science and engineering as well as a positive attitude toward it.

All of these factors—depictions, experiences, skills developed in play—are part of what gender studies scholars have called the social construction of gender. Parents, teachers, and—after a certain age—children themselves all use toys, clothing, and roles to create a child's gender, one of many things that will affect the child's way of being in the world. These others things will include class (buying LEGO sets requires significant money); race and ethnicity (LEGO's mainly (but not always) yellow minifigures do not succeed in excluding this as a factor, especially from their advertising[18]); and some disabilities (LEGO is accessible to many, but not all, children). Class, race, ethnicity, and disability combine with gender and other aspects of a child's life and social position to create a complex web that shapes their experiences. For example, the tendency of children's books to depict scientists as white men creates a stereotype that excludes some children from imagining themselves in a science-related occupation.[19] Within the complex web of identities, a child's assigned gender (whether they are being raised as a boy or a girl, usually based on observation of the genitals at birth but sometimes on chromosomes) is taught through language and action—including play.

One of the things children in our culture are taught as part of their gendered socialization is to regard school subjects or academic disciplines as gendered. Language-focused skills such as reading and writing are gendered feminine and thought of as girls' subjects, whereas science and physical education are considered masculine and treated as boys' subjects. Adults both expect to see this pattern and perpetuate it, often unconsciously, by the ways they talk to children and the messages they send when children play with the "wrong" toys. Children of both sexes might play with LEGO sets (although in a study of favorite toys among three to five-year-olds, LEGO appears on the boys' list and not the girls').[20] However, girls are encouraged by their caregivers as well as by LEGO's marketing to take an interest in stories and characters.

One Small Step for LEGO, One Giant Leap for Women in Science?

Teaching children that their gender does and should affect the toys they play with, the subjects they choose at school, their intellectual abilities, and the careers they will end up in obviously has a significant effect on the children themselves. The (often subconscious) decision to teach this also affects the marketing of toys like LEGO and the behavior of adults toward children.

It is possible that the gender of people going into science as a career has an effect on the progress of science itself. Science is often conceptualized as an independent thing, unaffected by who undertakes the work, but is it possible that the women of the Research Institute set have real-life counterparts who can discover things male scientists cannot?

To explore this possibility, let's look at a case study from the field of biology. In looking at the ways human anatomy is described, Emily Martin, an anthropologist, noticed a curious pattern in descriptions of eggs and sperm. She says that scientific texts "have an almost dogged insistence on casting female processes in a negative light" and that while eggs are described in feminine terms as "passive," sperm are "invariably active."[21] This way of speaking perpetuates ideas about how women and men are, by reading gendered traits into biological processes that do not have any connection to the social world in which gender is created. Among other things, it mirrors the distinction between active/masculine and passive/feminine which we saw in many toys, even LEGO's own themes. Lest we think that this is simply the way things are, more recent research has pointed in other directions: the egg could equally well be described as choosing which of the many available sperm will be opened and used.

It is not automatically the case that only female scientists can come up with new ways of looking at these issues, but it is the case that the majority of scientists in history and labs today are men, and that describing female biology with images—often negative images— usually applied to women is an ongoing and problematic tendency.

When we are looking at LEGO products, this pattern can be seen when women or girls are shown engaging in passive or overtly feminine behaviors (such as doing their hair or caring for animals and children), while men and boys are seen as active and given roles which reflect that (such as fire fighters and police officers).

In a sense, we impose roles on small yellow plastic figures in much the same way that scientists impose roles on the eggs and the sperm. As mentioned earlier, in a basic City theme set such as the Fire Starter Set (set #60106), the four minifigures consist of three coded masculine and one coded feminine—you can tell because she's wearing lipstick and has eyelashes. It could be argued that the unmarked minifigure heads—where neither a beard nor makeup is present—could be read as either masculine or feminine. However, in practice these heads are read as masculine, and people assign the male pronoun to these figures unless something else, such as a skirt or a strongly feminine-coded role, suggests otherwise.

Challenging the Representation of Women in Science: One Brick at a Time

Encouraging women to take up science and science-related careers might not just be morally good, or good for women, but also important for the progress of science itself. Science requires the training of clever and creative minds. That training requires education—not just formal education but also informal training. LEGO sets are an important part of that training for the children who encounter them—and if girls who visit LEGO stores or play with LEGO sets are given the message that science is for boys, this will be one brick in a wall which prevents many capable girls from taking up science seriously. The narratives and information about science provided by the Research Institute set hopefully have the potential—especially if joined by other messages—to counteract this impression and teach girls that they have a role to play in scientific investigation. This is important because the questions and knowledge produced by science affect everyone.

However, the Research Institute, perhaps unintentionally, does still seem to replicate the gendered distinctions between men and women in science by engaging girls through largely passive, feminine role play even as it consciously uses LEGO to raise the profile of women in science. As we try to remove bricks from the extensive wall that blocks off access to scientific careers for many women, we need to remember that LEGO and other toys may be part of this wall. In the future, we hope that girls will spend more time with the Spaceport—and perhaps boys can extend their range to the Heartlake Hair Salon, too. For everyone, LEGO's role play potential shouldn't be allowed to overshadow its capacity to teach science and engineering.

Notes

1. Alatariel's Atelier. See http://alatarielatelier.blogspot.se/p/female-minifigure-set.html?zx=7fc735e0789785ac (accessed February 27, 2017).
2. Becky Francis, "Gender, Toys and Learning," *Oxford Review of Education* 36 (2010): 325–44.
3. Ibid.
4. Ian Sample, "Toys Aimed At Girls 'Steering Women Away from Science Careers,'" *The Guardian*, available at http://www.theguardian.com/science/2015/sep/04/toys-aimed-at-girls-steering-women-away-from-science-careers (accessed February 27, 2017).
5. Sherry Turkle, *Objects in Mind* (Cambridge, MA: MIT Press, 2008).
6. LEGO 21110 Research Institute Building Instructions, available at http://cache.lego.com/bigdownloads/buildinginstructions/6107021.pdf (accessed February 27, 2017).
7. Ibid.
8. LEGO Online Shop, available at http://shop.lego.com/en-GB/Research-Institute-21110? (accessed February 27, 2017).
9. The World Bank, *World Development Report 2012: Gender, Equality and Development*, available at https://siteresources.worldbank.org/INTWDR2012/Resources/7778105-1299699968583/7786210-1315936222006/Complete-Report.pdf, 88 (accessed February 27, 2017).
10. See Rebecca Gutwald, "Girl, LEGO Friends is not your Friend! Does LEGO Construct Gender Stereotypes?" in this book, 103–12.
11. Maaike Lauwaert, "Playing Outside the Box—On LEGO Toys and the Changing World of Construction Play," *History and Technology: An International Journal* 24 (2008): 221–37.
12. Ibid.
13. "Lego's Consistency Has Been the Key to Its Success: Getting Girls was the Tricky Part," *AdWeek*, available at http://www.adweek.com/news/advertising-branding/legos-consistency-has-been-key-its-success-148553 (accessed February 27, 2017).
14. Jodi O'Brien, ed., *Encyclopaedia of Gender and Society* (London: SAGE, 2009), 359.
15. Becky Francis, "Gender, Toys and Learning," 332–7.

16. M. Gail Jones, Anne Howe, and Melissa J. Rua, "Gender Differences in Students' Experiences, Interests, and Attitudes toward Science and Scientists," *Scientific Education* 84 (2000): 180–92.
17. David Wade Chambers, "Stereotypical Images of the Scientist: The Draw a Scientist Test," *Science Education* 67 (1983): 255–65.
18. See Roy Cook, "Ninjas, Kobe Bryant, and Yellow Plastic: The LEGO Minifigure and Race" in this book, 91–102.
19. LSE Impact of Social Science blog, "Male, Mad and Muddle-headed: The Portrayal of Academics in Children's Books is Shockingly Narrow," available at http://blogs.lse.ac.uk/impactofsocialsciences/2014/02/14/academics-in-childrens-picture-books (accessed February 27, 2017).
20. Francis, "Gender, Toys and Learning," 329.
21. Emily Martin, "The Egg and the Sperm: How Science has Constructed a Romance Based on Stereotypical Male-Female Roles," *Signs* 16 (1991): 489.

12

Real Signature Figures

LEGO® Minifigures and the Human Individual

Robert M. Mentyka

From its interlocking pieces to its high degree of imaginative customization, the LEGO® brand is iconic in many ways, but one of its most recognizable features is the adorable and highly interchangeable character pieces known as "LEGO minifigures" or "minifigs" for short. Beginning with just a few pieces, the simplicity of the minifigures' design masks the sheer depth of customization available to them. By merely swapping out a different head, torso, pair of legs, or hat/hairstyle, inventive LEGO Maniacs can create a cast of thousands to inhabit the plastic worlds of imagination they create with LEGO bricks.[1]

For all of their versatility, however, minifigures have long been stumbling blocks for LEGO builders the world over. Despite the sheer number of variations possible using even the most basic of character pieces, LEGO minifigs tend to be rather homogenous components in a hobby that prides itself on creativity and difference. Whereas the castles, spaceships, and other inventions built using LEGO bricks are as unique and varied as the people who create them, these constructions are all inhabited by a crowd of strikingly similar plastic figures. Even *The LEGO Movie* referred to this issue by casting a relatively plain minifig with few distinguishing characteristics as its main protagonist while relegating more recognizable licensed characters to side roles and small cameos.

Given that these little toy figures are, for the most part, meant to represent human beings, it should really come as no surprise that

LEGO® and Philosophy: Constructing Reality Brick By Brick, First Edition.
Edited by Roy T. Cook and Sondra Bacharach.
© 2017 John Wiley & Sons Ltd. Published 2017 by John Wiley & Sons Ltd.

minifigs struggle. After all, similar problems arise within the philosophical study of the human person. Although humanity has always been a central concept in philosophy, many modern thinkers have begun to place a renewed emphasis on examining the nature and role of the individual in a world dominated by industry, mass society, and increasingly impersonal technology. Much like his blocky minifig counterpart, the human individual often struggles to distinguish himself from the crowd and provide an adequate explanation for just what makes him "special."

Laying the Foundation

In this chapter, we'll use the versatile LEGO minifigure to introduce three major themes, questions, and problems tackled in the "philosophy of the human person." We'll begin with the question of just what parts are involved in making a human person. After that, we'll consider the problems surrounding any individual's continued existence over time, and we'll end by discussing the philosophical view according to which our own acts of decision-making and imaginative creation are the very things that make us who and what we are. The cheerful yellow LEGO minifig presents a wonderful tool for exploring the human person, who similarly appears unique within the complicated systems of reality.

Gathering the Right Pieces

Like the entire LEGO system, the ingenuity of the minifigure lies in its construction out of numerous interchangeable pieces. Although the variation of styles for these simple components has grown exponentially over the course of LEGO's history, the basic combination used to bring them together has remained largely unchanged. By swapping out different standardized pieces for the legs, torso, head, and hairpiece, builders can construct individual characters to place within the inventive creations (often referred to as "My Own Creations" or "MOCs").

Just what, exactly, gives these characters their respective individuality? The same interchangeability that allows for so many permutations on the classic LEGO minifig also obscures the features that distinguish one LEGO character from another. For instance, say you recognize a particular female character (we'll call her "Eliza") by the fact that her minifigure has the black-colored ponytail hairpiece. Now suppose that you pick up another black-colored ponytail hairpiece and you use it on a brand new minifig (whom we'll call "Beth"). Obviously, Eliza and Beth will be distinguished from one another by differences in their remaining pieces, but what if no such differences are present? If both Eliza and Beth are made up of duplicate copies of the same pieces, can we really claim that there are two different characters represented instead of two copies of the same individual character?

One of the core problems plaguing any examination of the philosophy of the human person is the foundational question of just what goes into making a specific person. While we certainly encounter many different individuals in our day-to-day experiences, the systematic explanation of this phenomenon is one that has baffled thinkers for generations. The obvious answer, as it also seems to be with our minifig creations Eliza and Beth, is to focus on the distinguishing characteristics that separate one person from another. Though infinitely more complex when dealing with living human persons, the same basic method of separating individuals based on component elements such as hairstyle, facial expression, and other such attributes seems to hold true.

This simplistic response falls apart, however, when we encounter individuals who are physically identical, like identical twins. Even when considering friends who are merely similar in several aspects, we see how difficult it can be to separate the one from the other. While there most certainly is a difference between identical individuals, our normal methods for differentiating them are useless and we are forced to dig deeper for what we really mean when we separate one person from another.

Our quandary here is tied into the philosophical concept of "supervenience." This can be logically summed up by the phrase, "There cannot be an A-difference without a B-difference," which proclaims that if one object ("A") supervenes on another ("B"), then any change in the one is going to necessarily entail a similar change in the other.[2] If our minifigure creation Eliza "supervenes" on the component pieces that were used to build her, then swapping out any of those pieces will result in Eliza changing in that way as well. Replace the generic blue legs piece with the Pirate-themed peg-leg piece and Eliza will similarly go from having two legs in blue to sporting a fashionable wooden leg, ready for life on the high seas. While these examples make it sound relatively minor and straightforward, supervenience is quite the big deal, as it unites separate attributes with the same type of necessity found in mathematical truths like "2 + 2 = 4" or the Pythagorean Theorem.[3]

Human persons, like LEGO minifigures, certainly supervene on the parts that compose them. Whether it be a small change like getting a shorter haircut or a major one like amputating a limb, changes to our physical makeup also impact who we are as persons. The problem arises when we reduce human existence to this relation, believing that there is nothing more to a person than the physical parts that make them up and the changes that occur to those parts. There is nothing inherently wrong with identifying someone based on a defining characteristic like a certain style of hair, memorable scar, or unique manner of speaking, but reducing who that person is to such malleable physical characteristics is a gross injustice to their nature as a human person. It might be fine and, perhaps, unavoidable to categorize and differentiate people based on their personal physical traits, but such traits are a kind of "shortcut" used to describe their identity, not their actual identity itself. Physical characteristics are, indeed, a part of the equation, but they cannot be the end-all explanation for what defines a particular individual as who they are.

Interestingly, this conclusion also seems to hold true for LEGO minifigs, as there doesn't seem to be any inherent reason why two minifigs composed of all the same components could not, in fact, represent two distinct characters. We'll return to this idea, but for now, we must investigate further the central concept of identity.

My Own Creation Over Time

Returning to our example of Eliza and Beth, suppose the meticulous Adult Fan of LEGO ("AFOL") doesn't want any identical minifigs in a particular MOC. He therefore chooses to swap out Eliza's black-colored ponytail hairpiece for a spare Egyptian headdress he has available nearby. Eliza no longer looks the same as Beth, but, given that her hairpiece was her distinguishing characteristic, what exactly has happened to the character of Eliza? If one takes away or swaps out the feature that makes a certain minifig unique, does that same LEGO character persist, or is it replaced by an entirely new one?

Taking the problem further, suppose that Eliza's new headdress makes her identical to yet another minifig in the display. To correct for this, our diligent AFOL replaces her torso (an attractive red dress top) with a generic astronaut uniform torso, a move which, in turn, matches her up with yet another figure in the MOC. The same process is repeated again and again, with our seemingly unimaginative AFOL switching out piece after piece until Eliza is again a singularly unique minifig among her companions. If this process leads to every one of her pieces being replaced (perhaps several times), can we really say that it is the exact same character we started out with? If nothing of the original Eliza is present in the minifig currently bearing that name, what links the two constructions into the same character?

These examples draw attention to the problem of identity, particularly identity over time. More so than any other philosophical conundrum, this issue served as the catalyst for the philosophy of the human person. Put simply, identity deals with the person's existence as one, unified whole despite the changes that occur both within and outside that person over the course of their existence.

The question of personal identity was made famous by the philosopher John Locke (1632–1704), who speculated that memory was the glue that tied together the discrete bits of experience that go into every human life. This claim caused quite the controversy, spawning a lively exchange with the philosophers Joseph Butler (1692–1752) and Thomas Reid (1710–1796) that developed into a centuries-spanning debate. The lines of this battle would eventually coalesce into a conflict between those (like Locke) who believed that personal identity was maintained by some aspect of the human mind and those who claimed that a material continuation of our physical selves was necessary for the persistence of one's identity through time.[4]

Our second example described above, wherein Eliza sees all of her pieces replaced again and again, is lifted directly out of this grand tradition of personal identity. Her story recreates a famous thought experiment concerning the "Ship of Theseus" that began as an investigation into the nature of objects existing over time and has since developed into one of the major points of debate in the arguments concerning personal identity.[5] Indeed, LEGO minifigures seem particularly apt for discussions about this topic, as their ability to be easily put together and quickly taken apart can be readily equated to the questions concerning death and rebirth that first spawned discussions about personal identity. Locke's initial work on the subject, and much of the literature that has followed since then, struggled to come to terms with the Christian notion of death and the afterlife, especially the "Resurrection of the Body" that stands as such a central concept within this tradition. Again relying on our faithful LEGO minifigs, if we pull apart Eliza, throw her pieces into a pile of spare bricks, then come back several hours later and attempt to recreate her "block-for-block," what are the chances of successfully putting the original pieces of our minifigure back together again?

As you can see, the issue of personal identity is as problematic as it is important for understanding our nature as human individuals in an ever-changing world. This has led some contemporary philosophers, most notably Derek Parfit, to despair of ever solving such problems and, instead, to focus on the lasting impact we leave behind us.[6] Under such a view, Eliza's existence or non-existence is a moot point, relatively unimportant so long as the bricks which constituted her continue to be used to build new minifig characters. As we shall see in the next section, however, such a bleak response is hardly the definitive conclusion to the argument.

The Signature Figure of Philosophy

By now, our faithful minifig Eliza has gone through numerous transformations, to the point where, materially speaking, she shares nothing in common with the plastic figure we first talked about near the beginning of this chapter. Her identity, including the assorted changes to her component composition, is directly determined by the decisions and actions undertaken by the AFOL building and rebuilding her as part of his newest MOC. The reason why she has not dipped out of existence, to be replaced with another fictional character, is because her builder still views this particular minifig as "Eliza," the same character he has been diligently working on this entire time.

In many ways, the LEGO minifigure is given a distinguished position within the construction system by differing so dramatically from the rest of the bricks and other components utilized within it. Whereas LEGO, as a whole, is perhaps best represented by the classic four- or six-stud brick, the minifigure is composed of elements like the yellow head or hairpiece—individual bricks which are molded into fairly detailed recreations of the features they were built to mimic. While most LEGO bricks lack complex parts or moveable bits, these features come as standard for minifig torsos and legs that are intended to be posed in any number of imaginative ways.

Some philosophers have begun to place a similarly unique emphasis on the position of human persons within reality, even going so far as to claim that personal existence is the central concept and defining measure of the world in which we find ourselves. Encompassed under the umbrella term "personalism," these thinkers and movements seek to bring a renewed focus to the singular role of personal existence within philosophical discourse.[7] Rather than viewing human persons as problems to be hammered out through rigorous debate, they see personal life as the key to explaining all things, as the measure by which all other ideas and theories must be judged.

One of the major elements of personalism is an increased emphasis on the role of human action and choice in determining the nature of human existence. Confronted by many of the questions discussed in previous sections, personalists have chosen to avoid the philosophical pitfalls we've reviewed by focusing less on the static, unchanging nature of a person's being and more on their efficacious nature as willing actors making various choices. Put more simply, it isn't that who you are determines what you do; rather, what you do shapes precisely who you are.

Within the LEGO community, prolific builders traditionally use LEGO minifigures as a sort of "artist's signature" in their MOCs. These unique minifigs are referred to as "signature figures" (or "sigfigs") and often blend elements from both reality and fantasy to showcase the AFOL who created them. While many of these sigfigs mimic the physical traits of their creators, they can also showcase fantastical elements like a singular costume or unique accessory in order to capture a defining characteristic of their creator that might not be obvious from physical appearances alone. For instance, a sigfig for your diligent author could be a plain, brown-haired minifig with a goatee and a tacky sweater (representing how I usually look in real life) or a jetpack-equipped robot figure with an Egyptian headdress and a pizza (representing some of my other hobbies outside of LEGO and philosophy).

Sigfigs are what they are simply because their creators have chosen them to be so. It doesn't matter how much or how little they actually look like the AFOLs who put them together, just so long as those builders intend to represent themselves using that particular combination of LEGO pieces. The identity of these sigfigs rests on their builder's decision, which is precisely why the same figure can vary between MOCs and why an individual builder can have an entire collection of sigfigs to represent herself.

Whereas LEGO minifigures get this unitive narration of their lives from the decisions and actions of their builders, human persons combine these two aspects in one self-creating whole. The human person, in other words, is both the builder constructing his sigfig and the unique minifigure meant to represent such a creator. I, the author of this chapter, am both the actual writer of these words and the agent who determined that these particular words be written as opposed to any others. This powerful combination of both willing agent and active doer unites the discrete elements of human life into the coherent whole of the acting human person. As the prominent personalist philosopher Max Scheler (1874–1928) puts it, "[T]he person is the concrete and essential unity of being of acts of different essences," which renders him, basically, as "the 'foundation' of all essentially different acts."[8]

Far from being an assured thing, humanity's personal freedom is a gift that must be constantly guarded and maintained. While the average LEGO minifig is most often destroyed by having its pieces pulled apart and thrown back into the bin, authentic human personhood is largely lost by the apathy and lack of care exhibited by those who possess it. The Danish philosopher Søren Kierkegaard (1813–1855) was among the first to highlight this fact. In works such as *The Single Individual* and *Concluding Unscientific Postscript to the Philosophical Fragments*, Kierkegaard made passionate appeals for individuals to set themselves apart from the crowd, to actively choose the kind of existence they wished to live rather than merely settle for the common tripe loved by the masses.[9] Such rhetoric closely matches many of the opening lines from *The LEGO Movie*, which not-too-subtly lampoons the consumerism of a mass society wherein no one aspires to anything higher than watching the latest episode of "Where Are My Pants?"

Putting It All Together

Just as the LEGO minifigure stands out as a particularly noteworthy element in its building system, so too does the human person hold a unique place within the seemingly infinite complexity of actual existence. Fittingly, we've examined some parallels between these two and used these blocky little figures to help us better understand some of the most important, albeit difficult, questions surrounding our lives as human persons.

Although it can be tempting (and relatively simple) to reduce different persons to their distinguishing physical characteristics, such a simplistic course of action ultimately fails to do justice to their nature as unique human individuals. Rather, we must investigate further the nature of each being's identity, itself an issue full of nuance and seeming contradiction. While debates over personal identity are contentious, to the extent that several thinkers now believe that we need to abandon the notion completely, a promising solution to many of these quandaries can be found in the personalist emphasis on the human person's active, volitional character.

Alas, this chapter only scratches the surface of many of these issues. While a fuller exposition could be given, the real joy of both these disciplines, philosophy and LEGO, is the chance for every person to jump in and learn through experimentation. While one certainly needs to take the time out to study philosophy systematically, this shouldn't be one's only means of "philosophizing." Rather, one must join in the debate, testing new theories and trying to discover what fits, just as one must do when presented with a pile of LEGO bricks. Go out and choose to experiment, remembering, of course, the LEGO cry of "leg godt," play well.

Notes

1. The experienced LEGO builder will be quick to point out that there are, in fact, other ways to customize the LEGO minifigure. As long as one is careful, it is possible to remove and replace the individual hands, arms, and legs from the torso and leg assemblies, respectively. Although this is a common practice among the community of LEGO builders, I have chosen to focus on the main minifigure components simply because they are more accessible to the universal LEGO audience. This level of customization requires a bit of experience and care, and many builders (particularly younger ones) may not yet be familiar with this practice.
2. Brian McLaughlin and Karen Bennett, "Supervenience," in Edward N. Zalta (ed.), *The Stanford Encyclopedia of Philosophy* (Spring 2014 edition), available at http://plato.stanford.edu/archives/spr2014/entries/supervenience/ (accessed February 28, 2017).
3. For a much more thorough discussion of supervenience in philosophy, see Stephan Leuenberger, "LEGO® and the Building Blocks of Metaphysics" in this book, 197–206.
4. For a thorough summary of this entire debate, as well as many of the seminal texts that have helped to shape it, see John Perry, ed., *Personal Identity* (Berkeley: University of California Press, 2008).
5. For the very first mention of this particular thought-experiment, see Plutarch, "Life of Theseus," in *The Rise and Fall of Athens: Nine Greek Lives*, trans. Ian-Scott Kilvert (London: Penguin Books, 1960), 13–42.

6. See Derek Parfit, "Personal Identity," in John Perry, ed., *Personal Identity* (Berkeley: University of California Press, 2008), 199–223.

7. Kevin Schmiesing, "A History of Personalism," unpublished paper for the *Acton Institute for the Study of Religion and Liberty*, available at http://papers.ssrn.com/sol3/papers.cfm?abstract_id=1851661 (accessed February 28, 2017).

8. Max Scheler, *Formalism in Ethics and Non-Formal Ethics of Values: A New Attempt toward the Foundation of an Ethical Personalism*, trans. Manfred S. Frings and Roger L. Funk (Evanston: Northwestern University Press, 1973), 382–3, quoted in Peter H. Spader, *Scheler's Ethical Personalism: Its Logic, Development, and Promise* (New York: Fordham University Press, 2002), 104.

9. D. Anthony Storm, "A Primer on Kierkegaardian Motifs," in *D. Anthony Storm's Commentary on Kierkegaard*, available at http://www.sorenkierkegaard.org/kierkegaard-primer.html (accessed February 28, 2017).

Part IV
LEGO®, CONSUMPTION, AND CULTURE

13

LEGO® Values
Image and Reality

Sondra Bacharach and Ramon Das

LEGO® is more than just a toy. It's a lifestyle commitment, an attitude to life, a package of values. These values embody our conception of a good, wholesome childhood. Playing with LEGO is naturally educational—it supports free play, imagination, and creativity. The LEGO Group's mission is to "inspire and develop the builders of tomorrow" and their vision is "inventing the future of play." LEGO is forward-thinking—it was one of the first toys to promote gender equality, including letters in LEGO sets arguing that "The urge to create is equally strong in all children. Boys and girls."[1] LEGO has built working partnerships with educational institutions (they are sponsors of the MIT Media Lab and of a LEGO professorship of play at the University of Cambridge's Faculty of Education!), and LEGO provides educational resources to schools to integrate LEGO into the curriculum.

Everything really is awesome at LEGO—there seems to be no aspect of this company that doesn't contribute in some positive way to making LEGO an inherently good toy produced by an inherently good company, and their inherent goodness spreads widely through the community. For parents who want only the best for their children, LEGO offers a fantastic product that is grounded in wholesome goodness.

LEGO® and Philosophy: Constructing Reality Brick By Brick, First Edition.
Edited by Roy T. Cook and Sondra Bacharach.
© 2017 John Wiley & Sons Ltd. Published 2017 by John Wiley & Sons Ltd.

A Problem: The Greenpeace Video

At least, that's what the LEGO company tells us. Greenpeace, however, sees through the LEGO advertising and marketing ploys and
seeks to expose LEGO's dirtier underbelly. In a now-famous video
lasting just under two minutes, Greenpeace literally and metaphor-
ically drags LEGO's image through the mud (or oil, to be precise),
tarnishing its squeaky clean façade as a perfect company selling a
perfect product.[2] This video suggests that LEGO's image does not
square with its reality. With LEGO's upbeat pop hit "Everything is
Awesome" playing in the background, the Greenpeace video shows
what appears to be a beautiful, pristine Arctic landscape made out
of LEGO: a snow-filled wonderland where bears and huskies, fisher-
man and hockey players, birds and soccer players all blissfully frolic
together. True to the spirit of the song's call to collective and mind-
less happiness, the scene presented is just your average everything-is-
awesome-kind-of-moment in the Arctic LEGO landscape—everyone
is part of the team, side by side, living out a dream, sticking together,
and working in harmony. The music and images work together to construct an exaggerated and idealized conception of humanity's relation
to nature.

Against this naïve and idyllic LEGO background scene, the video
cuts to a stark contrast: a large Shell oil rig, whose "big boss" in a
fancy suit stands tall, dominating over his industrial terrain, enjoying
his cigar, and relishing his apparent power over nature. This big boss
looks remarkably like President Business, the president of the oil company Octan in LEGO's fictional world. President Business is a control-
ling person whose secret alter ego, Lord Business, has an evil plan to
control the world—the similarities between this boss, Lord Business,
and the CEO's of big industrial companies are not to be missed.

Unfortunately, the big boss in the scene is so self-absorbed that he
doesn't notice the small oil leak below. Slowly a mass of black oil
begins to spread, suffocating and engulfing everything in its path. The
reality of this image undercuts the naïveté of the theme song. As the
lyrics pathetically try to persuade us that everything is better when
we work together as a team, we are presented with the ugly truth—
innocent people and wildlife slowly being engulfed in oil leaking from
the rig. As the lyrics encourage us to work in harmony, we see helpless
children slowly drowning, and animals dying. The video ends with a
close-up shot of a polar bear trying to escape the oil on an iceberg
with the Shell flag on it. Slowly, the black oil engulfs not only the one

remaining bear clinging to the last chunk of iceberg but also proceeds to fill the entire screen in darkness and destruction. We are left staring straight at the culprit responsible for this horror: the Shell flag against a black screen.

Clearly, in the Greenpeace video, we are meant to believe that not everything at LEGO is as it claims to be. Rather, LEGO's relationship with Shell is tarnishing the clean and pristine image that LEGO wants to portray. The video ends by commanding viewers to "Tell LEGO to end its partnership with Shell," implying that Shell's oil drilling efforts are ruining the Arctic for all of its inhabitants. LEGO had profited from a merchandising contract with Shell involving Shell-branded toys being sold at Shell stations. The Greenpeace video suggests that this contract links LEGO to Shell's destruction of one of the last pristine environments in the world.

Given that LEGO advertises itself as a wholesome lifestyle choice whose values include being part of a team that educates people, living the dream where people do the right thing, this video poses a serious threat to their image—maybe also to the reality behind the image. The video undermines the entire ideology behind the LEGO brand and everything it stands for. As the title of the video reminds us, "everything is *not* awesome."

Everything is *Not* Awesome? A Philosophical Assessment of LEGO

The Greenpeace video is very powerful and extremely persuasive, but what exactly was this campaign *about*? The video hints at many possible criticisms of LEGO's relationship with Shell, and it's worth thinking through the video in more detail to get clear about the precise criticism being raised, and whether it is legitimate. In particular, from an ethical standpoint, how should we think about LEGO's relationship with Shell? And more generally, how should we think about a clean, green, and ethically upstanding toy company's relationship to other, dirtier, morally questionable companies?

Taking the Greenpeace video at face value, the imagery constructs a compelling metaphor in which the big boss at Shell oil stands alone, solitary and powerful, triumphant (and triumphantly ignorant!) over his drilling station, which is slowly flooding the Arctic with oil and destroying everything in its wake. Of course, nobody thinks *that* is a good thing, and we don't need a video to convince us.

However, we can find a different worry being articulated in the video's words (rather than its images) at the very end, when the Shell flag emerges out of the blackness of the oil, alongside Greenpeace's accusation: "Shell is polluting our kids' imaginations." What does this mean? One way of understanding this accusation is this: Greenpeace wants us to believe that when children play with LEGO toys with the Shell logo, LEGO pollutes our children's imagination. But, if that's the problem, then why aren't they also targeting Exxon and Esso, whose product placement appeared in LEGO sets as early as 1979? Surely both brands pollute our children's imagination equally, if they do so at all. And, it's not particularly obvious that they do: does Shell *really* pollute our children's minds by mere association with LEGO? That seems unlikely: *how* toys are made—whether it's in a socially responsible way, or not—does not literally affect the minds of the children who play with those toys. Likewise, the so-called pollution by association with Shell also does not seem as if it would prevent LEGO toys from doing what they are meant to do, namely to support free play, imagination, and creativity. After all, even unwholesome and evil people engage in free play, imagination, and creativity (even if Lord Business can't figure out how to do so). Whatever Greenpeace's complaint is with Shell, it's not about polluting children's minds.

A more plausible way to articulate Greenpeace's worry comes from the final plea in the video when Greenpeace commands us to "tell LEGO to end its partnership with Shell." This makes sense—Shell's attempts to drill in the Arctic were getting closer to being realized, and Greenpeace saw a strategic opportunity to leverage the LEGO name to criticize Shell.[3] Greenpeace made the video to put pressure on Shell by raising awareness within the LEGO community about LEGO's connections with Shell. Greenpeace's video was extraordinarily successful in targeting Shell via the LEGO community. The video went viral immediately, causing a massive uproar within the LEGO community and beyond. Indeed, within three months of the video's release in July 2014, LEGO agreed not to renew its contract with Shell.

All's well that ends well, right? Not exactly. Although LEGO agreed not to renew its contract with Shell, LEGO *did* honor the final years of its already existing contract. Still, the renewal would have seen $116 million U.S. dollars' worth of Shell-branded LEGO products at Shell gas stations around the world. But that's neither here nor there. The more lasting effects of the Greenpeace campaign are that it has heightened awareness amongst LEGO consumers regarding the morality of the LEGO brand and what LEGO stands for.

The philosophical challenge is to consider whether it is ethically problematic for LEGO to be connected to companies like Shell, and if so, why. How should LEGO fans respond when a seemingly clean, green, and wholesome company like LEGO is financially involved with Shell, a company whose activities are in direct opposition to everything that LEGO claims to stand for?

LEGO, Politics, and Values

These concerns are all part of a larger issue: examining the relation between one's ideology and politics, on the one hand, and one's status as a consumer of LEGO toys, on the other.

In the past, corporate values were usually treated as the private personal affair of the Board of Directors or CEO, but not relevant to the consumer. These days, however, consumers aren't willing to put up with that attitude. We care a lot more about corporate responsibility— the responsibility of companies to produce, market, and distribute their products in an ethically responsible manner. Parents care especially about the corporate responsibility of the products they purchase for their children, which has resulted in a proliferation of environmentally friendly, consumer-conscious, ethically sound toy companies. Not to be left behind, LEGO has engineered an entire marketing strategy to present an image that embodies wholesome goodness. LEGO advertises itself as a lifestyle choice whose values include being part of a team that educates people, that does the right thing, and that prides itself on its wholesomeness. This image is rather different from the reality of LEGO as a for-profit company, however, as we shall see.

Consider, first, LEGO's long-standing and problematic partnership with Shell. Shell, of course, is one of the world's largest and most profitable oil companies. And, like any major oil company, Shell is (and has been for a while) enmeshed in ethically problematic relationships, not least its relationships with various repressive governments on which its access to crude oil often depends. A notable example is its long relationship (beginning in 1958) with the Nigerian government, particularly its murky role in the government's brutal backlash against the Ogoni people and their non-violent campaign against Shell in the oil-rich Niger delta. The government's military repression left some 2,000 Ogoni dead and 30,000 homeless, culminating in the hanging of nine protesters in 1995, including environmental activist Ken Saro-Wiwa. In 2009, Shell agreed to pay $15.5 million to the Ogoni as part of a "humanitarian settlement," in the face of compelling evidence that it had been complicit in the Nigerian government's military repression. LEGO was undoubtedly aware of the Ogoni resistance campaign, which was notably supported by Greenpeace. Thus, one might think that LEGO had more than ample grounds to cut ties with Shell twenty years ago. However, in those pre-YouTube days, the Ogoni campaign never gained enough support or exposure to put sufficient pressure on LEGO to do so. No doubt this is an object lesson in the power of social media, but in terms of basic morality, it would be hard to deny that LEGO had at least as much reason to end its relationship with Shell twenty years ago as it does today.

Nor is everything awesome with LEGO's labor practices, which have followed a fairly typical trajectory for a major multinational company over the past decade. In 2006, amid falling sales numbers, LEGO decided to cut its U.S. and Swiss production and massively scale back its production in its home country of Denmark, laying off thousands of well-paid workers in the process. At the same time, it outsourced production to plants in poorer countries such as Mexico and the Czech Republic, where wages are much lower and environmental regulations comparatively lax. These practices are morally problematic if being a socially responsible company includes demonstrating loyalty to the workers who contributed to the very success of the company to begin with.

Two years later, LEGO ended up taking back control of its production from its outsourcing company (Flextronic). This has become a textbook case study in the business literature with respect to whether outsourcing is always "worth it." Largely overlooked, however, is the fact that even after ending the outsourcing arrangement, LEGO retained its manufacturing operations in the low-wage countries and never returned to its prior employment or production levels in the higher-wage areas it had abandoned. Although it is not hard to find companies with worse labor practices than LEGO, even LEGO's practices serve as a useful reminder that in business "social responsibility" is always subservient to the bottom line.

Finally, consider the key aspect of LEGO's social responsibility program, which centers around its stated commitment to the environment. This brings us back to the central issue raised by the Greenpeace video. LEGO made a public commitment to reducing carbon emissions at its production plants by 10 percent by the end of 2016, for which it deserves praise. Unfortunately, however, the actual manufacturing of LEGO components accounts for only 10 percent of the total emissions created in the production of LEGO, where this includes everything from extracting the necessary raw materials to bringing the finished product to market. The vast majority of harmful carbon emissions, about 90 percent, occur at various points along this supply chain.[4] Thus, while LEGO's commitment to reducing emissions at its own manufacturing plants is laudable, the relatively small percentage of the total emissions that this represents points up the reality that the problem is larger than any one company's climate policy.[5]

These points highlight the ways in which the reality of LEGO as a multinational corporation is in tension with its image as a wholesome company that consumers can feel good about supporting. The money and effort spent on constructing and maintaining that image makes it easy to forget that in the end, LEGO is a company motivated by its financial bottom line. It also explains why the Greenpeace video was so threatening to LEGO and why it proved so effective: in just a few short months, the video threatened to undermine the wholesome image that LEGO spent decades developing at tremendous cost.

But does LEGO *really* believe that everything is awesome? We are not so sure. It may be that LEGO is more self-aware of its own ethically precarious position—perhaps we should be giving LEGO more credit than either its marketing agents or Greenpeace allow.

So far, we have considered two opposing conceptions of LEGO: the clean, green, pristine, perfect version of LEGO courtesy of LEGO's marketing team at one end of the spectrum, and the environmentally dirty, hypocritical, and morally problematic version of LEGO portrayed in the Greenpeace video, at the other end. It would be too easy to end this chapter by taking a middle ground acknowledging that both sides are exaggerating. Perhaps the truth about LEGO's complicated relationship to the oil industry's dirty business is best appreciated by escaping to the LEGO fictional world.

In the LEGO fictional world, LEGO has always had an on-again, off-again relationship with all sorts of oil companies, including Shell. Shell has appeared in sets as early as the mid-1960s, and as late as 2014 (until the Greenpeace video). LEGO, however, was never exclusive with Shell—it also had relationships with Exxon and Esso since the late 1970s. LEGO dumped all "real" gas companies in 1992 after introducing its own fictional oil company, Octan. Octan was ethically upstanding and morally upright, serving as the major sponsor for sports teams in the LEGO fictional world (such as the Moose Jaw Octan Oilers of the LEGO Major Junior Hockey League), investing in renewable energy with its wind turbine in 2009 (set #7747), and even focusing more efforts on the renewable energy with an updated logo on its 2013 Tanker Truck (set #60016).[6] This logo contains many stylistic elements that hint at the company going green: the logo includes the word "Energy" in a larger font than the word "Octan," the logo is now entirely green, rather than its former red and green, and the logo now includes three leaves.

So, the truth in the fictional world is that LEGO was involved in the good (Octan) as well as the bad (Shell, Exxon, and Esso) intermittently. Yes, LEGO eventually did end its relationship with Shell (even if it held up the remainder of the last contract). But whether this was due to a desire to do the right thing or a desire to undo the damage to its reputation caused by the Greenpeace video is an open question.

This relationship is also muddied when we remember that President Business, the seemingly benevolent CEO of Octan, has Lord Business as his alter ego, the nefarious evil ruler who wants to destroy the world. Even worse, Lord Business cleverly uses the catchy "Everything is Awesome" pop song to brainwash his workers into blindly and happily following Lord Business's orders and letting him rule the world through its catchy tune with doublespeak lyrics.[7] Here, too, we see LEGO tacitly acknowledging its ambiguous relationship to the oil industry, the oil industry's equivocal relationship to the world, and the ambivalent position that the CEOs of major companies have toward their consumers and toward the industry's impact on the world itself, environmentally, socially, and economically. The dripping satire in the song's lyrics reminds us that behind Lord Business's seemingly good-natured encouragement to be positive and to buy overpriced coffee lies a parody critical of rampant consumerism and blind acceptance of corporate values.

The fictional world of LEGO suggests a more realistic image of LEGO than the real world! Yes, LEGO has had rather questionable ties to the oil industry—and it has had problematic social, political, and economic practices as well. These facts are nothing to be proud of, but LEGO is not alone in this. Nothing that has been said so far puts LEGO in an especially harsh light *as compared to other for-profit companies*. Indeed, it is not hard to find companies that are ethically (much) worse than LEGO in terms of their marketing, labor, or environmental practices. Whatever problems consumers might have with LEGO, it remains a much better company, ethically speaking, than most others.

Of course, those other for-profit companies don't portray themselves in the ethically positive way that LEGO does, and very few for-profit companies enjoy the ethically positive public image that LEGO enjoys. As we have seen, LEGO markets itself as "not just another toy company," an image that many consumers seem to accept as accurate. This raises the question: is LEGO hypocritical when it projects an ethically laudable vision all the while engaging in less-than-perfect practices? It's a fair question whether a company that trades on such a positive image should, in turn, be held to a higher moral standard than a company that does not.

Although this is not a question that we can settle here, being held to a higher moral standard may well be a reasonable "cost" of profiting from an ethically positive image. But, if we are going to hold these companies to a higher standard, then we had better do so with our eyes open, recognizing that first and foremost, LEGO, like all toy companies, is a for-profit (privately held) company.

Even if we may be disappointed that LEGO's practices may not have measured up to its image, we should still be supporting LEGO for taking the lead in developing its socially responsible ethos. Moreover, if we want to encourage other companies to develop greater environmental and social responsibility, then we should be calling out other toy companies that don't even bother trying to have an environmentally and socially responsible approach. In this respect, LEGO has the chance to be a leader in the toy world: the first to construct a socially responsible ethos, and hopefully in the future, the first to be able to follow through in its practices as well.

Notes

1. This letter has gone viral over the internet, and can be found many places, including http://www.telegraph.co.uk/men/the-filter/11250366/Lego-letter-to-parents-in-1974-on-gender-equality-still-resonates-40-years-on.html (accessed February 28, 2017).
2. Watch it at: https://www.youtube.com/watch?v=qhbliUq0_r4 (accessed February 28, 2017).
3. Since the 2000s, Shell had been trying hard to develop a feasible plan for Arctic drilling, designed to be implemented around 2010 or 2011. Fortunately or unfortunately, Shell's attempts at realizing the plans faced numerous setbacks, including the 2012 incidents where the Kulluk drilling rig ran aground in Alaska and where the *Noble Discoverer* lost control in Alaska (after its anchor slipped), and the 2013 finding by the

U.S. Coast Guard of over sixteen serious safety and environmental violations on its Arctic drilling rig. See http://fortune.com/2015/10/01/shell-arctic-oil-drilling-myths/ and http://wilderness.org/article/shell-pulls-out-arctic-chukchi-summer-drilling-decision-could-be-permanent. (accessed February 28, 2017).

4. See   http://www.energydigital.com/renewableenergy/3411/LEGOs-ambitious-plan-to-reduce-its-carbon-footprint. (accessed February 28, 2017).

5. See   http://www.lego.com/en-us/aboutus/news-room/2013/november/climate-savers.

6. It's not clear when this set emerged. http://lego.wikia.com/wiki/60016_Tank_Truck suggests it was released in January 2013. However, http://lego.wikia.com/wiki/Octan (accessed 29 August 2016) suggests it was in 2012. Either way, the set referred to is set #60016 (Tanker Truck). (accessed February 28, 2017).

7. For a more detailed interpretation of the song, see http://www.ibtimes.com/how-lego-movie-everything-awesome-parody-creeping-everyday-fascism-1555165 (accessed February 28, 2017).

Small Farms, Big Ideas
LEGO® Farm and Agricultural Idealism

Craig Van Pelt

The farms in the LEGO® Farm theme are immaculate.[1] They feature sparkling clean tractors, pristine fences, and the complete absence of dirt. Heck, even some of the farm animals seem to be smiling, but that's probably because the animals aren't standing ankle-deep in their own manure. Everything really is AWESOME in LEGO Farm.

Whether it is on purpose, or a limitation based on the number of pieces that can be placed inside a box, LEGO Farm presents an agricultural utopia. The farms are smaller, less dependent on toxic inputs, and friendlier to animals than real-life commercial farms. In other words, LEGO Farm presents an image of farming to children (and adults) that is environmentally friendly and responsible, unlike mega-industrial farms. But is the LEGO Farm theme harmful because it conceals the truth about the "dirty" side of farming? Or perhaps, on a more subconscious level, is LEGO Farm positive because it presents an agricultural ideal?

What Can We Learn from a LEGO Farmer?

Should we follow the model of farming presented by LEGO Farm? Food and environmental activists like Michael Pollan[2] and Bill McKibben[3] would probably say yes. Michael Pollan in *The Ominivore's Dilemma: A Natural History of Four Meals* makes a strong argument for eating vegetarian as a way to save the planet. The transformation of solar energy into plants, and then plants into animal

LEGO® and Philosophy: Constructing Reality Brick By Brick, First Edition.
Edited by Roy T. Cook and Sondra Bacharach.

food, and animal food into human food burns a lot of calories. Either on purpose, or by accident, LEGO Farm appears to advocate for a mostly vegetarian, environmentally friendly diet.

Large industrial farms can become overly dependent on using a lot of fertilizer, a lot of pesticides, lots of pharmaceuticals for animals, and a lot of water. When it rains fertilizer and other chemicals can run off into nearby rivers and lakes. Smaller farms, like the farms in LEGO Farm, can mean a smaller impact on the environment. This makes for pristine rivers, and happy little trees, and buzzing honey bees.

LEGO Farm Animals

LEGO Farm often features animals that are clean and well fed. Some animals even appear to be smiling, and that's appropriate considering that they are viewed as living creatures rather than commodities. Animals have feelings, and these LEGO Farm animals seem to believe that everything is awesome. No worries about grandpa being shipped off to the slaughterhouse.

LEGO Farm does not feature construction sets for concentrated animal feeding operations. In addition, LEGO Farm sets allow lots of room for cows, sheep, horses, and pigs to move around freely and enjoy life. Concentrated animal feeding operations do not exist, toxic lagoons of feces do not exist, and the farms do not occupy hundreds of acres in the world of LEGO Farm.

Perhaps surprisingly, the animals do not appear to be eaten in LEGO Farm. Yes, LEGO Farm presents a vegetarian (although not vegan) diet. In LEGO Farm sets, the animals seem to be raised only for eggs, wool, or milk: *not for human consumption*. Such a diet means less impact on the environment, as livestock eat a lot of food and drink a lot of water to grow to the proper size for human consumption. By promoting a diet of primarily vegetables, LEGO Farm could be promoting a more efficient conversion of solar energy absorbed by plants. Instead of animals eating plants, and then humans eating animals, LEGO Farm is suggesting we cut out the middleman (animals) by simply eating the plants. At most, LEGO Farm promotes eating the eggs and milk.

LEGO Farm sets are toys, not a direct representation of reality. But one should still pause and consider what kind of message is being sent to young impressionable minds. Will children grow up eating chicken and hamburger, not realizing that chicken and hamburger were once living birds and living cows? This kind of sheltered upbringing is not healthy. It leads to a parent having awkward conversations at the dinner table, such as "Mommy, why does daddy say he likes his steak bloody? Where does the blood come from?" This type of question comes from the omission of what happens to animals on farms.

On the other hand, LEGO Farm can be seen as presenting a more idealized view of living on a farm. The animals are smiling because they are cohabitating with the farmers who feed and take care of them. The farmers are happy because the animals provide milk and wool, so the farmers treat the animals well. Perhaps LEGO Farm presents a vegetarian ideal.

Either way, the ambiguity in this message about where our food comes from is a problem. It's not that the LEGO Farm theme is attempting to participate in a global conspiracy to hide where meat comes from. LEGO is not intentionally trying to hide the chemicals that are used to grow crops. This is not some weird iteration of the *X-Files*. But unlike the fantasy car represented by a *Hot Wheels* toy, for example, food is a very immediate issue for many people. Everyone must eat to survive. *Hot Wheels* can represent a car that people dream about having, but may never have. The dream *Hot Wheels* car is never part of everyday life for most people. LEGO Farm, on the other hand, brings many people close to sometimes hidden parts of the food system in which they participate every day. For that reason, perhaps LEGO Farm should be held to a different standard than other LEGO sets and other toys.

What Else Is Misleading about LEGO Farm?

In LEGO Farm, environmentally destructive farming practices are minimized or simply do not exist. These LEGO farmers are not bent on exploiting animals by raising them in grotesque living conditions. They are not focused on destroying the soil to make a profit now, at the expense of future agricultural productivity.

Similarly, LEGO Farm does not accurately convey the economic issues associated with farming. While there is some reference to food markets within the theme, the stress of agricultural work in the United States is not properly conveyed. Paying loans on tractors, buying seed and fertilizer, and paying the mortgage on the farm are anxious moments not fully embodied by LEGO Farm. Although parents may play with LEGO Farm with kids to help them learn the names of animals, it is unlikely that impoverished immigrant farmworkers are part of LEGO playtime.

Another real-world farm issue left out of the LEGO Farm theme is that size really does matter. Small is good. But when farms are too small, they can lose environmental friendliness. This happens because small farms might use a single pick-up truck to make ten deliveries to the market instead of one large truck.[4] Or the small farm may have one hundred customers drive out to a farm individually, instead of having one large farm truck deliver community-supported agriculture boxes to one location in the city.

The LEGO Farm theme doesn't even engage with the idea of food waste. One-third of all the food grown and raised in the world will end up in the trash.[5] There are various reasons for this. One is that food is a product for farmers to sell. If the food does not meet a certain standard, it is not worth the farmer's time to attempt to sell it on the market, even when that food is still edible. Leaving food in the field to rot is cheaper than donating it to a food pantry. Philip Ackerman-Leist writes that the United States is one of the biggest food wasters in the world, sending 40 percent of its food to the trash. *Many farmers don't have enough money to give food away, so they save money by leaving food in their fields to rot while people around the world go hungry.* But this lesson of basic farm economics is not part of LEGO Farm. That's probably not a fun conversation for parents to have with their kids. Nor is it a pleasant reality for farmers to deal with. Farmers aren't evil, but many of them just don't have enough money to give unsellable food away.

None of this means LEGO Farm is bad. These issues are a reflection of the larger conversations about where food comes from. Most people don't know where their food originates, or if they do know, they say something like: "My food comes from the grocery store." Bill McKibben and Michael Pollan advocate that people should know the source of their food, and how it is being grown or raised. None of this is LEGO's fault. LEGO, in this instance, is reflecting reality: People either don't know where their food comes from, or people don't really *want* to know.

Kids playing with LEGO Farm sets know they are growing food. However, LEGO Farm sets don't make the connection from farm to fork, meaning these sets miss a critical link in the chain of events that happens to many farm animals. This is actually a teachable moment for the proactive parent, not a moment to avoid the messy details of the food system.

LEGO did produce a collectible minifigure called Butcher, but there is no butcher shop set. The Butcher is advertised as knowing a lot about meat, but answering the question of where meat comes from is left vague.[6] The closest LEGO sets come to admitting that meat comes from animals is the retired LEGO Thanksgiving Feast (set #40056), which features a turkey on the dinner table. In addition, LEGO Heartland Food Market (set #41108) has a small sticker of a cow, but the food items included for sale in this set are bread, vegetables, and fruits.

So where does meat come from? It's difficult to make the farm-to-table connection using LEGO Farm. For example, there is no way to fully connect LEGO Pig Farm and Tractor (set #7684) to where the pigs go after they are fully grown. Perhaps questions about cows can be deflected as being raised for milk, and sheep for wool. But pigs? Pigs aren't raised for eggs, milk, or wool. This type of food connection could be made by enterprising individuals who create their own MOC cities, but it is absent in the small-scale individual LEGO Farm sets that most children play with. LEGO Pig Farm and Tractor comes with a tractor, a wagon, one male and one female minifigure, as well as a pig pen with water trough. There is plenty of room for the pigs to move around. The pigs and their environment are very clean. This is different from the grotesque environment in which many pigs have been raised where they stand ankle-deep in their own feces with very little room to maneuver.[7] The absence of the negative aspects of the reality of farming in the LEGO Farm theme is so prevalent, that it's unlikely to be accidental. What are the pigs for in this farm set? It's unlikely the pigs are merely pets.

So what message is LEGO Farm sending?

Let's Piece Together the Truth

So, as we have seen, the LEGO Farm theme does not appear to be comfortable engaging with meat in the food system. This means, also, that builders can skip over the meat-processing aspect of how meat goes from farm to table. Along with the messiness of food processing, the economic factors like mortgages and profit are often left out of LEGO Farm. This is not merely a LEGO message. LEGO is not creating the message, but is in fact accurately reflecting truth. As we have discussed, many people don't want to know their cows may have been raised in poor conditions, or that their berries may have been picked by exploited immigrant farm workers. In other words, they want to enjoy eating food but don't really want to think about where their food comes from.

On the plus side, LEGO Farm presents pristine farms, with ultra-clean tractors and animals, along with glistening crops. This might not be a terrible message. With LEGO, kids and adults can imagine farms as they would ideally make them. The beauty of LEGO is that anyone can be a Master Builder, building their own MOCs. As a Master Farmer the possibilities for representing environmentally friendly agriculture are endless. LEGO Farm does not present industrial agriculture with a business-as-usual model; it presents agricultural idealism. But this idealism is not in the farm sets themselves. The idealism exists within the creative freedom LEGO allows for Master Farmers to construct answers to problems.

Billie, do you use pesticides to keep the crops healthy? *No*, Billie replies with a roll of his eyes. *I built solar-powered drones to pick the bugs off the crops.*

Chris, do you let crops you can't sell rot in your fields? *Of course not*, Chris answers in disgust. *I built a high-speed electric train that goes from the city to the farm every day. People can come to my farm and get as much unsellable food as they want.*

Sarah, aren't you afraid of the toxic carbon emissions your tractor and combine are putting into the atmosphere? *Don't be stupid*, Sarah laughs. *I put conversion panels on the tractor and combine so they can operate on zero-point energy.*

The LEGO Farm theme isn't just about avoiding reality. It can inspire better realities. Yes, the farms in the LEGO Farm theme may be small. But the ideas and the inspiration for the creative future of sustainable agriculture remain big.

Notes

1. "LEGO Farm" is the name of a particular LEGO theme focusing on farm-based sets. It does not refer to any one individual LEGO farm set.
2. Michael Pollan, *The Omnivore's Dilemma: A Natural History of Four Meals* (New York: Penguin Press, 2006).
3. Bill McKibben, *Deep Economy: The Wealth of Communities and the Durable Future* (New York: New York Times Books, 2007).
4. Philip Ackerman-Leist, *Rebuilding the Foodshed: How to Create Local, Sustainable, and Secure Food Systems* (Santa Rosa: Chelsea Green Publishing, 2013).
5. Ibid.

6. "Butcher."   See   http://www.lego.com/en-us/minifigures/characters/
   butcher-4dd6e82873f74f4aaa60081bbe12402e (accessed   May   26,
   2016).
7. Bob Edwards and Adam Driscoll, "From Farms to Factories: The Environmental Consequences of Swine Industrialization in North Carolina,"
   in K.A. Gould and T.L. Lewis, eds., *Twenty Lessons in Environmental
   Sociology* (New York: Oxford University Press, 2009).

15

The Reality of LEGO®
Building the Apocalypse

David Lueth

LEGO® bricks, once primarily considered a toy for children, have spread in popularity to include many adults among their fan base. This trend has seen the formation of distinct sub-communities of adult fans of LEGO, or AFOLs, centered around different building themes. Many of these LEGO communities have at their base the premise of the MOC, which stands for "My Own Creation," a term describing any object designed and built by fans, as opposed to official LEGO sets.

Self-directed LEGO play has always been an integral part of the appeal of LEGO bricks. However, over the years official LEGO sets and brick molds have become more elaborate; this (along with the advent of product licensing, such as Star Wars® sets) has meant that following the directions included in purchased sets has increasingly gained importance. At the same time, this has allowed for a wider range of personalized creations. A set of basic bricks can be opened and put together by the most inexperienced user, but many current sets include pieces whose function is not obvious to the novice, and often have technical aspects to their use which require an instruction manual or prior knowledge—for instance, increasingly sophisticated "studs not on top" (SNOT) techniques.

Regardless of whether the advent and spread of MOCs is a push-back against the idea of following the directions, or a natural out-growth of increased possibilities inherent in the expanded selection of LEGO bricks and techniques, or some of both, it has become an

LEGO® and Philosophy: Constructing Reality Brick By Brick, First Edition.
Edited by Roy T. Cook and Sondra Bacharach.
© 2017 John Wiley & Sons Ltd. Published 2017 by John Wiley & Sons Ltd.

important part of the experience of LEGO bricks. AFOLs have connected through online photo-sharing sites like Flickr, LEGO blogs
like *The Brothers Brick*[1] and *From Bricks to Bothans*,[2] and LEGO
User Groups (LUGs—building clubs which can be regionally based
or online). Although some AFOLs primarily focus on official LEGO
themes like Star Wars, or are content to follow online forums but do
not design or build their own creations, many center on MOCs. These
communities are varied. Some are broad, while some are more narrow,
such as ones that exclusively deal with LEGO trains of a certain width,
or castles, or "neo-classic space," or post-apocalyptic scenarios. Usually being a member of one community does not preclude involvement
in another—it is common to find fans of both space and castle, for
instance—although there are occasionally schisms between, say, fans
of 7-stud-wide trains versus 8-wide.

The Basics of Baudrillard

LEGO bricks form one small arena in which culture is expressed.
Nonetheless, it is often possible to understand larger cultural issues
through focusing on one small element of that culture.

LEGO offers an example that can help understand a subtle and difficult cultural critique of society offered by Jean Baudrillard (1929–
2007), an influential French philosopher whose works contribute to
postmodern understandings of the world and our place in it. One element of postmodern theory is the claim that the world is linguistically
constructed and that an objective reality may not exist independently
of our ability to perceive it. Instead, our conceptual frameworks—the
way that we think about the world—organize our perceptions of the
world around us, creating reality as we perceive it.

Baudrillard elaborated on this theme with his concept of the *simulacrum*, the copy without an original. Baudrillard's work, in particular
his book *Simulacra and Simulation*,[3] largely concerns semiotics, the
study of signs (anything which represents other ideas or objects). He
wrote extensively on media and images, focusing on the relationship
between images and the things they represent. Baudrillard believed
that the sign as a representation of a meaningful, external reality was
breaking down as a result of the prevalence of media images and the
effect of these media images on culture at large. In *Simulacra and Simulation*, he argues that the relationship of signs to reality proceeded
through four historical stages of the image: "it is the reflection of a

profound reality; it masks and denatures a profound reality; it masks the *absence* of a profound reality; it has no relation to any reality whatsoever: it is its own pure simulacrum."[4]

Baudrillard's four stages are a model of the way the world works. It is often difficult to make the complexity of the world around us fit into categories meant to help us simplify and understand that complexity. LEGO bricks may not fit perfectly into Baudrillard's stages, but they can help us understand the four parts of his critique.

Stage 1: Basic Bricks Represent Reality

Many early LEGO sets appear quaint now. Through the early 1980s, most of the pieces consisted of basic plates and bricks in a limited selection of colors, and the builds were often correspondingly basic. Vehicles were boxy and, early on, even solid; buildings were often little more than rectangles with windows and roofs, occasionally sparsely furnished. It is precisely this basic, unspecialized quality that made these early sets correspond to Baudrillard's first stage, in which images represent a "profound reality."

These early LEGO sets had many of the same elements and themes of current LEGO offerings: there were castle, space, and town themes, for instance. Superficially, town sets appeared much the same as they do now, with police, fire, and other emergency services, gas stations, houses, and so on, with a large emphasis on vehicles. However, there was a key difference—there was little sense of narrative provided with these sets. Police officers, for example, did not have specific roles or functions. Most sets prior to the late 1980s consisted of a vehicle or two and a police minifigure or two, such as the 1983 Police Car (set #6623). There is no equivalent to sets like the 2008 Police Command Center (set #7743) and 2011's Mobile Police Unit (set #7288). Implicit in the early sets was the idea that police officers could be found patrolling the community, interacting with citizens, engaging in car chases, or acting much as any other minifigure, whether filling up the tank or eating a meal at home or at a truck stop. Even the yellow-skinned minifigures, although arguably not as racially neutral as some may claim, could still much more easily be interpreted as representing anyone than the flesh-colored minifigures found in later, licensed product lines.

This wide range of potential activities and roles allows these sets to be fairly accurate representations despite their basic, rough-hewn appearance. Indeed, the simple aesthetic allowed the form and function of the builds to stand in for real-world equivalents. In the real world, police officers, for instance, are complex humans with a multiplicity of personalities, activities, and social meanings; presenting the LEGO police in a very basic, unstructured way can reflect this clearly.

Stage 2: Conflict Play and Masking

LEGO sets experienced a shift in the late 1980s and early 1990s toward conflict-based, highly male-focused narratives which correspond to Baudrillard's second stage.[5] They no longer directly represented reality, but rather only *appeared* to represent it and instead began to "mask and denature" that reality (around the same time that LEGO made the move from relatively gender neutral themes to a supposedly more 'male' building perspective). Where previously, sets provided minifigures with vehicles and buildings, but no clearly defined narrative, now they began to have implicit or strongly suggested functions and roles, clearly and primarily targeted toward boys.

Early LEGO police sets often consisted of minifigures with cruisers or police stations and little in the way of a suggested narrative or objective—what role the accompanying police minifigures played in one's town was completely open—but newer police sets frequently included semi-trailers filled with elaborate surveillance equipment, and introduced an oppositional, conflict-based "cops and robbers" element, featuring masked thieves wearing prison stripes. Both the LEGO City Police Command Center and the Mobile Police mentioned previously include these elements. Furthermore, a police officer in a LEGO set from the 1980s could easily represent an actual police officer interacting with community members, and the basic smiley faces did not necessarily depict a particular gender. In more recent sets like the Swamp Police Station (set #60069) from 2015, they are portrayed almost entirely as gendered (male minifigures have stubble, female minifigures have long eyelashes and lipstick) agents of control, primarily concerned with arresting striped-shirt-wearing rings of thieves, whether in a city, forest, or swamp, and bringing them to jail—apparently without ever seeing a courthouse.

This last point is relevant to Baudrillard. Previously, sets were not presented as being somehow representative of actual urban settings, but instead served as little slices of life in no way meant to be comprehensive. This paradoxically allowed them to be *more* representative of reality, because any particular build did not allege to depict any more than one small element of our reality. A police car does not preclude courthouses from existing, but they are in no way a necessary part of the world of these minifigures. But having convicts wearing prison stripes means there is *necessarily* a justice system. To have police chasing criminals wearing outfits associated with prison, but to represent none of the legal mechanisms that send those criminals to prison, renders the legal and penal system invisible, or at least makes it appear unimportant. (The only judge released so far, wearing a powdered wig in the English style, came in the collectible minifigure line and not an actual city set.) This is very much part of how Baudrillard claimed images appear to be realistic while actually distorting the way we perceive reality. The same can be said for the increasingly gendered nature of both minifigures and LEGO marketing.

This is not to claim that these police minifigures were not still open to the same range of interpretation as before. In fact, that is also part of Baudrillard's second stage: representation of the real world as it actually exists is still *possible*, and this possibility makes it difficult for us to see the multitude of ways in which the narratives offered to us have broken with the real world. Because we *can* still use images or symbols, including LEGO builds, to represent reality as it actually exists, we may not notice that this seems to be happening with less frequency, and that official LEGO sets (and, presumably, MOCs made by recipients of those sets) are encouraging a view of the world in which some aspects of reality are emphasized while other parts of equal or greater importance are rendered absent or otherwise inconsequential.

Stage 3: Sky-fi and the Absence of Reality

LEGO builders of all ages have built entire communities and worlds relating to the creation of MOCs, and much LEGO play—since the earliest interchangeable bricks—has likely happened without following any instruction booklet or manual. The more recent trend of LEGO fan communities exchanging ideas, as well as the influence of licensed properties and the desire to build scenarios and vehicles that are included in these storyworlds (such as Star Wars) but not produced as licensed sets, best demonstrates Baudrillard's third stage, in which he argued that the proliferation of images "masks the *absence* of a profound reality." The application of Baudrillard's third stage to LEGO can be broken down into three parts: the proliferation of images, the absence of a "profound reality," and the fact that the former obscures the latter.

The proliferation of images can be seen by how LEGO MOCs, LEGO communities, the development of advanced building techniques, and a host of other LEGO-related image-building activities separate from official LEGO sets all interact with and build off each other. These activities even impact official LEGO sets. For example, LEGO Ideas is a way for LEGO users to get their MOCs produced as official LEGO sets. In other words, images made with LEGO bricks proliferate, with fans and the LEGO Group all influencing each other in myriad ways that lead to the creation of even more images.

As for the second part of Baudrillard's concept, in talking of an absence of a profound reality in the third stage, he did not mean that reality no longer exists. Instead, he was drawing attention to the increasing proliferation not just of images in general, but specifically of images that appear *similar* to real objects and settings yet are not representations of anything that actually exists. For instance, the "J-24 Katana" by Jon Hall skillfully recreates a color scheme often found in actual Japanese airplanes of WWII but does not represent any particular Japanese aircraft.[6] Many of this builder's other works have similarly realistic paint schemes and designations. *The Brothers Brick* highlighted a MOC by Stephen Chao of an airplane depicted in the animated film *Porco Rosso* by Hayao Miyazaki, the "Savoia S.21." While this is an airplane created by Miyazaki, there was actually a different airplane built in real life bearing the same designation.[7] The point is not that there is no distinction between fantasy and the real world, or between a MOC of a real World War II plane and a superficially similar original creation. The point is that this distinction between reality and fiction is becoming blurred so that the two are becoming difficult or impossible to distinguish from one another. The difference is becoming irrelevant.

Finally, Baudrillard argues that the proliferation of images obscures the absence of a profound reality—in short, these realistic but fictional images are referred to interchangeably with images of real-world equivalents, and often the two are used to play off each other— meaning that this process is self-perpetuating and self-reinforcing. So, for instance, the Savoia S.21 from *Porco Rosso* mentioned above is a MOC based on a fictional airplane which uses the designation of a real plane by a real airplane company. Undoubtedly this MOC will, in turn, influence new creations of realistic but fictional aircraft, perhaps referring to actual airplane manufacturers and designation systems and including realistic-sounding backgrounds and specifications.

Stage 4: ApocaLEGO and Self-Simulation

Baudrillard's explanation of his fourth stage, in which "[the image] is its own simulacrum," is, like much of his work, dense and difficult to follow. LEGO can illustrate this stage, but it will make more sense if we first consider Baudrillard's idea with an analogy from Jorge Luis Borges.

Borges wrote a short story called "Tlön, Uqbar, Orbis Tertius," in which the protagonists discover, in a single copy of an encyclopedia, an entry about the fictional realm of Uqbar, but cannot find the same entry in any other copy of the same edition.[8] As they track down more references to Uqbar, other people begin to construct their own geographical, historical, linguistic, and other references to this place. Importantly, the accuracy of new references is judged in terms of how well they fit with previous references, and not in terms of how well they accord with reality. As these references develop and expand, Uqbar slowly comes into being, eventually replacing our own world. The language and thought processes laid out in the invented entries for Uqbar become dominant, replacing the languages and thought processes which had arisen organically throughout the world. The fictional realm ultimately comes to be more real than the real world it originally was created in.

LEGO sky-fi does not quite correspond to Borges' story, because there are still original images—namely, WWII airplanes—that exist independent of their representations in LEGO and to which MOCs can be compared. However, post-apocalyptic scenarios have no real-world counterpart. Even those events which could be argued to have inspired apocalyptic scenarios, such as the two world wars, are not actually apocalyptic themselves, however horrible they may have been (not to mention that apocalyptic stories, such as H.G. Wells's *War of the Worlds* and, for that matter, the Biblical *Revelations*, precede the world wars).

Apocalyptic LEGO MOCs, or ApocaLEGO, began by combining various elements of the apocalyptic, as well as additional pop culture references such as zombies and steampunk. These images were themselves based on other cultural products such as film, video games, books, illustrations, and even Biblical references. At no point, however, do any of these cultural products *represent reality as we experience it*. Although it is possible to argue, with some merit, for some degree of symbolism in many of these texts, they do not explicitly refer to any real-world event or scenario. The key factor here is that ApocaLEGO, like other apocalyptic texts, is characterized by the way in which it remains in the realm of the fantastic or hypothetical, with each image referring primarily to other images. Countless MOCs refer back to each other, and to film, books, etc., endlessly.

An example of this can be found on the website *Bricks of the Dead*, which highlights a MOC based on *Metro 2033*, a novel by Russian author Dmitry Glukhovsky.[9] *Metro 2033* was subsequently turned into a video game, sold film rights, and has been turned into a major franchise. The original novel that inspired this *Bricks of the Dead* MOC is itself influenced by nuclear war scenarios, a common form of post-apocalyptic work since the 1950s. *Metro 2033* draws from nuclear war texts, but which ones? Glukhovsky lists the influence of Roger Zelazny, Ray Bradbury, and the video game *Fallout*, but even that only adds layers to the problem.[10] Authors may cite specific influences, but there are invariably other sources of unconscious inspiration, and what's more, Zelazny, Bradbury, and the makers of *Fallout* all drew their own ideas out of the culture they were immersed in. There is still an interchangeable aspect in which these texts very well *could have* referred to numerous other sources in ways that can never be parsed out. This may be what Baudrillard meant when he claimed that it is the "reality *principle*" [emphasis added] that is no longer intact, rather than reality itself. After all, we are still living beings that inhabit and interact with a world external to ourselves. But, Baudrillard argued, the distinctions between representations of that world and the world itself are no longer clear or even meaningful.

ApocaLEGO MOCs on *The Brothers Brick* feature references to the *Fallout* video game franchise, *The Walking Dead* TV show, the films *I Am Legend*, *World War Z*, and the *Mad Max* films.[11] This endless circularity of images referring back to each other, without ever representing the real world, illustrates Baudrillard's last stage. ApocaLEGO goes far beyond what creators of sky-fi did when they began to combine real-world WWII airplane styles and designations with steampunk sensibilities. While a sky-fi creation can be checked against the historical record, it would likely be impossible to point to any real-world equivalent, and difficult to even find inspiration, for ApocaLEGO MOCs: what actually existing house, or subway station, or deserted cityscape does a particular MOC refer to or even use as an influence? Certainly some may have specific, real-world references, but most do not—and even with those that do, it is rarely clear what that reference is. In the *Metro 2033* example, a book led to the creation of a video game and LEGO MOCs; MOCs influence other MOCs and even influence official LEGO sets (such as 2012's The Zombies (set #9465) in the Monster Fighters theme, which also shows a steampunk influence), which themselves will almost certainly influence further MOCs. Whether or not an ApocaLEGO MOC is judged to be accurate or good depends solely on its relationship to other fictional apocalyptic creations. This takes the interchangeable nature of reality and fiction demonstrated by sky-fi and eliminates even the appearance of referring to reality. Instead images refer only each other. Baudrillard would argue that reality is only something to compare to those images—as anyone who has heard or said, "that reminds me of [a particular movie]" could understand.

Baudrillard would find ApocaLEGO, like the rest of 21st-century culture, to be a hall of mirrors, everything reflecting off and influencing everything else and in the process modifying reality. To Baudrillard, reality is actually preceded by images: images come first and reality is simply a secondary function of them. His four stages merely describe the process from reality producing the image to the image producing reality. We can start with bricks that seem to effectively represent the real, but through subsequent developments the bricks have come to supplant the real. Baudrillard argues this happens throughout media-saturated culture. LEGO is just one example. If Baudrillard is correct, ApocaLEGO does not just consist of MOCs; it is, in a way, actually building the apocalypse. Certainly not in the sense that LEGO will cause an apocalyptic downfall of civilization, but rather in the sense that images and ideas that arise from MOCs and other cultural constructions end up modifying the culture they arise in. On one level this may seem commonsense, but Baudrillard's argument takes an important piece of received wisdom and turns it on its head—namely, that images or signs represent real-world objects and ideas. Like Borges' Uqbar, Baudrillard's work shows us that the proliferation of signs can actually produce reality.

Notes

1. *The Brothers Brick*, 2016, http://www.brothers-brick.com/ (accessed March 1, 2017).

2. *From Bricks to Bothans*, 2016, http://www.fbtb.net/ (accessed March 1, 2017).
3. Jean Baudrillard, *Simulacra and Simulation* (Ann Arbor: The University of Michigan Press, 1994), 1–42.
4. Ibid., 6.
5. For further discussion of the gender issues in LEGO, see Chapter 10 by Rebecca Gutwald and Chapter 11 by Rhiannon Grant and Ruth Wainman in this book.
6. "J-24 Katana," 2016, https://www.flickr.com/photos/25163007@N07/23622810814/ (accessed March 1, 2017).
7. "Version #5 – Audi.TW's Savoia S.21 from *Porco Rosso*," 2013, http://www.brothers-brick.com/2013/05/11/version-5/ (accessed March 1, 2017).
8. Jorge Luis Borges, *Everything and Nothing* (New York: New Directions Publishing Corporation, 1999), 12–30.
9. "Lego Creation: Metro 2033," 2014, http://bricksofthedead.com/2014/08/21/lego-creation-metro-2033/ (accessed March 1, 2017).
10. "Metro 2033 Interview," 2009, http://www.ign.com/articles/2009/12/01/metro-2033-interview (accessed March 1, 2017).
11. "Tag Archives: ApocaLEGO," 2016, http://www.brothers-brick.com/tag/apocalego/ (accessed March 1, 2017).

16

The American Archipelago
Touring the Nation at Miniland USA

Samantha J. Boardman

If you get the opportunity to go to one of the LEGOLAND® theme parks—go. Really. They're awesome. Not just because they're beautifully landscaped and full of LEGO® brick statuary, or because their "pink knuckle" rides offer additional entertainment for budding adrenaline junkies, but because they're wonderful places to contemplate how we—both Americans and non-Americans—imagine America and what it means to be American. No, really.

In LEGO fan parlance, the "Fan Developed Theme" or "FDT" (also sometimes referred to as a "Fan Created Theme") is a theme derived from the imaginations of LEGO enthusiasts rather than one officially sanctioned by LEGO HQ. In Miniland USA, the nation itself takes on many of the characteristics of the FDT: vignettes of LEGO bricks, thematically unified as "American," based on representations of locations throughout the United States. Unlike other areas in the park that use thematic elements from LEGO kits, the Miniland USA section is not a representation of any official "American" LEGO series, but instead an intersection where the LEGO enthusiast and the national imagination meet, a collective endeavor constructing a vision at once universally recognizable and wholly unique.

Miniland

Frequently referred to as the "heart" of the LEGOLAND theme parks, Miniland is a section made up of scaled-down versions of national

LEGO® and Philosophy: Constructing Reality Brick By Brick, First Edition.
Edited by Roy T. Cook and Sondra Bacharach.
© 2017 John Wiley & Sons Ltd. Published 2017 by John Wiley & Sons Ltd.

landmarks and icons, artfully arranged around winding paths. At the flagship LEGOLAND park in Billund, Denmark, the Miniland area is full of scenes from around Scandinavia (with a few outliers). Likewise, the UK outpost at LEGOLAND Windsor features a miniature Big Ben, London Bridge, and the like. At Miniland USA, this same strategy is adapted for an American audience, with individual sections corresponding to different regions or cities from across the United States. What sets the American location(s) apart is the way in which this racially diverse, culturally heterogeneous, and geographically expansive nation differs in its representation in the (older) Carlsbad, California location and in its (newer) version in Winter Haven, Florida. The evolution of Miniland USA between the two locations gives us an insight into the ways in which "America" is constructed—symbolically, at the level of the nation-state, and literally, in Miniland scale.

On their way to Miniland USA, visitors to LEGOLANDs East and West run a gauntlet of scenes based on current LEGO products and sets, each with a corresponding ride or display and a similarly themed gift shop. Interestingly, the sub-themes employed in these scenes—"The Knight's Table," "Pharaoh's Revenge," etc.—are established popular theming elements in American society.[1] In this context, the Miniland USA section designates "America" as a thematic device on a par with medieval and desert motifs and locates it on the same plane within the geography of the park.

The overall effect of Miniland USA is a pastiche of American iconography, culled from a touristic itinerary of the United States in the late twentieth century. Absent are scenes of mundane everyday life. Residential neighborhoods or workplaces are eschewed in favor of portrayals of already popular tourist destinations and the ludic celebrations—Mardi Gras parade, inaugural marching band, etc.—performed there. This is in keeping with the "view of the world" presented in the original LEGOLAND in Denmark, where designers purposefully constructed tableaux of life as a "comical pageant" in which "the work of the world" becomes "a carnival of quaint motions."[2] Accordingly, the designers of Miniland USA present an American landscape where this ethos is reflected and fulfilled through the visitor's encounters with the models. Also absent are any scenes from American history. The America of LEGOLAND takes place in a "now" that references a scant few historic sites and then only as components of the built environments of their contemporary locations.

America as Fan Developed Theme(park)

Miniland USA tells a semiotic narrative—that is, a story in symbols—of a modern nation at play rendered as a collection of scenes from largely affluent, urban, coastal areas. What unifies these discreet sections of Miniland into a representation of America is the visitor himself. Moving from one regional depiction to another transforms the tourist's body into the connective tissue that knits the miniature nation together.[3] Similarly, the visitor performs a simulation of national tourism, visiting each area of the Minilandscape in a manner that mimics the experience of travel in the jet age. Tourists in Miniland, like tourists in the life-sized U.S., can go directly from New Orleans to Las Vegas or from New York City to California without having to traverse even a simulation of the "flyover country" in between. The United States of Miniland is an archipelago of tourist destinations bound together by its "American" theme.

This America is encountered in a concentrated form (the miniature) in a space of concentrated experience (the theme park), rendering a heightened emotional effect on the beholder. Gaston Bachelard (1884–1962) in his *Poetics of Space* describes the relationship between miniaturization and time as one in which time slows down, asserting that one lingers over the miniature in order to savor its delicate detail.[4] However, in the setting of the miniature theme park, promotional literature touts the expediency of being able to see a variety of exhibits/replicas/environments in a condensed period of time, implying that the experience of the replica environment is more efficient than the real world.[5]

By definition, the miniature is a representation of something that already exists in larger form elsewhere.[6] The fidelity with which the model maker reproduces the referent structure, to be instantly recognizable to those familiar with its large-scale counterpart, is one of the measures of his skill.[7] The miniature America of Miniland USA assumes such familiarity on the part of its audience with the structures and landscapes represented and, accordingly, presents representations of those structures and landscapes most recognizable to the largest number of potential visitors.[8]

Geography is likewise manipulated to rearrange the literal landscape of the nation and bring far-flung metropolitan areas together. Given the vast geographical area of the United States, this spatial collapse is considered by designers and visitors alike as a value-added element, enabling attraction-goers to "see" more of the country by going to the miniature park than they would be able to if they literally, physically traveled to each destination portrayed. This idea that an ersatz version of a nation would be preferable to the "real thing" is a notion that recurs frequently in literature regarding tourist attractions and themed environments.[9]

Contemporary domestic tourism envisions the United States as several distinct geographic zones, differentiated by metropolitan centers and regional characteristics (primarily climate, food, and dialect). Tourist guides and maps reinforce this configuration, highlighting roughly the same delineation of regions: The Northeast, Mid-Atlantic, Southeast, Southwest, Midwest, and Pacific Northwest.[10] Echoing this conception of the national itinerary, LEGOLAND California's Miniland USA contains miniature versions of six different American locations: New York City, Washington DC, "New England," New Orleans, Las Vegas, and California.

Notably, each of these areas in the country at large is itself a popular tourist destination, which undoubtedly influenced its choice for inclusion. In order to fully appreciate the fidelity with which the LEGO replicas were reproduced, the visiting public would need prior acquaintance with images of the landmarks depicted. Thus, structures with images already circulating in the popular imagination as representative of specific American places would be most suitable for simulation in Miniland, and the mechanism of tourist imagery, its creation and circulation, would work to represent those areas as desirable.

America in Miniature: LEGOLAND California

Inevitably, this leads to idiosyncrasies. At LEGOLAND California, the American Midwest, Southwest, Northwest, and South are almost entirely absent from the tableau. This is an America of locales that, while overwhelmingly urban, does not include Chicago, Atlanta, and other cities not coastally located. The "New England" section is a curiously curated "harbor," in which the region is portrayed as primarily agrarian, lacking any sort of metropolitan area or even colonial architecture. No natural wonders are in evidence. This is an America without a Grand Canyon or Niagara Falls, or the need for them.

The New York City skyline of Miniland USA has a number of faithfully reproduced iconic skyscrapers, oriented in a peculiar geography. The "Freedom Tower" and 9/11 memorial located at the tip of "Manhattan" are of a prototype architectural design rejected years ago, becoming literal embodiments of the "simulacrum"—i.e., a copy for which an original does not exist.[11] The iconic Brooklyn Bridge originates in "Manhattan" and terminates in an empty, grassy "Brooklyn." Times Square is sandwiched in between the Woolworth Building and a less-defined "downtown" area. The Statue of Liberty rises in a lagoon just across from Mount Rushmore.

This is the modern tourist's view of New York City, as well as the New York City most recognizable to consumers of movies, television, and other images in circulation. In order to represent the location "New York City," LEGO assembled a set of images—an itinerary— that recreates the tourist's experience of Gotham in a scaled-down form. Places left off this itinerary include the outer boroughs (less frequented by tourists and less frequently portrayed in movies and television shows set in the city), primarily residential sections of Manhattan (the Upper and Lower East Sides, for instance), and neighborhoods that serve as concentrations of labor rather than leisure.

Popular tourist destinations and quirky geography also abound in the other American cities depicted in the Miniland assortment. The iconic architecture of Washington, DC makes it a perfect subject for reproduction. The orientation of the monuments and the dearth of explanatory signage as rendered in LEGO bricks present a decontextualized nation's capital, with the Olympic proportions of the buildings only reinforced by their miniaturization. Las Vegas aptly lends itself to LEGOization as the scale models of the whimsically themed casinos on the strip attest.[12] New Orleans features a Mardi Gras parade, complete with Rex and Zulu Krewe floats, passing the wrought-iron railing balconies of a mini French Quarter.

The "California Coast" section features scenes from popular Northern and Southern California tourist destinations (though notably absent is any reproduction of Disneyland® or, indeed, any other themed tourist attraction).[13] Also absent are any representations of Carlsbad itself. Though a popular tourist destination since the turn of the century for its mineral springs (the "bad" in Carlsbad is German for "bath"), there is no trace of the town, historical or contemporary. Ironically, the Miniland California in LEGOLAND California erases Carlsbad from the itinerary of U.S. tourist destinations even as LEGOLAND proper seeks to make it one.

Rebuilding America: LEGOLAND Florida

A continent away, the locations portrayed in the Miniland USA of LEGOLAND Florida skew more local. While the New York and

Washington DC replicas follow the modus operandi of using well-known locations to highlight the versatility of the LEGO bricks and the talent of their designers, other locations and landmarks depicted are of sites much closer to the attraction itself. The "Florida" of Miniland

> encompasses the entire state from Mallory Square in Key West to Bok Tower in Central Florida and antebellum mansions in the Panhandle … Kennedy Space Center and an interactive Daytona International Speedway®.[14]

The Kennedy Space Center as depicted is a peculiar scene, with a Space Shuttle from the now discontinued NASA program sitting on a launch pad, awaiting a blast-off that will never come. The addition of the antebellum mansions and life-sized replicas of the hoopskirted "Southern Belles" who once greeted guests to Cypress Gardens (the defunct theme park that has been repurposed as LEGOLAND Florida) make it somewhat difficult to locate the LEGO version of "Florida" in real time.

As in the California version of Miniland and in addition to the Florida section, Washington DC, New York City, and Las Vegas are all figured as locations essential to the American itinerary so depicted.[15] According to Marcy Harrison, the personal assistant to LEGOLAND Florida General Manager Adrian Jones, the criteria for the areas included in this version of Miniland were: "areas that have proved popular in other attractions," areas that gave "the opportunity to re-create models we have made before but [which we could] 'enhance' with more lights and effects," and areas that would "follow existing plans [which] is also cost-effective."[16] So, in addition to the budget efficacy of recreating models popular elsewhere, we see the evolution of the American tourist itinerary as New England and New Orleans fall out of favor. Whether this is due to the somewhat lackluster presentation of "New England" as a section in the California version or the region's inescapable synonymy with early American history (itself a theme we see falling out of favor in tourist preferences), the area is gone from the scene. Likewise, New Orleans's deletion from this mapping could be for any number of reasons—the lingering aftermath of Hurricane Katrina or the BP oil spill being the most immediate associations with the location in the current popular imagination, for example.

While the Washington DC area of Miniland Florida contains mostly the same models (right down to the marching band performing in front of the Capitol) and the casinos on the Vegas Strip remain largely unchanged, the New York City section reveals some striking departures from its Carlsbad counterpart. Most notable is the complete omission of the Freedom Tower, 9/11 Memorial and, indeed, much of Lower Manhattan below Wall Street. In its place, the island just terminates into a very narrow harbor, almost immediately abutting Liberty Island, with the Statue of Liberty a stone's throw from the Manhattan skyscrapers. Where LEGOLAND California anticipated the replacement of the Twin Towers with a building that ended up not being built, the designers of LEGOLAND Florida's Manhattan deftly avoided the matter by simply leaving the entire site out. Other notable differences in the Florida version of New York include a Rockefeller Center with fountains instead of ice skating (in a nod to the Florida climate), and a Times Square whose logos have changed to Pepsi and Ford (instead of Coke and Volvo) in honor of the exclusive sponsorship deals brokered with these companies at the East Coast site.[17]

Information as to which sections had proved popular before was based on "mostly guest feedback." But model builders were given "creative license ... particularly for unique zones like Pirates and Florida."[18] The addition of the Florida section was seen as essential since "at every LEGOLAND attraction we take on the 'Face of the Place' [giving] the Park/Discovery Centre a unique identity and [making] it relevant to the local community."[19] The repurposing of the Cypress Gardens site added an extra level of local pride as LEGOLAND took pains to preserve the infrastructure of the park and maintain beloved entertainment features like the water-skiing shows, along with two roller coasters and, among the native botanical elements, a banyan tree planted in 1939.[20] As with the Carlsbad location, LEGO sought to make tourists of the locals themselves, both in choosing a location demographically suited to supporting the park long term and in the design of the "American" themed Miniland section in which visitors experience the postmodern dislocation of leisure tourism in a miniature replica cross-country trip.

Diorama Americana

The appeal of LEGO is, at its root, the promise of boundless, unbridled creative potential. LEGO bricks present opportunities to build and rebuild worlds, limited only by the imagination of the creator. Conversely, the appeal of the themed environment is the order it imposes on chaos. The landscape is tightly scripted, with the flow of visitors moving through a planned route in a predictable way.[21] The path through which a tourist winds his way through Miniland USA provides a spatially choreographed and physically experienced series of nationally themed vignettes with which to engage. In the tension between the boundless potential of the LEGO element and the controlled environment of the theme park, Miniland USA emerges as a negotiated space—built by designers, but created by touristic expectation—the nation-state rendered as Fan Developed Theme.

Notes

1. See Mark Gottdiener, *The Theming of America: Dreams, Media Fantasies, and Themed Environments* (Boulder: Westview Press, 2001).
2. Henry Wiencek, *The World of LEGO Toys* (New York: Harry N. Abrams, Inc. Publishers, 1987), 147.
3. For an interesting discussion of how motion—specifically walking—effects the way one constitutes and perceives of one's environment, see Edmund Husserl, "The World of the Living Present and the Constitution of the Surrounding World External to the Organism," translated by Frederick A. Elliston and Lenore Langsdorf, in Husserl, *Shorter Works*, edited by Peter McCormick and Frederick A. Elliston (Notre Dame: University of Notre Dame Press, 1981), 238–50.
4. Gaston Bachelard, *The Poetics of Space* (Boston: Beacon Press, 1969).
5. Here there is some interesting overlap between scholars of Tourism Studies, Semiotics and Themed Environments, see: Barbara Kirshenblatt-Gimblett, *Destination Culture: Tourism, Museums and Heritage* (Berkeley: University of California Press, 1998); Mark Gottdiener, *The Theming of America: Dreams, Media Fantasies, and Themed Environments* (Boulder: Westview Press, 2001); Scott Lukas, *The Themed Space: Locating Culture, Nation, Self* (Lanham: Lexington Books, 2007).
6. See Susan Stewart, *On Longing: Narrative of the Miniature, the Gigantic, the Souvenir, the Collection*, 1st edn (Berkeley: University of California Press, 1984); John Mack, *The Art of Small Things* (Cambridge, MA: Harvard University Press, 2007); and Bachelard (1969).
7. Along with the amount of time taken to create the miniature and the process by which the model is built.
8. Here, Miniland USA fits Guy Debord's definition of a "spectacle" as "everything that was directly lived … moved into a representation." See Guy Debord, *Society of the Spectacle* (Detroit: Black & Red, 1983), Section 3.

9. See: Kirshenblatt-Gimblett (1998); Lukas (2007); Mark Gottdiener (2001); and of course Jean Baudrillard who calls the idea that there is a "real thing" into question, wryly noting that "Disneyland is presented as imaginary in order to make us believe that the rest is real." Jean Baudrillard, *Simulations* (New York: Semitext(e) and Jean Baudrillard, 1983), 25.

10. For a contemporary example, see *Frommer's USA*, Kathleen Warnock, ed., (Hoboken: Wiley Publishing, 2009). Interestingly, the "islands" that make up the archipelago of LEGOLAND's Mini USA also follow along this metropolitan/regional representational strategy.

11. Jean Baudrillard, *Simulacra and Simulation* (Ann Arbor: The University of Michigan Press, 1994).

12. In what Scott Lukas refers to as a "meta moment," see Scott Lukas, *Theme Park* (London: Reaktion Books, 2008), 170.

13. This is almost certainly due to the complex copyright issues inherent in recreating trademarked properties. Disney's litigiousness is legendary enough to inspire Michael Sorkin to represent its Anaheim park with a photo of a bright blue sky, devoid of any Disney imagery whatsoever, in his chapter on the subject. See Michael Sorkin, ed., "See You In Disneyland," in *Variations On A Theme Park: The New American City and the End Of Public Space* (New York: Hill and Wang, 1992), 207.

14. LEGOLAND Florida Fact Sheet 2012, 3, available at https://www.yumpu.com/en/document/view/18878567/legoland-florida-2012-fact-sheet (accessed March 2, 2017).

15. A California section was added in 2012.

16. Personal correspondence with Marcy Harrison via Tina Froberg Mortensen, Records Manager, LEGO Group Archives, November 11, 2011.

17. "Grab a Pepsi at Legoland," *The Ledger*, Winter Haven, December 14, 2010, C4.

18. Personal correspondence with Marcy Harrison.

19. Personal correspondence with Marcy Harrison.

20. "Pieces in Place for Florida's New Legoland," *Daily Herald*, October 9, 2011.

21. Miodrag Mitrasinovic, *Total Landscape, Theme Parks, Public Space* (Burlington, VT: Ashgate, 2006), 156.

Part V
LEGO®, METAPHYSICS, AND MATH

The Brick, the Plate, and the Uncarved Block

LEGO® as an Expression of *Dao*

Steve Bein

One of the great virtues of LEGO® is that it has the potential to make any one of us a Master Builder. By itself, of course, the brick is silent. It offers potential, not guidance. For that we can turn to instruction booklets, or the MOCs of other creators, or even to the greatest sculptors of history. Auguste Rodin (1840–1917) was a Master Builder if ever there was one, and many a LEGO fan has recreated his famous *Thinker*. What can Rodin teach us about making our own masterpieces?

When asked for his secret to sculpture, Rodin said it was quite simple: "I choose a block of marble and chop off everything I don't need." That may leave you wondering: has Rodin said nothing about sculpture, or has he said everything?

"Both," says the Daoist sage. It's the sort of answer that makes the most famous figures of Western philosophy want to pull out their hair. From their perspective, the problem with the answer is its lack of clarity. By contrast, from an Eastern perspective, such imprecision can be a virtue. Indeed, the founding texts of Daoism are riddled with indefiniteness. In one of its most quoted passages, the *Daodejing* says that in order to be a good ruler you have to "return to being the uncarved block."[1] That's it. We get no further context. Now what in the world is that supposed to mean? And if it means anything at all, why not spell it out it more clearly?

LEGO® and Philosophy: Constructing Reality Brick By Brick, First Edition.
Edited by Roy T. Cook and Sondra Bacharach.
© 2017 John Wiley & Sons Ltd. Published 2017 by John Wiley & Sons Ltd.

It's an Invitation, not a Toy

The *Daodejing* is billed as a work of political philosophy, but paradoxically it says almost nothing about governance in any direct fashion. Even when it does address the subject directly, its advice is about as clear as Rodin's:

> "Governing a large state is like cooking a small fish."
> "Look at the state through the state; look at the empire through the empire."
> "Bring the common people back to keeping their records with knotted string."[2]

At this point the skeptic might ask what makes this a philosophical position, and not mere mumbling? If it's to be political *philosophy*, and not just political *advice*, it's got to give us some specific principles to build upon, hasn't it?

Those questions are founded on an unspoken assumption: that open-ended, imprecise language is incompatible with philosophical argument. Clearly, the Daoists challenge that assumption. This challenge itself is pretty audacious—as audacious, perhaps, as expecting children to enjoy a box of parts when you could just as easily have bought them a toy. That, of course, is exactly the challenge the LEGO Group set out for itself: to sell not toys but parts, and then let the kids do the assembly themselves.

One LEGO brick by itself isn't a toy, though, is it? It doesn't *do* anything. What it really is, when you get right down to it, is an invitation. Get a pile of them and you can create any toy you can imagine—and not just toys, but architectural models, works of art, even prosthetic limbs. The only way the brick can do this is by having no standing of its own. It's *because* it's not a toy that it can be the greatest toy ever. By being nothing, it can be anything.

In that way it's actually a perfect model for understanding the *dao*. It also encapsulates what makes open-endedness valuable even when you're trying to do some really important philosophical work, like figuring out what the ideal state would be like and who its ideal ruler would be.

"It's Super Serious, Right, Babe?"

Before we get to the value of open-endedness, let's take a moment to consider the alternative. We shouldn't just *assume* that precision in language is inherently better, any more than we should assume that building a LEGO X-Wing according to the instructions is inherently better than building a spaceship of your own design.

In *The LEGO Movie*, Wyldstyle and Batman® present a case study in the value of precision in language. Every time she says their relationship is "super serious," we see he's on edge. He agrees a little too quickly, doesn't he? And he's a little too convincing when he runs off with Han, Chewie, and Lando on the *Millennium Falcon*. Yes, he's duping everyone so he can steal the hyperdrive, but the only reason the deception works is that it's totally in character for him to bail on his girlfriend. When Wyldstyle says "super serious," she's trying to get Batman to commit—that is, to agree on the precise nature of their relationship. It's that drive for precision that gives Batman cold feet. He'd prefer to leave things vague, and in that way he's a bit like the early Daoists.

On the other hand, Wyldstyle's approach is much closer to the dominant traditions of Western philosophy, which you can trace all the way back to ancient Greece. The Greeks were obsessed with precision in a way you don't see in many other places in world history. Plato (427/9–347/8 BC) writes entire dialogues dedicated to defining a single concept: courage in the *Laches*, piety in the *Euthyphro*, friendship in the *Lysis*, virtue in the *Meno*. He seems to have inherited this fascination with precision from his mentor, Socrates (469/470–399 BC), and he certainly passed it on to his pupil, Aristotle (384–322 BC). It's a popular theme throughout Greek philosophy: precision is better than imprecision. Why this preference, and not the other way around?

Here's one reason: in ancient Athens, choosing just the right words could be really good for your career. Unlike most of the ancient world, Athens was a democracy. A young man could make himself immensely powerful if he could convince others to agree with him. Hence the rise of the Sophists, who made quite a name for themselves (and quite a lot of money too) educating wealthy young men in the arts of argument and persuasion. Plato's mentor, Socrates, had little time for sophistry. For him, the purpose of philosophical debate was to find truth, not to score points. He never claimed to have found truth—in fact, he famously insisted he knew nothing at all. He did a lot of thinking about how best to govern, though, and he concluded that you'd have a very hard time knowing how to rule *justly* if you didn't know how to define *justice*.

Like the LEGO brick, that Greek distaste for imprecision has proven to be nearly indestructible, such that two thousand years after Socrates, the American philosopher William James (1842–1910) would define philosophy as "the uncommonly stubborn attempt to think clearly." Yet the *Daodejing* has had remarkable staying power too. This may come as a surprise given its famously enigmatic approach, but there's a big difference between Daoist philosophy and the way Batman deals with Wyldstyle: Batman is being deliberately evasive and non-committal, whereas Daoist imprecision is actually a highly nuanced philosophical stance.

"Actually it's a Highly Sophisticated Interlocking Brick System"

The unsettledness in the *Daodejing* (also spelled *Tao Te Ching*[3]) starts not from the first chapter, nor from the first page, nor even from the first line. Scholars can't even agree on the title. In one English translation it's *Te-Tao Ching*, and in fact the traditional title is simply the *Laozi* (also spelled *Lao Tzu*).[4] That's supposedly the name of its author, but one of the few things scholars can agree on is that no one named Laozi ever existed.

So in a sense our springboard is a book without a title or an author. Laozi himself is built up out of history's LEGO, and so is the *Daodejing*. In Laozi's case, the bricks and plates are a bunch of stories, remarks, and references in other works, all pointing at whoever it was that wrote the passages we now call the *Daodejing*. Similarly, there isn't an "official" or "original" *Daodejing*, but rather a series of constructions made by various contributors. What we have today is a received text that can be traced back to a number of different documents—its bricks and plates, so to speak—and over the years, different scholars have stuck them together in different arrangements.

Little wonder, perhaps, that we can apply this composite philosophical tradition to the composite brick system that is LEGO.

"No Government, No Babysitters … and There's Also No Consistency"

The *Daodejing* is a challenging text, and one of its many challenges is that it never concretely defines *dao*. *Dao* is usually translated into English as "way" (or "Way," or even "the Way"), and that's not a bad translation so long as you keep in mind all the meanings "way" has in English. In *The LEGO Movie*, Princess Unikitty would be able to show you the way to Cloud Cuckoo Land (a geographical route), the way to remove a bushy mustache (a technique), the way to create an entire realm without rules or consistency (a system of techniques), or the way to be happy all the time (a philosophical approach). *Dao* can be any of those ways. Notice that those ways aren't *things*. They're closer to *activities*, and this highlights two important concepts in Daoist thought. First, a way isn't a permanent, unchanging entity. As any backpacker knows, the way from A to B is really more like an ongoing process, changing season by season and sometimes even day by day. Second, there's not *one* way. For any given destination, there's probably more than one path to get you there, and for any given path there's more than one way to walk it.

That's the message of the very first sentence of the *Daodejing*: "Way-making (*dao*) that can be put into words is not really way-making."[5] The early Daoists were leery of any attempt to define *dao* in specific terms. Definition is a kind of limitation, and *dao* defies all limits. We'd encounter a similar problem if we tried to fully unpack the "awesome" of "everything is awesome." It's hard to define "awesome," but not because you don't know what you're talking about and not because you have nothing to say. The problem is quite the opposite. No matter how much you say, you'll always have left something out. That's the only way definition can work—*this* is only *this* if it's not *that*. So if the thing you're talking about is broad enough, and casts its influence widely enough, any attempt at definition must always fall short.

Throughout the *Daodejing* we find a willingness to describe, but a deep reluctance to define. For example:

> As a thing the way [*dao*] is
> Shadowy, indistinct.
> Indistinct and shadowy,
> Yet within it is an image;
> Shadowy and indistinct,
> Yet within it is a substance.
> Dim and dark,
> Yet within it is an essence.
> This essence is quite genuine
> And within it is something that can be tested.[6]

The concept of awesomeness works the same way. Can you define it concretely? No, not without leaving something out. But can you test it? Absolutely. If I say "that ski slope is awesome" you can go ski it and see for yourself. The same goes for awesome restaurants, awesome jiujitsu instructors, awesome LEGO sets, you name it: if you're open to the experience, you can test it for yourself. So it is with *dao*. There is *dao* latent in the snowy mountainside, and if you align yourself with it, you can ski it beautifully. There is a *dao* of cooking, and of jiujitsu, and of designing with LEGO. Those who understand this *dao* can do things that amaze and delight and make the rest of us marvel.

The artist Nathan Sawaya is a case in point. He began by recreating masterpieces of classical art in LEGO: Hokusai's *Great Wave off Kanagawa*, Leonardo's *Mona Lisa*, Michelangelo's *David*. Had he reproduced them in their original medium, he'd be little more than a mimic, but Sawaya understands the *dao* of LEGO. His Hokusai is five layers thick, so his *Great Wave* has a texture and depth beyond what the original woodblock can deliver. He doesn't just imitate; he evokes, then delivers something entirely new—and the most stunning part is, you could have done it yourself if only you'd thought of it first. The pieces were always there. The possibility was always there. Sawaya was the sage who put them together.

In Daoism, the sages were masters who had aligned themselves with the *dao* of their chosen vocation. Here's how the *Daodejing* describes the sages of ancient times:

> Those of old who were good at forging their way (*dao*) in the world:
>   Subtle and mysterious, dark and penetrating,
>   Their profundity was beyond comprehension.
>   It is because they were beyond comprehension
>   That were I forced to describe them, I would say:
>   So reluctant, as though crossing a winter stream;
>   So vigilant, as though in fear of the surrounding neighbors;
>   So dignified, like an invited guest;
>   So yielding, like ice about to thaw;
>   So solid, like the uncarved block;
>   So murky, like muddy water;
>   So vast and vacant, like a mountain gorge.[7]

Notice two images here: first, the uncarved block we've seen already; second, the vast and vacant mountain gorge. It turns out both of these are also images of LEGO.

Let's examine the gorge first. It's a fitting image for *dao* because it is inexhaustible. You can use it all day long and never wear it out. Why not? Because the part of the gorge you can see—the cliffs that wall it in—is actually the least important part. What makes a gorge gorgeous is all the empty space. This amazing power of emptiness is perfectly exemplified by the LEGO brick. At its most basic level, your standard two-by-four brick is more nothing than it is something; that is, by volume there's more empty air than there is plastic. Why is it awesome? Because it marries the something to the nothing. If it didn't, the bricks couldn't stick together. But because of this perfect marriage of something and nothing—*yin* and *yang*, in Daoist terms—it's the greatest toy ever.

But the brick isn't just physically empty; it's also empty of *meaning*, just like the uncarved block. Suppose you're a sculptor and I hand you an ordinary block of wood. You're now holding limitless possibilities. The block can become *anything*, right up until the moment you shave off a piece. After that, there are some shapes it can't take anymore. The more you take off, the more you limit what's possible: once it starts to look like a person, it's pretty hard to make it into a spoon or a spaceship.[8] We can think of the LEGO brick in the same way. By itself it's empty of meaning, and that's exactly why it can be anything you want it to be: because by itself it's nothing.

If your basic two-by-four brick is the "uncarved block," LEGO makes "carved" ones too: cockpits, irregular minifig heads, all those cool bits. But the more an element is designed to look like something specific, the less versatile it becomes. Print a design on it or put a sticker on it and you end up with less, not more. As the *Daodejing* describes it, "Thus a thing is sometimes added to by being diminished, and diminished by being added to."[9]

"They're Expecting Us to Show Up in a Bat-Spaceship"

Here's where we get to political philosophy. In the case of the LEGO brick, the less it's like a toy, the better you can play with it. According to the Daoists, government is no different: the less it does, the better it works. That doesn't entail abdicating responsibility altogether. Rather, the goal is to be as effective as possible with as little intervention as possible. There's a Daoist term for this: *wei wu wei*, literally "doing without doing." Water is especially good at this. It's gentle, not coercive. It flows, it doesn't hammer. It always follows the path of least resistance, and because it's like this, it's one of the strongest forces on the planet.

As such, water itself is not just an inspiration for the Daoists; it's actually a role model. Effortless power is just one of its many virtues.

Water is beneficial to everyone, seeking nothing in return. It's non-competitive, always happy to sink to the lowest places. It doesn't play favorites. And it expresses all of these virtues through *wei wu wei*.

Emmet Brickowski is by turns a total doofus and a master of *wei wu wei*. (This is perfectly in keeping with Daoism. One of the themes of the early texts is that it's often hard to tell the difference between a fool and a sage.) Everyone wants him to devise some ingenious plan to break into Lord Business's tower, but instead of designing a Bat-spaceship, a pirate spaceship, or a rainbow-sparkle spaceship, he designs ... well, nothing. Better to build what's already there: a plain old Octan delivery spaceship, so ordinary that it might as well be invisible. No inspiration, no ingenuity, no cleverness at all—and that's exactly why his plan works. Keep It Simple, Stupid.

This is the point of that cryptic line we considered earlier: "Governing a large state is like cooking a small fish."[10] The trick to cooking a small fish is to handle it as little as possible. Fuss with it too much and it falls apart in the pan. The best spatula in the world can't help you; what you really need is highly skilled attentiveness to very subtle changes. After that, it's all *wei wu wei*: minimal intervention for maximal effect. One flip and you're done.

For the sage, statecraft is no different: legislate well and you won't have to legislate often. This approach is anything but standoffish; a ruler needs to be every bit as attentive and skillful as a master chef. The ideal result is that "with the most excellent rulers, their subjects only know that they are there."[11]

The objection, of course, is that this is still too imprecise. Yes, we ought to *try* less and *do* more, but to what end? After all, this *wei wu wei* stuff can be used for evil just as easily as for good, can't it? Lord Business had several options when it came to beheading poor Vitruvius. He could have built an elaborate decapitating device, maybe something like a Micromanager. Instead he just threw a penny at him. Does this make Lord Business an evil sage?

No. It's true that he stepped outside of the conceptual confines within which everyone else operates. That much looks like sagacity. And it's true that he found the path of least resistance, and in doing so accomplished exactly what he sought to accomplish. But he's missed the most important part of *wei wu wei*: the whole point is to be non-coercive, to benefit everyone, to be fair-minded—in short, to flow like water. Instead, Lord Business's every effort is to coerce the world into the shape he wants it. Thus while he may be a genius, he's not a sage.

That said, the initial worry still remains: the problem of imprecision. If the Daoist says the ruler should take a minimalist approach, we must still ask how. Which laws do we keep and which do we repeal? Which areas should this unassuming government watch closely, and which should it leave entirely to the people? And if we can't find an answer to any of those questions, is this minimalist approach so minimal that it says nothing at all?

"Everything Is Awesome!"

As we've seen, one of the most telling differences between ancient Greek philosophy and ancient Chinese philosophy lies in their attitudes toward imprecision. It was anathema to the Greeks, yet the Chinese were quite comfortable with it. A philosopher like Plato or Aristotle will say—rightly, I think—that without more detail, it's hard to tell whether the *Daodejing* supports Democrats or Republicans, Greens or Libertarians (or for that matter, red ants or black ants). On the other hand, the authors of the *Daodejing* are also right to be suspicious of specificity. Too often one-size-fits-all means one-size-fits-poorly. What works for King A might not work for Queen B, and what worked last year might not work next year. Thus it's better for rulers to take *wei wu wei* as their default position and then judge each novel situation on its own merits.

LEGO Master Builders understand this. Perhaps you've seen the video that went viral of a young woman building her own prosthetic leg out of LEGO. She doesn't have an instruction booklet; she only has a goal. Through time-lapse photography we watch her test the fit of the new LEGO limb, see how well it bears weight, pull a few pieces off, stick a few on, test-fit it, modify it, test it again. This is the Daoist model of government: commit yourself to the goal (in this case, a harmonious nation of flourishing citizens), be willing to be flexible, and *voilà*, you've freed yourself of the tyranny of the instruction booklet. Will you make mistakes along the way? Sure, but that's exactly why you don't want to take a heavy-handed approach. Like Rodin, chop away all the parts you don't need. Be empty in your politics: throw out parties, platforms, and ideologies, aligning yourself instead with the *dao*.

Or don't. Sit at home with your LEGO and build to your heart's content. That's another teaching of the *Daodejing*: "There is no crime greater than having too many desires; there is no disaster greater than not being content."[12] For millions of adults and children around the world, sitting down to a big pile of LEGO is the very picture of contentment. The fact that it appeals to so many, of so many ages, in so many cultures, over so many decades, is arguably due to its *dao*. Because it's empty, it contains infinite possibilities; because it tries to be nothing, it's capable of being anything; because you can't contain its awesomeness in words, it expresses awesomeness to everyone, everywhere, in every language.[13]

Notes

1. *Tao Te Ching* 28, translated by D.C. Lau (London: Penguin, 1962).
2. *Daodejing* 60, 54, 80. Chapters 60 and 54 are D.C. Lau's translation, and Chapter 80 is Roger T. Ames and David L. Hall's translation (*Daodejing: Making This Life Significant* (New York: Ballantine, 2003)). In this chapter I'll switch between the Hall and Ames translation, which is the most philosophically accurate, and D.C. Lau's, which is the more accessible.
3. *Tao Te Ching* is how it's spelled following a Romanization transliteration system called Wade-Giles. Spelling it *Daodejing* follows the pinyin system, which most scholars use these days, and which I'll be using throughout this chapter. Pronunciation is identical in both systems— so, for example, *tao* should be pronounced with a "d", not a "t", and one reason many students of Chinese prefer pinyin is that it looks closer to the proper pronunciation.
4. Robert G. Henricks's translation is called *Te-Tao Ching* (New York: Ballantine, 1989). Lao Tzu is the Wade-Giles spelling of Laozi.
5. *Daodejing* 1, Hall and Ames translation.
6. *Tao Te Ching* 21, Lau translation.
7. *Daodejing* 15, Hall and Ames translation. For purposes of consistency I've taken the liberty of replacing "unworked wood," their translation of *pǔ*, with Lau's "uncarved block."
8. Spaceship!
9. *Tao Te Ching* 42, Lau translation.
10. *Tao Te Ching* 54, Lau translation.
11. *Daodejing* 17, Hall and Ames translation.
12. *Daodejing* 46, Lau translation.
13. I'm indebted to David Levy and Myrna Gabbe for their helpful insights on Greek philosophy.

18

LEGO®, Impermanence, and Buddhism

David Kahn

Growing up, I found myself in a relentless battle between appreciating my LEGO® masterpieces and adding a coat of superglue to preserve them for the ages. If this sounds unusual, my eight-year-old self would tell you that what is really unusual is creating a work of art only to destroy it at cleanup time. In the end, I conceded to take it apart, but this was always done begrudgingly and not without my mom first taking a picture for posterity.

Thirty years later, I watch in amazement as my kids spend hours building a LEGO tower only to knock it down in a fit of laughter. No qualms. No pouting. No pictures to reminisce for all of history. They enjoy the construction and the destruction.

The battle between my childhood disposition to preserve and my kids' disposition to destroy is typical. *The LEGO Movie* explores this idea when Finn is reprimanded for "ruining" his father's elaborate LEGO structure. Once Finn's father realizes that the villain in his son's scenario is based on him and his use of Kragle (Krazy Glue), the lesson of the movie (and of LEGO) emerges—nothing is static, life is in a state of perpetual change.

Change is commonly resisted. When leadership Professor John Kotter researched this idea in his book *Leading Change*, he found that 70 percent of all workplace change programs fail.[1] Likewise, when studying dietary changes, food psychologist Traci Mann discovered that 66 percent of people claiming to desire to lose weight regained more weight post-diet than they started with, and when studying

LEGO® and Philosophy: Constructing Reality Brick By Brick, First Edition.
Edited by Roy T. Cook and Sondra Bacharach.
© 2017 John Wiley & Sons Ltd. Published 2017 by John Wiley & Sons Ltd.

changes resulting from New Year's resolutions, psychologist Richard Wiseman observed an 88 percent failure rate.[2]

Accepting change can be difficult, but not changing can be fatal. A company's long-term survival is based on its ability to evolve in an ever-changing industrial landscape. Someone with unhealthy eating habits must be able to alter their diet to match their lifestyle. And resolutions are an indicator that you are not satisfied with some aspect of your life and feel the need to make a change.

Despite our best efforts, every aspect of life is in a state of flux. To adapt is to survive. That is why we must learn to embrace the Buddhist philosophy of impermanence.

What Is Impermanence?

According to Buddhist teachings, all things have a transient nature. Whether that thing is tangible or intangible, organic or inorganic, it is undergoing a constant process of change. This is the essence of impermanence—reality is never stagnant but is dynamic throughout.

In the traditional Buddhist scripture Digha Nikay ("Collection of Long Discourses"), Buddha (circa 563–circa 480 BCE) is quoted as saying:

> Impermanent are all component things,
> They arise and cease, that is their nature:
> They come into being and pass away,
> Release from them is bliss supreme.[3]

This can be translated for the LEGO aficionado as:

> Impermanent are all aspects of LEGO,
> They assemble and are dismantled, that is their nature:
> The creative things you build come into being and are put away,
> What we gain from LEGO is bliss supreme.

If we cling to something (the current state of a relationship, a time in our life, a particularly impressive LEGO configuration), we will feel anxiety when it changes. If we can avoid clinging, there is no anxiety. We will more quickly accept the change, thereby experiencing a painless assimilation (allowing relationships to evolve, aging gracefully, discovering new LEGO configurations with which to shock and amaze).

People who hold on to ideas feel stress when they are wrong or when the idea becomes outdated. They typically come up with reasons and excuses to rationalize their decisions, adhering to behavior patterns or to a self-image even when it no longer benefits them. We all experience this to some degree; it can be difficult to change once we've found something that works. Buddhist philosophy, however, teaches that clinging is always unfavorable, even when the thing to which we cling has a positive effect. In his book *Positive Addiction*, famed psychiatrist William Glasser argues that compulsive habits such as jogging and transcendental meditation "strengthen us and make our lives more satisfying."[4] Yet, while these activities enhance health, creativity, and feelings of self-efficacy, Buddhist thought warns against becoming dependent.

If you cling to daily meditation or exercise, you will feel anxiety on the days you are unable to do it. To avoid this counterproductive stress, impermanence helps us eliminate our attachments. By removing these attachments, we remove the delusions and trappings of false security, thus equipping ourselves for life's barrage of rapid-fire change and getting us closer to the Buddhist idea of nirvana.

When we look at LEGO bricks, their impermanence is evident. For instance, the materials that make up a LEGO brick changed from Cellulose Acetate to Acrylonitrile Butadiene Styrene (ABS) in the 1960s. Some bricks have thinner walls with different-shaped tubes when compared to their 1980s predecessors. Instructions are much more complex than they were twenty years ago, with some booklets containing hundreds of pages separated into multiple books. Even the LEGO logo has gone through multiple variations over the years— twelve at last count.

The process of change can be slow and incremental, yet it is constant and inevitable in all aspects of existence. While many transformations take place without our ever noticing, impermanence is verifiable through direct observation. It may require patience, but it is there. A LEGO piece left in direct sunlight will take months before you realize its color has faded, and even then you may need another LEGO brick to discern the contrast. However, since LEGO utilizes aerospace-like industry standards to mold their bricks, it is improbable that they will undergo significant physical changes. More likely, your perception of these bricks will evolve long before the pieces themselves do.

Consider the way you perceive a particular LEGO piece. The one-by-four blue brick with bow that was once associated with the roof of the LEGO Cinderella's Dream Carriage (set #41053) is now unidentifiable in a Tupperware container of assorted sets. And the structure you once believed to be the Da Vinci of all LEGO works is a pale comparison to what you are able to create today. Skills evolve, experience accumulates, and every LEGO project raises the bar for your next endeavor.

Benefits of an Impermanent Mindset

Understanding impermanence is necessary if we are to lead fulfilling, productive lives. In our relationships, how often are friendships made in the LEGO aisle of a store? How often do alliances deteriorate because one of the people involved refuses to share his LEGO blueprints? How often does a significant other evolve from a Non-LEGO spouse (NLS) into a LEGO enthusiast? And how often does an adult fan of LEGO (AFOL) become the parent of LEGO-loving kids?

Our relations with others are entirely marked by impermanence. When we fight this, we tend to put others in a box. We get locked into who someone is without allowing them room to grow and change over time. Then, when the change becomes too noticeable to ignore, we call them a fraud because they no longer match the person we antecedently decided they were always going to be. Their growth was always happening, yet we feel betrayed because we are fixed on their illusory permanent state. This is true when we write off our LEGO building buddies for only wanting to spend half of their free time on LEGO-related activities, and when we do not accept a newbie to the LEGO life because they haven't enjoyed LEGO as long as we have. In both instances, we are not allowing change, thereby alienating ourselves from reality and more meaningful bonds. Here we can learn a lesson from Buddhism.

Even in death, Buddhist practices celebrate the ever-changing nature of the world. At funerals, flowers and lit oil lamps are ceremonially placed before the statue of Buddha. This is not intended to be a prayer to Buddha but to acknowledge that as the flowers wilt and the flames subside so does the state of all things. As the Buddha said:

> Life is like a floating cloud which appears.
> Death is like a floating cloud which disappears.
> The floating cloud itself originally does not exist.[5]

Funeral attendees are then asked to "remember death" for this will discourage excessive desire and remind us of our own ultimate impermanence. From the moment of birth, we move inexorably toward death. It is easy (and understandable) to view this as bleak, but Buddhist philosophy does not emphasize death to depress us. Instead, the certainness of death is intended to motivate us to make the most of our time by not getting fixated on petty, unimportant items. LEGO is no different.

From the moment a new LEGO set goes on sale, it is one step closer to being discontinued. The set may still exist on eBay, but the opportunity to buy a new set will never be available again. Once you purchase it, the LEGO set progresses inescapably toward the land of misfit toys. You can do everything possible to preserve them, but the unventilated attic will not allow your LEGO to remain in "good as new" condition. Even if the LEGO bricks manage to retain their freshness, the pieces will quickly decay once you pass your LEGO collection on to your children.

Finally, impermanence is key to understanding the ultimate nature of life. With all things being perishable, we begin to see their lack of substantial existence. This is true for ourselves and for the world around us. In a sense, impermanence is the property of "not-self." To explain, self is a convenient term for a collection of your physical and mental personal experiences. It is no different than using the name "LEGO Star Wars® Death Star" for a collection of LEGO pieces that when assembled, creates the iconic Star Wars structure. The grey, rectangular plates are not the LEGO Star Wars Death Star (set #10188). Neither is the hallway structure, the elevator pulley, or the Darth Vader figure.

The LEGO Star Wars Death Star illustrates the basis for the Buddhist rejection of the self. To disagree is to believe in the existence of something that does not exist, an independent, permanent entity. There is no core of personal experience apart from the ever-shifting, inter-reliant, transitory elements of our beliefs, and behaviors, and judgments, just as there is no LEGO Star Wars Death Star without its 3,803 pieces.

By denying self, we begin to recognize that personal experience is like our aforementioned LEGO Star Wars Death Star. When we dismantle it brick by brick, systematically examining each piece, we find that the self, like the Death Star, lacks any substantial permanent essence, that it is bereft of the sum of self. Then, once we remove the delusion of seeing things as permanent, wisdom to comprehend our true purpose, motivations, and needs occurs. And when this wisdom occurs, personal experiences can be fully experienced. So let's dismantle our personal experiences.

Aggregates of Impermanence

We are all made up of a collection of our personal experiences. This assortment of experiences makes up the five aggregates of Buddhism. As per Buddha's teaching in the Samyutta Nikaya, "When you understand that form, sensation, perception, formations, and consciousness are impermanent then you understand right view." The aggregates— form, sensation, perception, formations, and consciousness—serve as the impermanent elements that work together to produce the mind-body entity of a person. One is not more important than another and, like the various pieces needed to construct a LEGO creation, all play a part in the various ways we experience life.

The aggregate of form serves as the initial way we observe the world. This encompasses the ways our five senses enable us to experience material objects. Form is how we *see* the studs on a LEGO brick, how we *hear* two pieces snap together, how we *smell* a bowl of LEGO figures melting in the microwave (this was a childhood experiment that I would not recommend), how pieces *taste* when dipped in pudding (another inadvisable experiment), and the way a stud *feels* when you run your finger across it. Each experience is a momentary observation with no judgment or interpretation. That comes with the next few aggregates.

With any personal experience, the aggregate of sensation dictates that it can take on one of three emotional tones—pleasure, pain, or indifference. Ever try to interlock four dozen LEGO pieces into your hair to create a multi-colored mohawk? No, just me? The cool sensation of the plastic on my scalp was pleasant; taking it out, however, was unpleasant. I write this not to brag about my LEGO hairstyling skills, but to demonstrate that the same object can lend itself to different sensations, which further exhibits its impermanence.

Just as sensation produces an emotional reaction, the aggregate of perception is based around recognition. Perception helps us formulate an idea about an object of experience and attach a name to it. It is like seeing your son's latest LEGO composition and not being able to figure out what it is—it could be a car, or a plane. Then, once he tells you that it is an elephant, your perception is formed and you are able to turn your indefinite perceptual experience into an established idea.

After an established idea has been formed, the aggregate of mental formation determines our response. This involves opinions, prejudices, and compulsions as learned from previous experiences. Unlike the emotional or identifying responses, mental formations take on a moral dimension—wholesome, unwholesome, or neutral. If you have a positive experience building the intricately detailed LEGO Eiffel Tower (set #10181), you will consider this experience wholesome and respond by intentionally challenging yourself to build another complex LEGO set. Conversely, if the experience was frustrating, you will consider this experience unwholesome and your mental formation may direct you to attempt a simpler LEGO project or leave you screaming at the site of the catastrophe.

The last of the five aggregates is indispensable in its influence on experience. Consciousness is our awareness of an object. It occurs by utilizing perception and mental formation to establish a holistic, meaningful impression of the entity. Consciousness enables you to envision a potential LEGO configuration without having to rely on the cover of the box. It allows you to compare your imagination-based blueprints with the available LEGO pieces, adjust your schematics, and work at a speed that takes into account how quickly your "friend" is using the pieces you need.

The five aggregates of impermanence help us discern the rapidly changing interconnected acts of cognition. Together, they produce personal experiences and reinforce the ephemeral nature of existence. For instance, let's say you walk into your daughter's room. As you enter, your eyes come into contact with a visible object. As your vision focuses, your consciousness becomes aware of the as-yet indeterminate object. Perception will identify that object as your limited edition Taj Mahal LEGO set (#10189) that, until today, was in new, unwrapped mint condition. You then respond with the sensation of displeasure. Finally, mental formation leads you to react by crying or, if you can regain your composure, perhaps helping your daughter with the finishing details.

The physical and mental factors of our personal experience, the objects all around us, our minds and ideas are continually changing. They are processes, not enduring things. You were trying to keep the vintage LEGO set in a permanent state, but it was aging regardless of whether your daughter tore open the box. Even your perception of the Taj Mahal set was changing—what you once considered a "cool toy" transformed into "an investment that will one day pay for my daughter's college tuition" until you saw your daughter's enjoyment and perceived it as a "bonding activity." To gain a deeper understanding, let's move beyond a ten-year-old limited edition LEGO set and explore a much older art form.

The LEGOs of Impermanence

Thousands of years before the advent of LEGO, Tibetan Buddhist monks were mastering the MOC (My Own Creation). LEGO enthusiasts recognize the MOC as a LEGO creation that they designed and built (as opposed to using the provided instructions). The monks, however, were doing it with mandalas.

Mandalas are an ancient, sacred form of Buddhist art. They are similar to LEGO in that both are colorful, imaginative displays of creativity. Where they differ is in how the multi-colored plastic pieces are replaced with multi-colored sand.

The mandala is meant to represent impermanence. If imagining the creation and destruction of the universe sounds overwhelming, these elaborate exhibitions of artistic talent bring the abstract idea of temporariness into a more tangible, bite-size depiction. They also offer ways to further enhance our LEGO building experience.

Per the ancient Buddhist traditions that are still practiced today, the monks begin a mandala by determining its intention. The theme, which can focus on such topics as compassion or wisdom, is aligned with particular deities and geometric patterns to infuse the unique spiritual and sacred qualities that each mandala possesses. Once a theme is decided, the monks consecrate the site through music, meditation, and mantra recitation.

With a mental blueprint of the mandala, the monks then begin to draw the lines for the design on a table, which will serve as the base for the mandala. They measure out the architectural lines using a straight-edged ruler, a compass and a white ink pen. Because every detail is deliberate from the design to the colors to the placement of symbols, this preparatory process can take days to complete.

Once the outline is complete, the team begins to gently place the sand granules along the drawing. Using small tubes, funnels, and scrapers, they create vibrations with the tools that cause the sand to slowly spill out, almost grain by grain, until the entire pattern is covered. Nothing holds the sand in place and there is no room for error; even a small sneeze would ruin it. The finished product is approximately the size of a queen-size bed, and will take days or weeks to complete based upon the precision of the work.

Unlike most art that is intended to last for the ages, after all the time and effort has been exerted to create the mandala, this stunning display of artistry is destroyed. In a Dissolution Ceremony the monks ritualistically dismantle the mandala, removing the colored sand. Some of the sand is distributed to the audience as a blessing for health and healing; what remains is collected and released back into nature.

How much of the mandala process sounds like your use of LEGO elements? Let's break it down. Both begin with a mental picture of what you want to create. Your LEGO build's theme may not be as altruistic as to embody world peace, but you don't begin building without some intention of what you would like to create. Plus, who's to say your LEGO Batman®'s Batboat Harbor Pursuit (set #76032) is not as impactful or as life altering as the mandala that the Dalai Lama commissioned depicting the paradise of Avalokitshevara, the Buddha of Compassion?

Once you have an idea of what you will be making, it is time to prepare. We do not need to draw the sophisticated diagrams that the monks require, but that does not mean the planning stage should be overlooked. How much space do you have to work? How much time can you dedicate to it? And the question I rarely ask but always regret not asking, do I have the LEGO pieces needed to fulfill my expectations? You cannot make a mandala without a few pounds of sand just as you cannot build a life-size Kermit the Frog without a generous supply of green LEGO bricks.

Now that you have your schematics and have taken inventory of the needed materials, construction begins. As the monks scrutinize every grain of sand, you vigilantly choose each LEGO piece. A round brick cannot replace a cone just as pre-2003 light grey plates are not synonymous with their more bluish post-2003 "light bley" brethren. Minor details? Maybe, but art is intentional and purposeful.

With meticulous craftsmanship, your structure is finally complete. This is the perfect time to bask in the glory of your fine work. Rope off a viewing area so others can stop by to check it out. Take stock of what you've accomplished. Then, once you've received your share of accolades, it is time for your LEGO creation to follow in the ways of the mandala and for its ceremonial demolition to begin.

We all follow a different method for disassembling LEGO. Some take a set apart piece by piece so as to sort each bit into its respective plastic bag, thereby preserving newness and keeping it systematically organized for next time. Others take a more Godzilla-like approach where the structure is punched, swatted, kicked, and beaten into dismantled mess. Either way, the creation is no more.

Like my childhood obsession with supergluing LEGO bricks, some have tried to fight the mandala's temporariness. Back in 1992, Robert Jacobsen, the curator of Asian Art at the Minneapolis Institute of Arts, led an experiment where adhesive sand could harden into a "permanent" mandala capable of being hung on a wall. While technically a success, Jacobsen seems to miss the point—destruction of a mandala, like dismantling LEGO creations, demonstrates that beauty is only meant for this world for a short time.

By wittingly putting effort into a temporary piece of art, we reveal the fleeting nature of all material life. This is the very core of impermanence. It is a reminder that existence has a beginning, middle, and end. Then, once we've accepted the unremitting cyclical changes, it frees us to return to a mindset of infinite possibility where we no longer search for finality but rest in unbound awareness.

The creation of art, transitory or otherwise, involves skill acquired through practice and effort. An eye for detail separates a casual pastime from the creation of your chef d'oeuvre. If the particulars can be overlooked, at what point does your LEGO project become a mishmash of rainbow warrior-like chaos where you no longer attempt to coordinate colors?

Once your efforts become infused with lackluster motivation, it is a slippery slope to an inner monologue of, "Why bother starting a LEGO project if it is just going to be taken apart anyway." This nihilistic reaction toward impermanence not only runs counter to Buddhist philosophy, but can only lead to a dissatisfied life. After all, with all things being momentary, a "Why Should I Care?" attitude would expand beyond LEGO, a mandala, or any other form of art you use to express yourself. You'd be left in a state of never bothering to do anything because it will inevitably come to a close.

Impermanence is not an occasion for sorrow, but rather recognition for the unavoidable realization that reality is in a perpetual state of change. It is a time to acknowledge that all things will end, appreciate the time spent doing it, and celebrate how it has enriched our life. This frees us from trying to "superglue" our worldview through failed attempts to keep everything as is or becoming overly fixated on any one goal or object. We can then adopt a renewed vigilance to remain open to new experiences, for as every LEGO project ends, another is soon to follow.

Notes

1. John Cotter, *Leading Change* (Cambridge, MA: Harvard Business Review Press, 2012).

2. Traci Mann, *Secrets from the Eating Lab: The Science of Weight Loss, the Myth of Weight Loss, and* Why You Should Never Diet Again (New York: Harper Wave, 2015). "Blame It on the Brain: The Latest Neuroscience Research Suggests Spreading Resolutions Out Over Time is the Best Approach," *The Wall Street Journal*, December 26, 2009, available at http://www.wsj.com/articles/SB10001424052748703478704574612052322122442 (accessed March 6, 2017).
3. Wijesekara, O.H. DeA, *The Three Signata, Anicca, Dukkha, Anatta* (Buddhist Publication Society, Kandy, Sri Lanka, 1981).
4. William Glasser, *Positive Addiction* (New York: HarperCollins, 1976).
5. Seung Sahn, *Only Don't Know: Selected Teaching Letters of Zen Master Seung Sahn* (Shambhala Publications, Colorado, 2013).

19

LEGO® and the Building Blocks of Metaphysics

Stephan Leuenberger

LEGO® allows each of us to do something traditionally thought to be reserved for God: to create a world. In fact, we can even create more than one world, a privilege rarely attributed even to God.

Calling LEGO creations "worlds" prompts a question: how similar are LEGO worlds to the real world? On one level, the answer will differ for each LEGO world, and will depend on the intentions, the skills, and the resources available to the builder. But there is another level at which the question can be asked, where the details of a particular LEGO world do not matter. How similar is a LEGO world in its fundamental structure to the real world—specifically, in the way in which the world as a whole relates to the parts out of which it is made?

The Metaphysics of LEGO

Our question relates to a central area of philosophy called "metaphysics," which is concerned with the fundamental categories of being and the basic structure of the world. Typically, the metaphysician wants to know what *kind* of world we live in. She takes an interest in its most general features, and abstracts away from the vicissitudes of its history. But we can also ask about the metaphysical features of a LEGO world. In addition to being interesting in its own right, this might provide us with a good model for the true metaphysics of the real world.

LEGO® and Philosophy: Constructing Reality Brick By Brick, First Edition.
Edited by Roy T. Cook and Sondra Bacharach.
© 2017 John Wiley & Sons Ltd. Published 2017 by John Wiley & Sons Ltd.

Consider a creation—a My Own Creation, or MOC—made from a traditional, pre-1978 LEGO set, not containing any minifigures. Such an object has a few features that seem hardly worth mentioning because of their familiarity, but which are nonetheless remarkable from a philosophical point of view. The first thing to observe is that the MOC is a complex object made up of many atomic building blocks—LEGO bricks. (They are atomic in the sense that they cannot be broken down further—at least not while playing by the rules.) This is a fundamental difference between the metaphysics of LEGO and the metaphysics of Play-Doh, for example. Play-Doh is "gunky," in the jargon of contemporary philosophy: each part of a bit of Play-Doh is made up of smaller parts (at least on a macroscopic level of analysis, though quantum physics may offer a different perspective).

Further significant characteristics become apparent when we consider LEGO's atomic building blocks themselves:

- They fall into a small handful of different kinds, all of whose members have exactly the same properties (shape, color, size, density, and surface texture).
- They are homogeneous: they have exactly the same properties (color, density) at every region of space they occupy.
- Their different kinds differ from each other only along a very small number of dimensions, such as shape and color. They are the same with respect to density, surface texture, and often even size.

Of course, LEGO worlds also contain houses, towers, bridges, fences, and other features. These items differ in their characteristics from the atomic building blocks:

- There is no limit to how many different kinds of them there are.
- They are heterogeneous: they have different properties, notably different colors, at different regions of space that they occupy.
- Their different kinds differ from each other along a good number of dimensions, such as shape, size, and color.

Still, all the features of the complex objects are the result of putting the bricks together in a certain pattern. The LEGO houses are nothing over and above the bricks, arranged in some specific way. Heterogeneity arises out of homogeneity, through complexity.

Worlds can be strikingly different from each other, even though they are made from the same kinds of ultimate building blocks. This is obvious to any builder: the blocks are arbitrarily re-combinable. Every block can stand on its own, or can combine with every other one. Each one is the key to every other's lock. Again, this may seem obvious, but it is not something the metaphysician takes for granted. It represents a fundamental difference between LEGO bricks and the pieces of a jigsaw puzzle. There is typically only one way for the latter to fit together into a picture. On the spectrum between full re-combinability and the complete lack of it, they are at opposite extremes.

Well, there is a small complication: bricks cannot be combined *completely* arbitrarily. They do not have studs on each side, and a stud does not fit together with another stud. Studs Not On Top (SNOT) techniques achieve a greater degree of re-combinability.

LEGO Bricks and Fundamental Properties

So much for the metaphysics of LEGO. How does it compare to the metaphysics of the real, actual world—our universe? As with many other philosophical questions, there is no consensus view. For a long time, the world was believed to be made up of four elements—Earth, Water, Air, and Fire. On that view, the world bears very little resemblance to a MOC. But according to the view that has perhaps been most influential in metaphysics in the last few decades, our world is strikingly like a LEGO world. The view is called "Humean supervenience" and was formulated and defended by the American philosopher David Lewis (1941–2001). Roughly, it is the claim that basically, the world is just an arrangement of fundamental properties.

A fundamental property is a property whose presence is not to be explained in terms of any other properties. Weight is not fundamental, since it is to be explained in terms of mass and gravitational attraction; the latter is in turn explained in terms of masses of other bodies. Plausible examples of fundamental properties are those that play a role in fundamental physics, such as mass, electric charge, and spin.

On Lewis's view, the things of which the fundamental properties are properties are not familiar extended things like you or me. They are very small: points of space, or more precisely, of space-time. The fundamental properties obey a principle of re-combination: the instantiation of one of them is fully independent of the instantiation of another one, either by the same or by different points. This is sometimes expressed by the slogan that "there are no necessary connections"—things could be arranged differently.

Lewis introduced Humean supervenience as follows (using the term "qualities" for fundamental properties):

> Humean supervenience is named in honor of the greater denier of necessary connections. It is the doctrine that all there is to the world is a vast mosaic of local matters of particular fact, just one little thing and then another. ... We have geometry: a system of external relations of spatiotemporal distance between points. ... And at those points we have local qualities: perfectly natural intrinsic properties which need nothing bigger than a point at which to be instantiated. For short: we have an arrangement of qualities. And that is all. There is no difference without difference in the arrangement of qualities. All else supervenes on that.[1]

The "greater denier of necessary connections," after whom the view is named, is the Scottish philosopher David Hume (1711–1776). To say that something supervenes on something else is simply to say that you cannot change the former without changing the latter.

If Humean supervenience is true, then our world is fundamentally like a LEGO world. Space-time corresponds to the base plate, and the bricks correspond to fundamental properties. It is obvious that in a LEGO world, everything—how many houses and chairs and windows there are, for example—supervenes on how the bricks are arranged. To make another house, you will have to add to or modify the arrangement of bricks.

Lewis himself liked to compare the world to a mosaic or a dot matrix. But a LEGO world would be an even more apt comparison, because it is three-dimensional rather than two-dimensional. (His own passion was model railways, not LEGO creations. Perhaps this is why the LEGO metaphor did not occur to him.)

What reasons are there to believe that Humean supervenience is true? There is no particular observation to support it. Rather, the view is recommended by a very general methodological principle called the principle of parsimony or "Ockham's Razor" after the fourteenth-century friar William of Ockham (1287–1347): "entities are not to be multiplied beyond necessity." In other words, we should not believe in more things than we need to. Now it can be argued that we need to believe in the existence of fundamental properties and in space-time anyway—metaphysicians are ill-equipped to challenge the authority of physics on that point. If we accept Humean supervenience, then we do not acknowledge the existence of any further things beyond those. Hence we comply with Ockham's Razor by accepting Humean supervenience.

This provides us with an argument for Humean supervenience only if rejecting the view is not also compatible with Ockham's Razor. A metaphysician who rejects Humean supervenience would in effect accept further things beyond the fundamental properties and space-time. His or her view would violate Ockham's Razor unless these further things need to be accepted. Lewis argued at length that there is no such need—there are no features of the world that could not be explained using the resources of Humean supervenience.

But why, in turn, should we accept Ockham's Razor as a methodological principle? This is actually a really difficult question, even though the principle is widely accepted in science as well as in philosophy.

We could motivate this principle if we saw the world as a testament to the skill of an ultimate master builder—traditionally called God. Suppose you are instructed to build a real-life scene. Would it take more skill to do that if you had only simple LEGO bricks at your disposal, or if you already had ready-made figures? Clearly the former. So the simpler the elements, the more glory to the creator.

This justification only works if you take it for granted that there is a builder. Once that is in question, Ockham's Razor can be wielded against the existence of God. A theory that just says that there is a world, and describes it, appears to be simpler than one that says the same thing, and adds that there is also a God that created it. On Lewis's view, at any rate, our world was not created by a God: it just is. This does not make the world in and of itself different from a LEGO world, however. Though LEGO worlds are built by someone, their builders do not belong to those worlds as parts.

Counting Worlds

We might think that for all their similarity, LEGO worlds and real worlds at least differ in how many there are: there are many LEGO worlds, but only one real world. Not so, on Lewis's view. He maintains that there are many, many more real worlds than LEGO worlds. Our world—the universe, the things whose size cosmologists are investigating—is just one among a multitude of worlds.[2] In fact, he holds that there are infinitely many worlds. In this respect, the LEGO worlds as we know them are not a faithful model of his possible worlds: the number of actually created LEGO worlds is finite, and even the number of different LEGO worlds that could be made from all actual bricks is finite. (If Lewis is right though, and there are infinitely many possible worlds, there will likewise be infinitely many possible worlds which contain LEGO worlds as parts, just like our world.)

According to Lewis, there are worlds in which you were saved from entering the dark ages. There are worlds where you have a billion bricks at your disposal. But there are also worlds where LEGO has never been invented. More generally, everything that could have happened—everything that is possible—does happen in some such world. As mentioned before, Lewis thinks that the building blocks of the world—the fundamental properties instantiated at space-time points—are re-combinable. Accordingly, he accepts a principle of re-combination for worlds: for every possible arrangement of such properties, there is a world where they are arranged in this way. So, in particular, every LEGO world that you may build will be an accurate model of a genuine world, spatio-temporally separated from all other worlds. There is a sense in which you are replicating rather than creating.

On Lewis's view, other worlds are just as real as the actual world. They are concrete universes, typically very large ones. It is tempting to think of them as distant galaxies. But strictly speaking, worlds are not distant. For them to be so, they would need to belong to a common space, or space-time—a very large base plate. But there is no such thing. Things in different possible worlds do not stand in any spatial or spatiotemporal relations to each other.

If you find Lewis's claim that there are infinitely many parallel universes incredible, you are not alone. When Lewis made it clear to other philosophers that he seriously believed this, he often met with an incredulous stare. On the face of it, asserting the existence of all these other worlds violates Ockham's Razor.

But Lewis had a nice reply. He argued that if the principle is understood correctly, it favors theories that are parsimonious with respect to how many *kinds* of things they posit. A theory according to which the fundamental particles are protons, neutrons, and electrons is better, other things being equal, than a theory according to which the fundamental particles fall into thousands of different kinds. But a theory that says that there are five trillion protons is not better, on that account, than a rival that puts that number at ten trillion. Lewis argued that his theory just posits more things of a kind that everyone believes in—namely, universes—and that it is therefore quite compatible with Ockham's Razor.

Be that as it may, Lewis's plausible thesis of Humean supervenience need not be combined with his extravagant claim that there is a real world for any possible arrangement of the fundamental building blocks. Whether it is so combined or not, there remains a difference between the number of real worlds and the number of actual LEGO worlds. The number of actual LEGO worlds is fairly large but finite. The number of real worlds is either one—as most philosophers think—or infinite—as Lewis and a handful of others think. Nobody holds that there 17, or 5,874,764 worlds—any finite number apart from one would look hopelessly arbitrary.

LEGO Worlds, Change, and Causation

At this point, we have a sense of why it might be plausible that Humean supervenience is true, that is, that our world is fundamentally like a LEGO world. But many philosophers have found even that incredible, quite independently of the further question of how many worlds there are. Change, a pervasive and obvious phenomenon of our world, is absent in a LEGO world. Things change—cars move, babies grow, coffee goes cold, leaves turn brown. In contrast, a LEGO world is an utterly static world. (Remember that we are talking about creations from old-style LEGO sets, where no Krazy Glue is needed to keep things at rest.)

Lewis has a response on behalf of Humean supervenience: change, on his view, is variation along a fourth dimension. The world is four-dimensional, and we are four-dimensional space-time "worms" in it. Just as I have spatial parts—my head or my left arm, for example—I also have temporal parts. Change consists in the part located at one time having different properties from the part located at another time.

The idea that an extra dimension can, in a sense, account for change is familiar. In an old-fashioned slide show, images that are two-dimensional (if we ignore their small depth) are stacked upon each other, and shown in sequence. If there are more than 16 shown per second, our eyes can no longer discriminate the individual images, and we see the slide show as a continuous film.

The sequential display of the slides is still a process that involves change: at one time one slide is being projected, at another time another. For this reason, an extra dimension can account for change "in a sense." Change seems to be presupposed in the slide show case.

For this reason, Lewis and other four-dimensionalists need to say more to justify their claim that they can account for change.

Though it is debatable, let's grant Lewis that our world is four-dimensional, and return to the question of how similar it is to a LEGO world. Since a LEGO world is three-dimensional, we have identified another important respect in which they differ. But this is arguably a relatively superficial difference, and does not detract much from the fundamental similarity of LEGO worlds and the real world. A proponent of Humean supervenience can think of the real world as being like a sequence of LEGO creations, stacked upon each other in a fourth dimension. This would account for the fact that things change.

But according to critics of Humean supervenience, this way of thinking about the world still leaves out one of its crucial features: that some things *cause* others, and correspondingly, that some things are the *effects* of others. If I step on your toe, and you subsequently feel pain, there are not just two things happening in succession. Rather, my stepping brought the pain about—or so it seems. But even if LEGO creations are stacked upon each other in a fourth dimension, what is the case in one of them does not in any way bring about what is the case in the next one. They are, in that sense, all independent from each other.

This issue marks a fundamental divide in contemporary metaphysics between Humeans and non-Humeans. Hume denied that there are necessary connections, by which he meant causation. Watching football, I observe feet approaching and then touching a ball, and the ball subsequently moving away. I do not observe any mysterious connection between the two things—I do not observe the one thing causing the other. I think that there is causation merely because I observe kicking regularly being followed by ball movement.

Lewis does not deny outright that there is causation in the world. But like Hume, he does not take it to be one of its fundamental features. His idea is that causation is a matter of what happens in similar worlds. Here the other possible worlds that he controversially believes in turn out to be useful for him. My stepping on your toes causes you pain because in those worlds in which I do not step on your toes, and that are otherwise maximally similar to our world, you are not in pain. The idea is that a cause is something that makes a difference, with respect to the effect, between our world and a similar world.

Whether Lewis turned this idea into a successful theory of causation is, again, a large and contested issue. If he is successful, then that also vindicates the idea that our world is fundamentally like a LEGO world. We can then use our judgments about which LEGO worlds are similar to which other ones to make claims about what causes what in a four-dimensional LEGO world.

In his ingenious defense of Humean supervenience, Lewis has shown that LEGO worlds might be very much like the actual world, and thus when we create a LEGO world, we might be making a toy model of the actual world that captures its metaphysically significant features.

Notes

1. David Lewis, *Philosophical Papers*, vol. II (New York: Oxford University Press, 1986), ix–x.
2. David Lewis, *On the Plurality of Worlds* (Malden, MA: Blackwell Publishers, 1986).

20
What Can You Build?

Bob Fischer

You have pile of LEGO® bricks in front of you. What can you build with them?[1] A natural answer is: *whatever you can imagine!*

It's so natural an answer that representatives of the LEGO Group have actually given it,[2] and they've used this refrain in their catalogs to advertise certain sets.[3] Obviously, the LEGO Group's representatives aren't doing philosophy, as they're too busy making billions of dollars. Still, it sure *sounds* like a good answer. Is it true?

Well, maybe not *whatever* you can imagine. I'm pretty sure that I can imagine a three-headed LEGO guy—and I'd guess that you can too. Just imagine the torso being a bit wider, three head posts instead of one, the legs suitably far apart, and so on. Then, there will be room for all three of his heads to sit happily beside one another. Of course, we know you can't build such a figure—the LEGO gods don't allow it—but he's no less imaginable for that.[4]

Did that feel like a cheap move to you? If so, you're probably thinking something like this: "It's not that you can build whatever you can imagine *period*—instead, you can build whatever you can imagine *with stock pieces*." Fair point. This nicely solves the three-headed guy problem, since extra-wide torsos certainly aren't stock pieces. But there are other problems. If you're like me, you've imagined structures that really *seemed* like they were going to work. Then you start pressing pieces together, and you find that the arch you're making can't quite support its own weight, or you can't quite get the curvature you wanted, or whatever. But that means you imagined something that

LEGO® and Philosophy: Constructing Reality Brick By Brick, First Edition.
Edited by Roy T. Cook and Sondra Bacharach.
© 2017 John Wiley & Sons Ltd. Published 2017 by John Wiley & Sons Ltd.

you couldn't build with stock pieces. Again, your imagination let you down.

Perhaps we can live with fallibility—perhaps we can accept that the imagination is merely an OK guide to what we can build, getting things right only sometimes. The worry with this move is that it leaves us with an uncomfortable question: for any particular imagining (a life-sized three-toed sloth, a MINI Cooper replica, an Escher-inspired castle), why think that *this* is one we can trust? If the imagination isn't usually trustworthy, why trust it at all?

So we could keep tweaking. Maybe you can't build whatever you can imagine, or even whatever you can imagine with stock pieces, but only whatever you can imagine *in detail* with stock pieces. In other words, you can build whatever you can *completely* imagine, brick by brick. Which is probably true. Unfortunately, it's also pretty useless, since we never imagine anything but the simplest structures so thoroughly. (There might be a few especially brilliant designers who do. Odds are, you aren't among them. I know I'm not.) The upshot: if we know what we can build by imagining-in-detail-with-stock-pieces, then we don't know very much.

All that said, it doesn't seem crazy to say that our imagination helps us figure out what we can build. It just isn't clear *how*. Can we tell a better story?

Modal Epistemology

I think so. Before we try, though, let's get some perspective on what we're doing. When we start wondering what we can build, we're starting to think about LEGO modal epistemology. Modal epistemology is the study of how we know how things could and must be—ideas that take a bit of unpacking.

Let's begin with the "modal" bit. Consider these truths: I drink a pot of coffee every morning, sharks aren't mammals, two and two is four, there are no LEGO plates with exactly 4,289,387 studs on them. But not all truths are made equal: some are *contingent*, others *necessary*. Contingent truths could have been false. I might not have coffee tomorrow (I can quit anytime I want!), and the good folks in Billund could have made a plate with exactly 4,289,387 studs—they've just never had a reason to do it. Necessary truths, by contrast, *couldn't* be false. Two and two, for example, could never equal five.[5] Contingency and necessity are two *modes* of truth, and they're the modes we care about when we do modal epistemology.

Epistemology is the study of how and what we know. On the "how" side, we ask questions like: what does it take to know that Ole Kirk Christiansen founded the LEGO Group? Presumably, you're going to acquire that knowledge via *testimony*—that is, someone's going to tell you about Christiansen's exploits. Seems straightforward, but there are puzzles nearby. What if the person's a pathological liar? *OK: the person's got to be a reliable witness.* Do you have to know that he's a reliable witness? Does that mean you can't learn things from strangers? *No: you can definitely learn things from strangers. You just can't have any evidence that the guy is a pathological liar—that's what would undermine knowledge.* So… does that mean you *can* know that Christiansen founded the LEGO Group based on the testimony of a pathological liar—as long as you don't have any evidence that he isn't a liar? As you can see, things get messy pretty quickly.

On the "what" side, we ask questions about particular cases. Earlier, I said we know that the good folks in Billund could have made a plate with exactly 4,289,387 studs. Is that true? Maybe it isn't: a brick with that many studs would be awfully large, and perhaps there are limits to the mold-size that their machinery can handle. Or perhaps their machinery could handle it, but the size would require breaking their rules about plate thickness (3.2mm, vs. 9.6mm for bricks). And if they did that, would they still be making a true LEGO plate?

Anyway, modal epistemology has the same two parts. Some of it is the study of how we know that some things are contingent and others necessary. Let's assume that we *do* know that the good folks in Billund could have made a plate with exactly 4,289,387 studs. How'd we figure that out? The other part of modal epistemology concerns how *much* we know about what's contingent and necessary. To date, the tallest LEGO tower is just over thirty-five meters high. How high could you go? A hundred meters? Very likely. A thousand? Maybe. Ten thousand? Well, at some point, it's going to collapse under its own weight—the base will be crushed by the weight of the superstructure—and if I had to bet, the last number crosses that line. In any case, even if we know that we *couldn't* build a ten-thousand-meter tower, there are plenty of numbers in between a thousand and ten thousand where we aren't sure what to say. And so we've found one gap in our modal knowledge, at least where LEGO towers are concerned.

Imagination Revisited

Now we can be a bit more precise about what went wrong with the imagination-based story. That story does pretty well, actually, on the "how" part. We might not know everything there is to know about the imagination, but it isn't a completely mysterious mental faculty—like the one that would enable ESP, were ESP real. (Sorry, Psychic Hotline!) Instead, the imagination-based story falls down on the "what" part. There's a mismatch between what we can imagine (the three-headed LEGO guy; the arch that seems fine in the imagination, but in fact can't support its weight) and what we take ourselves to know about what we can build. Or if you prefer the fortune cookie version, which is from an actual fortune cookie that I got while writing this essay: "He who has imagination without learning has wings with no feet."

We can fix this problem by tweaking the imagination-based story to the point that it doesn't have these mismatches. But then we find out that we don't know much at all about what we can build—which is just another mismatch, since we *do* know a fair amount about what we can build.

What can we learn from all this? First, the "how" part of a better theory needs to be at least as good as the one we get from the imagination-based account. In short: explain how we know by using something we understand fairly well. Second, the "what" part is a *constraint* on a good theory—which is just to say that we have to get the cases right. A theory isn't any good if it says we know stuff we don't, or that we don't know stuff we do.

Working Knowledge

So let's start over. And as we do, let's notice that, at least when you first began playing with LEGO, you really *didn't* know what you could build. You probably didn't even consider that question. You just tinkered: snapping bricks together, pulling them apart, configuring and reconfiguring them endlessly. In other words, you *experimented* with these brightly colored playthings, slowly developing a feel for how they could and couldn't be arranged, how you'd need to balance a structure to keep it from toppling, how much lateral pressure the stud connection could bear, and so on. Very little of this was explicit knowledge—you couldn't articulate much of it. But it was knowledge nonetheless.

Ignoring all this is one of the deeper problems with the imagination-based story. What's so wonderful about the imagination is that it isn't constrained by our background knowledge—by all those things we've learned about how the world works. (And it's a good thing too: if it were so constrained, fiction would be a whole lot more boring. Consider a version of *The LEGO Movie* in which LEGO people behave just as they actually do in the real world—which is to say, not at all.) But we need those constraints when we're trying to figure things out about the world. After all, we don't make up the facts about what we can build; they aren't ours to stipulate. What you can build is determined by the facts about the bricks. So whatever our story about how we know what we can build, it had better be one that factors in our background knowledge, since that's what makes the imagination useful.

In fact, my guess is that you've already seen this constraint at work, though you probably didn't recognize it at the time. Recall my question about whether there could be a three-headed LEGO guy. I'll bet you didn't even consider the possibility of an extra-wide, tri-posted torso, since you know that there aren't any. Of course, you *could* have imagined such a torso—so it isn't the case that you can build whatever you can imagine—you just *didn't* imagine it, and this is precisely because your background knowledge spared you from an implausible answer.

This line of reasoning leads us to a better proposal. What you can build is determined by the facts about LEGOs; so, you come to know what you can build by getting a better handle on those facts. It's your working knowledge of those little pieces that allows you to make judgments about what can and can't be done with them.

Crucially, there are various ways to make those judgments. Sometimes, the imagination plays an active role, guided by our background knowledge. But not always. Sometimes it just *seems* to you that something is buildable. In other cases, it's a more abstract, conceptual affair: you *conceive* of a structure, and thereby come to know that you could build it. In short, there are lots of ways to extrapolate from what you already know—imagining, considering how things seem to you, conceiving—but they all work (when they do) because they're drawing out the consequences of what you already know about LEGO.

Beyond Working Knowledge

One nice feature of this view is that it explains the difference between the best LEGO builders and the rest of us. It's amazing to see gravity-defying builds—ones where you're just not sure why the thing doesn't collapse, no matter the angle you take. But it probably isn't amazing to highly experienced builders. I'd guess that they look at a life-size LEGO giraffe and think: "Nice."[6] They see that it's good work, of course, but it isn't stunning to them. Why not? Because they have a better understanding of LEGO, and hence of what's possible with it. LEGO experts don't have better imaginations than we non-experts; they just know more. (That's why we read their books.)

Nevertheless, working knowledge—at least of the implicit, unarticulated variety—doesn't always cut it. Think about the sort of question that I raised earlier: could you build a LEGO tower that's, say, a thousand meters tall? No one's got a "feel" for LEGO that lets him answer this question. Without some pretty detailed reasoning, you're not going to get an answer.

Instead, you have to make that working knowledge explicit. You have to start formulating some claims about the properties of different LEGO pieces, about the strength of the various connections between pieces, and so on. And if you want to think about any interesting cases—such as whether you can make a prosthetic leg (spoiler alert: you can[7])—you'll need to integrate those claims with things you know about ABS plastic (from which LEGO products are made), basic mechanics, and much else besides. The upshot: you have to develop a decent theory about LEGO, one that fits neatly with the other theories you take to be true.

None of this should be surprising, and I doubt that it is. A few years ago, some engineers got interested in a debate on Reddit about the tallest possible LEGO tower. They then went to work in their lab: first, they figured out how much force it would take to crush a brick; then, they calculated how many bricks it would take to exert that much force on the first brick in the stack. The answer? 375,000 bricks, which at 9.6mm each, means a height of 3,591 meters, or roughly 2.17 miles.[8]

What matters here isn't the answer, which may actually be wrong. (They're imagining a single stack, and you might be able to do better with, say, a pyramid.) Instead, what matters is that *they've obviously employed the right method.* That is, they took what they knew about LEGO, and made it play with what they knew about material science.

The fact that they obviously employed the right method might even suggest something about what our working knowledge really is: namely, the beginnings of a theory, a kind of implicit understanding of those rules that govern LEGO construction. As a result, we don't balk at the idea of bringing our LEGO knowledge into conversation with everything else we know, building better theories to help us build yet wilder structures. So my bet? It's theory all the way down—though we don't realize it until we start confronting weird questions.

For what it's worth, I think this is the way things work generally, in the non-LEGO world. (Yes, Virginia, there is a non-LEGO world.) You learn what could and couldn't be by developing better theories about what *is*—some of which you can articulate, but many of which you can't (at least not without some time and effort). If we want to give this view a name, we might call it *a theory-based epistemology of modality*.[9] Suitably dull, right?

Purism

Let's wrap things up by turning our attention away from modal epistemology and toward a segment of the LEGO community that might seem a bit fussy: purists.

Purists won't build with bricks not made by LEGO, they won't add stickers or apply paint to change the appearance of their work, and they won't grind down the studs to get a particular look or functionality. On the face of it, these people are (dare I say it?) missing the point. The LEGO Group makes toys. Toys are for fun. If tweaking some pieces makes playtime more enjoyable, then what's the harm? To each his own, of course, but it isn't clear what's gained by slavish devotion to a company's intentions (even if that company is Danish and generally wonderful).

But here's the thing. Suppose I'm right about how we know what we can build. Suppose that, as a result of spending a lot of time messing around with bricks and plates and minifigures, we develop a working knowledge of the LEGO world—knowledge that makes us pretty good at judging what we can and can't construct. And suppose we find—as so many of us have—that we fall in love with that world.

My guess is that we don't just love the aesthetic. It isn't that we're drawn to unusually blocky people, or have a special affection for primary colors. In large part, we love the possibilities and impossibilities of that world. The value of the possibilities might be more obvious, since we focus on them (or *hope* we're focusing on them!) when we imagine all that we might assemble. However, we love the limits, too—both that there are some, and that they take the form they do. Finding out what we can't make sparks our creativity. It brings out the determined engineer in us all—the one who says *there must be a way*. (What's better than getting lost in search of a solution?) At the same time, we value the way LEGO strikes a balance of possibilities and impossibilities. Too many of the former, and we wouldn't have toys. Too many of the latter, and we'd only have single-purpose toys.[10] Discovering that balance—and learning to build in light of it—is one of the pleasures of play.

So it isn't only the possibilities that contribute to our enjoyment. The impossibilities matter too. And this, it seems to me, is part of what the purist recognizes. The limits—the specific ones that the LEGO world involves—make building engaging and frustrating and fun. We love LEGO not in spite of them, but because of them.

Notes

1. We really ought to distinguish between *what's buildable* and *what you can build*, since the latter is relativized to your abilities in a way that the former isn't. But sometimes we don't do what we really ought to do.
2. See, for example, what one of LEGO's Event Managers said here: http://www.lego.com/en-us/aboutus/news-room/2014/april/btc-china (accessed March 7, 2017).
3. See, for example, http://catalogs.lego.com/Club/uk/2015/GB2015yell owbrick1/?Page=11 (accessed March 7, 2017).
4. LEGO has made a *two*-headed minifigure—the Ninjago® Fangtom minifig—though it has snakes rather than two standard heads.
5. At any rate, so many have thought. Of course, we could have used the word "five" to refer to the number four, in which case "two and two is five" would have expressed a truth—namely, that two and two is four.
6. I'm assuming that the giraffe wasn't made with some of the resources that LEGO professionals employ—e.g., special glue or a custom-built internal metal frame, both of which are used to stabilize models in stores and places like LEGOLAND®. Plainly, using such resources changes what you can build, and it would be massively harder—if not impossible—to build comparable structures without them. Thanks to Roy Cook for pointing this out to me.
7. Christina Stephens shows how at https://www.youtube.com/watch?v= W8fdXNN0irI (accessed March 7, 2017). But this just invites the next

question: can you build one that will last for more than a few minutes of normal use?

8. See http://www.bbc.com/news/magazine-20578627 (accessed March 7, 2017).

9. For details about the non-LEGO version of the view, have a look at my "A Theory-based Epistemology of Modality," *The Canadian Journal of Philosophy* 46 (2016): 228–47, or *Modal Justification via Theories* (Cham: Springer, 2017).

10. This is one reason why someone might object to the highly specialized pieces that have been produced in recent years. Thanks to Sondra Bacharach for this observation.

21

Playing with LEGO® and Proving Theorems

Fenner Tanswell

What's the point of LEGO®? Why do we want so much of it and to build so many models with it? One answer might be that we like having it as a material possession and that LEGO is about owning, building, and collecting as many models as possible, or the rarest models we can get, or our favorite sets, or some combination of all of those. Certainly this is entirely true for some people, and maybe a little true for all of us, but it doesn't seem like it can be the whole picture. Even the moral of the LEGO movie is that there is more to it than that: a lot of the joy of having LEGO models is the freedom to re-combine, muddle up, invent, and play with them.

There's a similar question that we can ask when doing math. What's it all about!? One answer that is pretty common among philosophers of mathematics is that it's about numbers, shapes, equations, and all that kind of stuff. But, as in the case of LEGO, this might be a limited answer, only getting some of the picture right.

The actual answers to both questions are closely connected. That is, just as LEGO isn't only about bricks, math isn't just about numbers and all the other mathsy stuff. They are also both about what we *do* with the objects in question—the *activities* and *actions* to which we put those objects. In LEGO we can build sets following the instructions, or alternatively dump a whole bunch of LEGO on the floor and build whatever we like. In math, we have a similar freedom to create new things, solve problems, and play around.

LEGO® and Philosophy: Constructing Reality Brick By Brick, First Edition.
Edited by Roy T. Cook and Sondra Bacharach.
© 2017 John Wiley & Sons Ltd. Published 2017 by John Wiley & Sons Ltd.

Plato against the Geometers

It's fairly obvious that for LEGO a large part of the fun is in the activities, but this idea is not as obvious when it comes to math. The blame for this attitude, I think, can be traced all the way back to Plato (427/8 BC–347/8 BC). In Book 7 of the *Republic*, Plato has Socrates (469/70 BC–399 BC) say the following:

> Now, no one with even a little experience of geometry will dispute that [geometry] is entirely the opposite of what is said about it in the accounts of its practitioners. [...] They give ridiculous accounts of it, though they can't help it, for they speak like practical men, and all their accounts refer to doing things. They talk of "squaring," "applying," "adding," and the like, whereas the entire subject is pursued for the sake of [...] knowing what always is, not what comes into being and passes away.[1]

The accusation here is that when we focus on the activities of mathematics, we lose sight of the very nature of the subject. Math is precisely about the mathsy objects like numbers and shapes; these mathsy objects are independently existing abstract objects. This means that they are real things that don't exist anywhere concretely. This view, known as (surprise, surprise) *Platonism*, holds that objects like numbers are eternal and unchanging—and thus we can't *do* anything to them. For a Platonist, the idea of focusing on mathematical practice might well be "ridiculous" because any activities we might engage in cannot have any effect on that mathematical stuff which math is about. In other words: in doing mathematics we want to find out about these eternal and unchanging mathematical objects themselves. Activities like adding up numbers and drawing circles are beside the point, because they can't affect the objects we are trying to find out about. (This might even be a strong disanalogy with the LEGO case, because with LEGO we are directly playing or building with the bricks themselves.)

But in our quick discussion of Plato we find two key components for switching the negative attitude around entirely, toward the idea that a focus on the activities of math is not ridiculous at all. Rather, these activities are *vital*. The first reason is this: the geometers' activities are about *demonstrating* the relations and truths of mathematics because these activities may be crucial for mathematical *proofs*. Indeed, Plato himself is concerned with knowledge, and one of the most important ways for us to come to know things about mathematics is through proving them to be the case. The second component is the fact that geometry in particular has caught our eye. Geometry makes far greater use of pictures and diagrams than tends to be the case for other areas of mathematics. So we'll focus on diagrammatic proofs—that is, proofs which are wholly or primarily comprised of pictures—as a key case where proofs guide us through a series of actions. Such processes or activities, with pictures to guide us through, allow us to draw a very close parallel between mathematics and LEGO, and to highlight the role that *following the instructions* has both in learning mathematics via the use of picture proofs and in taking us from a box of LEGO bricks through to completed models.

Proofs and the Logical Structuring of Mathsy Stuff

Let's contrast the two perspectives we have considered so far. On the one hand we have the Platonist idea that math is just about unchanging mathematical stuff like numbers and shapes, which our activities cannot influence in any way. On the other hand, we can see the importance of math as being bound up with the activity and creativity of the people doing it. In the second case, proofs and demonstrations can be seen as not being directed at changing the mathsy stuff, but as guiding us through a process of coming to know and understand how mathematics fits together. But on the first, Platonist point of view, what is the point of proving things?

Figure 21.1 Minifig Gottlob Frege and minifig Bertrand Russell chatting about LEGO and math. Created by the author using http://www.ldraw.org/.

Certainly, proofs are about coming to know things about the mathsy stuff, but the question is what we are coming to know exactly? Many modern Platonists tend to endorse a kind of *foundationalism*. We might attribute this idea to Gottlob Frege (1848–1925) and Bertrand Russell (1872–1970), although the latter famously changed his mind *a lot*. The foundationalist idea is that we can build math "from the ground up." If we want to be secure and rigorous in our reasoning and proving, then we want to make sure no bad assumptions sneak in. For this, you set out the basic principles that hold for the mathematical things you are interested in and the logical rules by which you can figure out new truths. Historically, an important reason for wanting to stop sneaky extra assumptions being used and for making everything explicit was to do with concerns about the use of infinity in math at the end of the nineteenth century and start of the twentieth century. This issue was becoming ever more crucial for analysis and calculus, both central to modern mathematics but relying at the time on potentially spurious uses of the notion of infinity.

I think one way to understand the point of proving for the Platonist is via an analogy to showing off a mighty structure made out of LEGO.

If you want your mighty LEGO structure to stand up, it needs to be built up solidly all the way from the base to the top. Each brick needs to support those above it and in turn be supported by those below it. For each brick, we can check exactly which others it is resting on and which bricks above depend on it. The full model that is built up this way is also a model of mathematics: for the foundationalist (and therefore also for the Platonist with foundationalist leanings) the

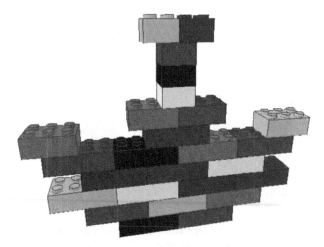

Figure 21.2 A mighty structure! Created by the author using http://www.ldraw.org/.

importance of a proof is that it shows the logical structuring of the math in much the same way the diagram above shows the structuring of our mighty LEGO build.

One big way in which the analogy between building a foundation for mathematics and building the mighty structure in LEGO breaks down is that you might well think we really need to build a model out of LEGO bricks for that model to exist. For the Platonist, the structuring of mathematics is already existent: it is simply the abstract objects and the relations between them. So the purpose of proving on this view is to see or reveal the structure, not to create it afresh.

Follow the Instructions!

One problem with the foundationalist take on proofs as showing off logical structuring of mathematical objects is that it doesn't do so well with picture proofs. Now, it should be emphasized at the outset that some philosophers believe that diagrammatic proofs can't truly prove anything, for various reasons. Of course, a major reason might be that picture proofs don't work well with the foundationalist take on proofs! Let's not go into this. Instead, you can judge for yourself through two simple examples.

The first is to show the following equality holds:

$$\frac{1}{4} + \left(\frac{1}{4}\right)^2 + \left(\frac{1}{4}\right)^3 + \left(\frac{1}{4}\right)^4 + \cdots = \frac{1}{3}$$

We can do this with the following diagram of an equilateral triangle:[2]

What!? How is that supposed to work? Well, imagine taking the whole triangle to have an area of 1. Then we can chop up the triangle into quarters as follows:

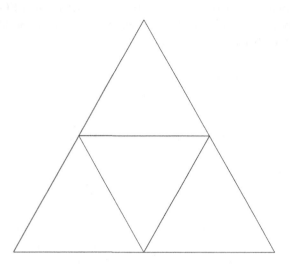

Well, if we take the top triangle and chop that into quarters again, each triangle is a quarter of that quarter, so will be (1/4) x (1/4) = $(1/4)^2$. In fact, we can keep dividing the top quarter to get higher and higher powers of 1/4, leaving us with a diagram like this:

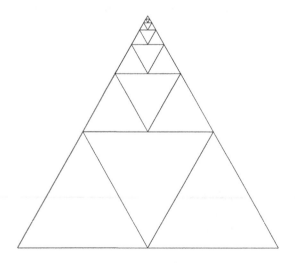

But then we can split this into three series of triangles: one along the left, one along the middle and one along the right, getting us our first diagram:

Each of the series (dark shaded, light shaded, and white) will now be of the form

$$\frac{1}{4} + \left(\frac{1}{4}\right)^2 + \left(\frac{1}{4}\right)^3 + \left(\frac{1}{4}\right)^4 + \cdots$$

But we also can see that the whole triangle is covered by these series and that they all have the exact same area, so each series must cover 1/3 of the triangle! As such it follows that

$$\frac{1}{4} + \left(\frac{1}{4}\right)^2 + \left(\frac{1}{4}\right)^3 + \left(\frac{1}{4}\right)^4 + \cdots = \frac{1}{3}$$

Voilà!

The foundationalist response to this demonstration could either be to deny that it shows what it appears to show, or to *logicify* it. However, it seems to me that no way of formalizing the idea in the above picture will maintain the elegance or intuitiveness that the original has.

Here is a second example, this time to prove the Pythagorean Theorem that $a^2 + b^2 = c^2$, where c is the length of hypotenuse of a triangle and *a* and *b* are the lengths of the other two sides. The proof is given by the following picture:

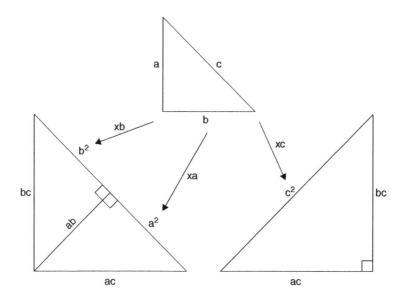

The idea is that we take the initial triangle, inflate it, and rotate it to get three different triangles. Furthermore, we can slot two of them together to get a new triangle (at the bottom left) which is identical to the third (at the bottom right). But for the two we slot together the length of the hypotenuse is a^2+b^2 while for the other it is c^2. Since these two triangles are the same size (in technical terms, they are *congruent*), the two hypotenuse lengths are equal, so the Pythagorean Theorem is proved!

What I love about this proof is that it brings to the fore the active nature of the demonstration. You must take the original triangle and *perform* three different actions on it, as indicated by the arrows in the picture. By manipulating the triangle in various ways we can then come to see the truth of the theorem. Here the parallels with LEGO are far stronger than they were with the foundationalists and Platonists. In LEGO instructions, we are guided through a series of actions that we must perform. Of course, the diagrams are on the printed page and so obviously cannot move. But having a series of pictures showing what changes occur between one step and the next, with occasional uses of arrows, manages to nonetheless successfully communicate a series of *actions* for us to build our model. In general, we are not interested in the pictures in the instructions for their own sakes or for what they show (after all, it won't be long before we have built the model itself so won't need pictures of it anymore).

Likewise in diagrammatic proofs, we are not focused on the picture for its own sake, but instead we are interested in the series of actions that it tells us to perform in order to construct the proof. In our first example, the actions are those of carving up a triangle in particular ways in order to mirror the infinite series we were dealing with. In the second example, we are scaling up the triangle in various ways, then rotating and re-combining the results.

We might call the idea underlying all of this the *LEGO account of diagrammatic proofs*. A similar analogy for another book could have led us to an *IKEA account of diagrammatic proofs*, comparing the activities directed by picture proofs to IKEA instructions for building furniture. (Any Swedes reading this may take comfort in the fact that they have an alternative to the Danish LEGO domination.)

The Geometers Strike Back

Thinking back to where we began, if we accept the LEGO account of diagrammatic proofs then we have strongly sided with the geometers against Plato. Where Plato thought that the geometers were ridiculous for using active, practice-based terminology for their demonstrations, on our LEGO account of proofs this is the *most important* aspect of those proofs. The main principle of departure from Plato is to not think so much in terms of mathematical objects but instead focus on *mathematical activities*. The same thought is meant to apply to LEGO: the particular bricks are only important insofar as they facilitate the things we can practically do with them.

It might even be possible to extend the LEGO account of diagrammatic proofs to a full account of proofs. For example, we might take all proofs to be describing a series of activities for us to undertake to come to appreciate the truth of mathematical theorems. The philosopher Ludwig Wittgenstein (1889–1951) puts the idea as follows: "The mathematical proposition says to me: Proceed like this!"[3]

On this view, mathematics isn't about the statements of truths, or arranging them into a neat logical structure as the foundationalist might think, but is instead about dynamic activities. The ultimate philosophy of mathematics we may end up with from here is one that values the practice of doing mathematics and according to which proofs are like a list of instructions to follow. Like the instruction booklets included with LEGO models, they must be seen not as the ends in themselves, but rather as a set of imperatives or guiding moves to follow in order to come to understand the wonderful realm of mathematics.

A final thought: we started out with parallel questions about LEGO and math. Why are they interesting? Why do we encourage kids to learn math and to play with LEGO? Well, with the LEGO account of proofs in hand we can tentatively suggest some answers. Though there are some aspects of both LEGO and mathematics that are about the objects (for example, we want to collect the awesome new Star Wars® LEGO sets and learn about the properties of triangles), we also want to concentrate on the activities that go along with them, like building, playing, proving, and discovering. These activities are interesting and useful precisely because they teach us how to solve puzzles effectively and play creatively. We can even solve problems with LEGO and play with mathematics, so the two are not so far apart after all. Maybe, with this in mind, we can throw away the old stereotype of mathematics as abstractly detached from reality, and see it as both important for doing things and fun in its own right.

Notes

1. Plato's *Republic*, trans. G.M.A. Grube, 2nd edition revised by C.D.C. Reeve (Indianapolis: Hackett Publishing Company, 1992), 527a–b, 199.
2. The two diagrammatic proofs are reproductions of proofs appearing in Roger B. Nelsen's *Proofs Without Words II: More Exercises In Visual Thinking* (Washington DC: The Mathematical Association of America, 2000). The first proof is credited to Rick Mabry and the second to Frank Burk.
3. Ludwig Wittgenstein, *Remarks on the Foundations of Mathematics*, eds. G.H. von Wright, R. Rhees, and G.E.M. Anscombe, trans. G.E.M. Anscombe (Oxford: Blackwell, 1956), Part VI, Section 72.

Glossary

Alice Leber-Cook and Roy T. Cook

Acrylonitrile Butadiene Styrene (or ABS): The thermoplastic used to produce molded products such as musical instruments, protective equipment, and LEGO® bricks.

Adult Fan of LEGO (or AFOL): A LEGO enthusiast who is at least 18 years old.

ApocaLEGO: A fan-created, minifigure-scale LEGO theme centering on zombies, postnuclear apocalypse wastelands, and steampunk.

Billund, Denmark: The location of the international headquarters of the LEGO Group.

Brick Separator: A wedge- shaped LEGO element specially designed for use in separating other LEGO bricks or plates.

Clone Brick (or brik, or knock-off): A construction toy designed to be compatible with LEGO bricks but not manufactured by the LEGO Group itself. Clone bricks are typically inferior in design and quality to official LEGO products, and are generally avoided by adult LEGO enthusiasts.

Color Change: A change which occurred in late 2003, when the older, brownish dark and light greys were replaced by bluish shades of grey (dark bley and light bley), and the older brown was replaced by a redder shade of brown (reddish-brown).

Dark Age: The period in an adult fan of LEGO's (AFOL's) life when LEGO products are temporarily set aside for other interests. Dark ages typically occur from sometime in the middle teen years to sometime in adulthood. Due to the fan community developed

LEGO® and Philosophy: Constructing Reality Brick By Brick, First Edition.
Edited by Roy T. Cook and Sondra Bacharach.
© 2017 John Wiley & Sons Ltd. Published 2017 by John Wiley & Sons Ltd.

online, as well as the formation of teen-friendly LEGO user groups (LUG)s, dark ages are becoming less common.

Dark Bley: The bluish shade of dark grey which, in 2003, replaced the older, browner version of dark grey in LEGO sets.

DUPLO® Bricks: LEGO bricks that are scaled up by a factor of two, and intended to introduce toddlers and preschool children to the LEGO System of Play (System i Leg).

Enfield, Connecticut: The location of the North American headquarters of The LEGO Group

Female Fan of LEGO (or FFOL): A female LEGO enthusiast.

FIRST LEGO League: An international robotics competition for participants aged 9 to 14, based on the Mindstorms® robotics LEGO theme. FIRST LEGO League is sponsored by the LEGO Group and FIRST (For Inspiration and Recognition of Science and Technology).

Fleshie: A minifig molded in pink or peach-colored ABS plastic, as opposed to traditional yellow-skinned minifigs. Fleshies were introduced in 2003 for use in licensed sets to distinguish figures representing real people from the more generic figures appearing in non-licensed sets.

Great Ball Contraption (or GBC): A collaboratively built LEGO machine. Each module takes LEGO soccer balls or basketballs into one end, transfers them to the other end, and then passes the balls off to the next module.

Kid Fan of LEGO (or KFOL): A LEGO enthusiast who is between the ages of 5 and 13. Kid fans of LEGO are the primary market for the LEGO Group, but are often not allowed to participate in online forums and other LEGO-related websites due to government regulations.

Kragle (short for KRAzy GLuE): The superweapon wielded by the villain Lord Business in *The LEGO Movie*.

LDraw: A freeware program which allows LEGO enthusiasts to create virtual LEGO creations. LDraw is constantly being extended and refined by members of the LEGO community.

"Leg Godt": A phrase which means "play well" in Danish and the source of the name of the LEGO Group. The LEGO Group also claims that "lego" translates as "I assemble" or "I put together" in Latin, although this is a somewhat strained translation.

LEGO Ambassador: Volunteer adult fans of LEGO (AFOLs) who work with the LEGO Group in order to foster communication and collaboration between the company and the LEGO enthusiast community.

LEGO Group (or **The LEGO Company,** or **TLC,** or **TLG**): The official name of the company that produces LEGO products.

LEGO Ideas (formerly **LEGO CUUSOO**): A program run by the LEGO Group where fans can submit their own designs and compete to have their creations produced as official LEGO sets.

LEGOLAND®: A series of LEGO-based theme parks. There are currently LEGOLAND parks in Billund, Denmark; Windsor, England; Carlsbad, California; Günzburg, Germany; Winter Haven, Florida; Iskandar Puteri, Malaysia; and Jebel Ali, Dubai.

The LEGO Movie (or **TLM**): A mostly animated, big-budget film distributed by Warner Brothers and released in 2014. The film won a BAFTA (British Academy of Film and Television Arts) award for best animated film, and a number of sequels are planned.

LEGOs: There is no such thing as **LEGOs**. The term "LEGO" should only be used alone to refer to the company, otherwise the term should be used as an adjective, as in "LEGO sets" or "LEGO elements."

LEGO Train Club (or **LTC,** or simply **train club**): A group of LEGO train enthusiasts, often restricted to adult fans of LEGO (AFOLs) and teen fans of LEGO (TFOLs), who meet regularly (either in person or online) to discuss railroad-related aspects of the hobby and participate in collaborative activities. Thus, a LEGO train club is a particular type of LEGO user group (LUG).

LEGO User Group (or **LUG,** or simply **user group**): A group of LEGO enthusiasts, often restricted to adult fans of LEGO (AFOLs) and teen fans of LEGO (TFOLs), who meet regularly (either in person or online) to discuss their hobby and participate in collaborative activities.

Light Bley: The bluish shade of light grey which, in 2003, replaced the older, browner version of light grey in LEGO sets.

Microscale (or **microfig scale,** or **pocket model scale**): Any LEGO creations that are built in a scale much smaller than minifig scale. Often, microscale creations are built according to a one-stud-brick equals one-adult-human scale, although this varies.

Mindstorms: A series of LEGO products which combine programmable bricks with motors and technic elements in order to create LEGO robots. Mindstorms products have been used by schools and other programs in order to teach the fundamentals of robot design and control.

Mini-doll (or **MDs,** or **Friends Figs):** The figures found in sets within the Friends, Disney®, Elves, and Fusion LEGO themes.

Minifigure (or **MFs,** or **minifigs):** The figures most often found in LEGO sets today. Typically approximately four bricks in height, minifigures have interchangeable hands, hair, legs, heads, torsos, and accessories.

Minifigure Scale (or **minifig scale):** This refers to LEGO creations that are built to the scale of minifigures. Minifigure scale is approximately 1:48.

Miniland: An exhibit featured at each of the LEGOLAND theme parks. Miniland consists of LEGO recreations of iconic buildings and landmarks, built on a miniland scale, which is approximately 1:20.

Miniland Scale: This refers to LEGO creations that are built on the same scale as the exhibits in the Miniland displays at the LEGOLAND theme parks. Miniland scale is approximately 1:20.

My Own Creation (or **MOC):** Any LEGO creation designed and built by a LEGO enthusiast.

Octan: A fictional gas station that appears in official LEGO sets. Occasionally the Octan brand has been abandoned in favor of corporate licenses with Shell.

Ole Kirk Kristiansen (1891–1958): Founder of the LEGO toy company—later the LEGO Group—in 1932.

Pick-A-Brick (or **PAB):** A service provided at LEGO retail stores where particular elements are stored in containers on a wall. Customers can buy as many elements off the wall as can fit into a plastic cup (or sometimes, special larger containers) for a fixed price.

Programmable Brick: A large LEGO brick containing electronics which allow it to be used in the creation of LEGO Mindstorms robots. Programmable bricks include the RCX programmable brick and the NXT programmable brick.

Purist: A LEGO creation is **purist** if it does not contain any paint, clone bricks, non-LEGO stickers, modified parts, or third-party parts or accessories. The term can also be used to refer to LEGO enthusiasts who restrict their building techniques in this way.

Seriously Huge Investment in Parts (or **SHIP**): A LEGO spacecraft that is at least one hundred studs in length. Building a SHIP is viewed as a rite of passage within the LEGO space community.

Serious Play®: A corporate team-building program founded by the LEGO Group where participants learn to foster their creativity and work together effectively through a series of activities focusing on building with LEGO bricks.

Signature Figure (or **sig fig**): A minifigure used by a LEGO enthusiast to represent him- or herself. Often, photographs of signature figures are used as avatars on online forums and other LEGO-related sites.

Smiley: A yellow minifigure head with a generic, gender-neutral smiley face printed on it. The first non-smiley minifigure heads appeared in 1989 in LEGO Pirates sets.

Studs Not On Top (or **SNOT**): A body of specialized building techniques that allow LEGO elements to be incorporated into LEGO creations on their sides or even upside down in order to obtain the desired shape or effect.

System i Leg (or **System of Play**): The idea that individual LEGO sets are not independent toys, but instead are compatible with one another, forming a single system of building and creativity. The first LEGO sets developed within the System of Play framework appeared in 1955.

Teen Fan of LEGO (or **teenage fan of LEGO,** or **TFOL**): A LEGO enthusiast who is between the ages of 14 and 17. Unlike kid fans of LEGO (KFOLs), teen fans of LEGO can legally participate in online forums and other LEGO- related sites, and are often allowed to join LEGO user groups (LUGs).

Index

References to notes are entered as, for example, 161n.

Printed and bound by CPI Group (UK) Ltd, Croydon, CR0 4YY

25/03/2025

14647350-0004